SOUTH WEST
FRANCE
AQUITAINE, GASCONY, THE PYRENEES

SOUTH WEST FRANCE

FRANCE

AQUITAINE, GASCONY, THE PYRENEES

Andrew Sanger

Second edition

Photographs by Joe Cornish

CHRISTOPHER HELM
London

© 1994, 1990 Andrew Sanger
Second Edition 1994

Photographs by Joe Cornish
Line illustrations by David Henderson
Maps by Oxford Cartographers

Published by Christopher Helm (Publishers) Ltd, a subsidiary of A&C Black (Publishers) Ltd, 35 Bedford Row, London WC1R 4JH.

ISBN 0-7136-3992-X

A CIP catalogue record for this book is available from the British Library.

The publishers invite readers to write in with comments, suggestions and corrections for the next edition of the guide. Writers of the most informative letters will be awarded a free Regional Guide of their choice.

Printed in Spain by Artes Gráficas Toledo, S.A.
D.L.TO:545-1994

Title illustration: the Grosse Cloche at Bordeaux.

For Joe and Hilda Sanger

Acknowledgements

With many thanks for the assistance, information and advice generously offered by the staff of the Comités Régionals de Tourisme of Aquitaine and the Midi-Pyrénées. Above all, my love and thanks to Gerry Dunham for being with me and for her immeasurable help at every stage.

Contents

1
Introduction

The immense tidal waters of the Gironde estuary, cutting deeply inland from the Atlantic ocean, place a great barrier through France's western départements. The traveller crosses its swirling, sandy current and finds, on the far side, that this is where the South really begins. The Garonne, principal tributary of the Gironde, continues the barrier far across France: from the great port city of Bordeaux, the river reaches round to the other South Western provincial capital, Toulouse; there it meets the Ariège pouring north from the Pyrenees mountains. These two rivers form the basic boundaries of our region, which must also be allowed to embrace the country on their right banks: the north side of the Gironde, and the départements of Gironde, Garonne, and Haute-Garonne. This rolling, hilly, varied land, blessed with southern sun and Atlantic freshness, is arguably the most exquisitely beautiful, rustic and satisfying region in France.

Whether for the visitor with a real interest in the history and culture of France, or for the *amateur* of good food and (especially) fine wines, or for the lover of sunlit sandy beaches and clean ocean waves, the South West proves to be a marvellous discovery. And while Biarritz and its Basque coast, as well as the new resorts of the amazing Landes coastline (the Côte d'Argent, 288 km of magnificent pale sand), and the cooler, airy towns of the Pyrenees, are certainly not unknown to tourists — indeed, they have been popular for years — yet they are a good deal less crowded than other parts of the South of France. These, in any case, are merely the fringe, the edges, of the South West. The whole of the interior of this vast area, its rich rural heartland, remains almost completely undiscovered except by a few wise connoisseurs who, no doubt, would prefer to guard their secret.

The South West, an evocative but rather nebulous and expansive-sounding title, encompasses several broadly overlapping historical regions. Some do represent considerable contrasts, but most are virtually synonymous: Aquitaine, Gascony, Guyenne, the Pays Basque, Armagnac, the Landes … it would be excusable to imagine that all these must be different places. In fact, almost the whole of France's South West was for centuries known as Gascogne, or Gascony. The fertile undulating farmland at Gascony's centre is called Armagnac, and from here comes the famous brandy of the same name; this area often still calls itself Gascogne. The original Gascony, largely taking over the territories of the Romans' Novempopulania ('the Nine Peoples',

1

or nine communities) which had been the early basis of Aquitania, came into being in the 7th century as an extension of the Basque's Vasconia; its southern boundary was, and still is, made up of a string of Pyrenean mountain districts — Béarn, Bigorre, Comminges, Foix. Today, some of these are occupied by Basques and some are not; the Pays Basque, a surprisingly small but gorgeously pretty area, is confined now to only the extreme western part of the Pyrenean chain. The sand-dunes and pine woods of the coastal Landes also came within Gascony's old frontiers, and so too, at times, when the term Gas-

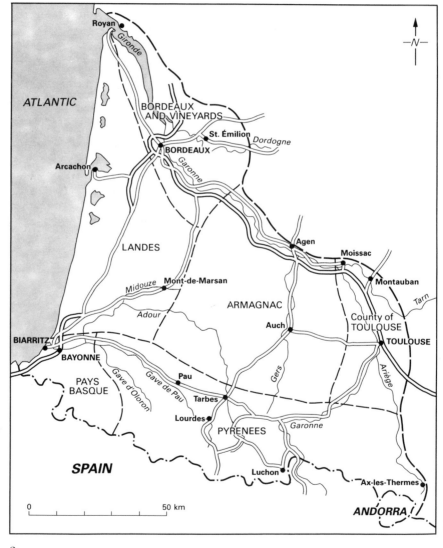

cony was used at its loosest, did the productive vineyards of Bordeaux. To the east though, Gascony is bordered by an altogether different region, formerly part of the domaine of the powerful Counts of Toulouse, whose lands and language were called Languedoc, and belonged more to the Mediterranean than the Atlantic.

Theoretically, to Gascony's north lay the separate province of Guyenne (pronounced 'Gweeyenne'), although the two encroached on each other's territory and the border between them was flexible. Every map of medieval France seems to show the two in a different position, and they appear to have edged round each other as if performing a stately dance. Originally, Guyenne was considered as none other than an alternative name — supposedly the English name, which first began to be used in the 12th century — for the duchy of Aquitaine.

Where, then, in the South West's complex mosaic of geography and history, was ancient Aquitaine? This, the Romans' 'water land', finally conquered in about 28 BC, was initially focused well to the south, around the Adour river and the inland Armagnac. Lapurdum (Bayonne) was its first major port town. Aquitania grew under Roman rule to become a vast and little-developed province which took in everything south and west of the Loire right down to the borders of present-day Spain and Languedoc. In time, Burdigala (Bordeaux) became its principal city. Growing too big to administer as a single unit, eventually Aquitania was divided into three sub-provinces (Prima, Secunda, Tertia). The area from the Garonne to the Pyrenees — Aquitania Tertia (later to become Gascony) — was the same area which had earlier

been known to its Roman masters as Novempopulania, named for the original Gallo-Roman settlements in Aquitania. The nine survive today as the towns of Dax, Lectoure, Tarbes, Eauze, Auch, and Bazas, and the hill districts of Béarn, Comminges (or Cominges), and Labourd (which includes Bayonne).

When, from the 3rd to the 5th centuries, the great onslaught of the nomadic barbarian armies — Vandals, Sueves, Huns, Goths — proved too much for the Romans to hold back, Aquitania continued to exist as part of a huge and unruly Visigothic kingdom. But the most powerful of these Germanic tribes, the Franks, was soon to seize Aquitania. The decisive Battle of Vouillé in 507 drove the Visigoths down into their more southerly strongholds, Spain and Languedoc, leaving Aquitaine as part of a Frankish empire which would eventually evolve into the French nation. Roman Aquitania had thus become a 'barbarian' kingdom (later, a duchy), owing allegiance to the French emperor. It did not cover the full extent that it had under Roman rule though. For even at this time, Gasconia (initially Vasconia) was becoming a recognisable, distinct region, as the people called Vascones (Basques) spread north over the Pyrenees from their homeland in northern Spain (from which they had been driven by the Visigoths) and took over the larger part of the old Novempopulania. By the 7th century Gascony had its own language (a dialect of the old Latin-based *langue d'oc* southern language, with a spice of Basque), its own culture and traditions, its own rulers.

This Gascon land, which even extended far enough east to include Toulouse at one stage, was incorporated into the larger Aquitaine duchy in

3

1036, while retaining a regional identity. The remainder of Aquitaine, at this time reaching north right up to the Charente river, was to become known as Guyenne. Aquitaine, like its cosmopolitan neighbours Languedoc and Catalonia, was incomparably more cultured and civilised than the austere Frankish kingdom to its north. The arts, education and trade flourished, and although religion was vitally important it lacked the stifling quality typical of some other provinces.

The key personality in the subsequent destiny of South West France was Eleanor of Aquitaine, granddaughter of the illustrious troubadour Guilhem IX of Aquitaine, and daughter of Guilhem X. Being in direct line, and the only child, she inherited the entire duchy of Aquitaine, which consisted of Gascony and Guyenne, as well the other provinces to their north and east: Périgord, Saintonge, Limousin, and Poitou. It was a formidable inheritance. Many kings and princes looked at both her and her lands with longing, and Eleanor was wooed and won at last by Louis VII of France (1137). Of course it was a marriage of state, of strategy, of politics. Eleanor was probably brought up to expect nothing else, and perhaps did not mind too much that she had no affinity with her lord and that the marriage was not a contented one. Eleanor had two daughters by the pious Louis, and may have been fully expecting to spend the rest of her life as Queen of France.

However, many at the royal court in Paris did not like the gay atmosphere which was generated by Eleanor's presence there. Under pressure from the ecclesiastics, Louis divorced Eleanor on his return from a crusade in 1152. The dowry which she had

brought him — the Aquitaine duchy — was honourably returned to her. Eleanor at once married Henry Plantagenet of Anjou, of whom she seems to have been rather fond already, and who was within two years of inheriting the crown of England. Thus she and Henry — a Gascon and an Angevin — who, incidentally, are said to have spoken the Gascon language to each other and in court, came to have sovereignty over the whole of England and Wales and much of Ireland and all of western France. Not surprisingly, they did not live in England, but made Poitiers their royal home.

When Henry died in 1189, Eleanor ruled the great kingdom herself, only handing over the crown to her eldest son Richard I in 1199.

Inevitably, in subsequent generations, the Plantagenet territories became more distinctly 'English' in character, with English-speaking traders and settlers coming to live in Bordeaux and the Gascon towns. To safeguard against any desire among the locals to revert to French rule, many civil liberties were granted to Gascony's wealthier classes by the English crown. They could look across without envy at their neighbours living under the yoke of feudal France.

Nevertheless, apart from the few urban areas, of which Bordeaux was the main one, England's control of its domain was weak. There was a tremendous overlap of French and English culture, and for the poorer rural classes there was no significant difference between one distant king and another. To achieve a stronger grip on their lands, the English, like the French and the Languedoc counts, instituted the building of many fortified new towns called *bastides* in the disputed, vulnerable Gascon terrain. Almost invariably constructed on a grid plan with a church and big arcaded market-place at the centre and the whole town enclosed within sturdy ramparts, the *bastides* were settled by English and locals alike. In the 13th century tension grew between the two kingdoms as the French flexed their muscles and wondered if they could retake Aquitaine — as well as the other English possessions on French soil. At the start of the century there were about 100 *bastides* in these vulnerable eastern reaches of Aquitaine; by the end of the century, there were almost 1,000: the picture of a growing sense of insecurity on both sides is clear.

By the start of the disastrous 14th century, there had already been a good deal of fighting between England and France, as the French tried to regain parts of their lost territories. In 1328, on the death of the French king, Charles IV, last of the Capetian line, Edward III of England at once asserted that he had the most eligible claim to the throne of France, having historically closer links with it than Charles IV's cousin, Philippe de Valois. Philippe was nevertheless crowned as Philippe VI. Edward invaded France with the clear intention of taking the whole kingdom. It was the start of the Hundred Years War. In Aquitaine, the Black Prince expanded the English dominion, savagely conquering new areas. However, at the same time the country was being ravaged by the Black Death and soon the population of fighting men was more than decimated. At the Treaty of Bretigny (1360), which ceded yet more of Aquitaine to him, Edward renounced his claim and allowed the French kings to keep most of the central strip of their country. Almost all of the original Roman Aquitania was therefore reunited under English rule, which was firmly centred on its Roman capital Bordeaux and based around the old south-western province of Gascony.

The Peace of Bretigny, as it was called, proved but a brief lull. As events progressed, the English began another period of expansion in 1415, with the arrival in France of Henry V. Within five years it appeared that the whole of France would soon belong to the English crown. Then, by marrying Catherine, daughter of Charles VI in 1420, Henry made himself legitimate heir to the French throne. Incredibly, it was not to be — Henry V died before Charles VI, but only by a matter of weeks. The cowed French, inspired by Joan of Arc, suddenly regained their confidence and fought back; by almost miraculous turns of fate (genuinely miraculous, Joan of Arc was claiming) France began to recover its power. Gradually the English were pushed back, even having to abandon their loyal Gascons. In 1453 the last important battle of the Hundred Years War was fought near Bordeaux at Castillon-la-Bataille (which takes its name from the event). The English were beaten.

With the French in control, many things had to change in Aquitaine, but the transformation was not particularly abrupt. To mollify its large bourgeois class, accustomed to English liberties, a *parlement* was set up in Bordeaux (like the one in Toulouse — see below), while out in the country districts, Armagnac and some smaller *domaines* were left in the control of their counts, and the remote Pyrenean provinces were allowed to be autonomous. One of the smallest districts under its own family of local *seigneurs* was Albret, north of Armagnac. The lords of this tiny *pays* had high ambitions, and through a policy of prudent marriages, were able to realise them. By the 16th century they held, in addition to their own Albret, the titles of Foix, Béarn, and Basse-Navarre — in other words, most of the Pyrenees and their foothills to the north. In 1527, Henri d'Albret married Marguerite d'Angoulême, sister of the French king François I (1515–47). Both were keen advocates of religious 'reform' — Protestantism. Their daughter Jeanne d'Albret succeeded to the throne of Navarre and, in what was to prove a turning point for the South West and for the whole of France, she officially renounced Catholicism and embraced Protestantism. She successfully repulsed an attempt by the French monarch Charles IX to reconquer the South West for Catholicism, and went on strongly to promote Protestant dominance in the region (see pages 172–3).

There had not previously been any widespread popular movement towards Protestantism in the South West, and there was a deep conflict between those who were loyal to Jeanne d'Albret and those who preferred to remain loyal to their old faith. The area had been strongly Christianised by the beginning of the 4th century. At that time it was one of the first few islands of the new religion in Europe. When the strong fresh wind of Protestantism began to blow through the corruption and hypocrisy of the Roman Catholic Church, the new ideas made little impact in Gascony. The Religious Wars were thus particularly damaging in this region.

Jeanne's son, Henri d'Albret brought up as a Protestant, married the king's sister, Marguerite de Valois. When the last of the king's sons, Henri III died in 1589, Henri d'Albret, already King of Navarre since Jeanne's death, succeeded to the crown of France as Henri IV. But there was one obstacle in his way — Protestants could not sit on the throne of France. After first attempting to assert his position by force, Henri decided, with the notorious explanation that 'Paris is worth a Mass', to be rebaptised as a Catholic. For all that, his reign was a good one for the population as a whole and especially for the Huguenots: his Edict of Nantes (1598) gave them freedom of worship in certain specified centres; all civil offices were open to Protestants; and tribunals were set up to ensure that they were given equal treatment.

Pau became one of the largest Huguenot centres, and in this climate Protestants increased in number and in influence throughout the native land of Good King Henri. Catholic discontent with the situation did not go away though; Henri was assassinated in 1610, and the persecution of Protestants was resumed. After the late 1670s, Louis XIV imposed a systematic regime of oppression and slaughter to destroy the new creed. Life became increasingly barbaric, culminating in Louis's revocation of the Edict of Nantes in 1685. The whole of South West France suffered severely from these measures — much of the population fled, literally for their lives, many settling in England.

Louis XIV died in 1715, having brutally enforced a degree of national unification and brought Aquitaine more into the mainstream of French life. The 18th century, most of it under the much more easy-going Louis XV, was to continue that trend. Tolerant and liberal thinkers

— such as Bordeaux's Montesquieu — began to emerge. Benevolent and forward-looking royal administrators in the provinces, such as Tourny in Bordeaux, and d'Étigny in Auch, reinvigorated the South West, and caused rebuilding on a grand scale, which still gives character to these towns today.

The end of the century, however, saw the discontent among the bourgeoisie which led to the Revolution of 1789. At first, the middle class in the South West advocated *Liberté, Egalité,* and *Fraternité* as loudly as any, perhaps more loudly, since Bordeaux had never lost the taste for personal freedom acquired under the English. As the Revolution passed through its various stages, each more tyrannical than the one before, the South West, particularly Bordeaux and its region, stood firm for the original, more moderate, objectives of 1789. This view was expressed in the new Revolutionary National Assembly of 1791 by all the representatives from the Gironde département, whose name — *les Girondins* — was given to the movement for a more libertarian, tolerant Revolution. But the extremist Jacobins, creating a bloodthirsty dictatorship pushing for a completely new order, won the day and instituted their notorious reign of terror (*le Terreur*). Despite coup and counter-coup within their own ranks, the hardliners succeeded not just in crushing the moderate viewpoint but in hunting out and killing every one of its advocates. The last of the Girondins were discovered hiding in St. Émilion, and were executed in 1794. Yet as things turned out, the Girondist approach was destined to prevail in modern times. Under Napoleon, France was in an expansionist mood, and had several great successes. However, Napoleon's efforts to extend his burgeoning empire into Spain met with opposition from Spain's allies, the British under Wellington. This Peninsular War, as it was known, involved direct conflict between the British and the French on French soil. There was fighting on the Basque coast and farther inland, and even at Toulouse. British officers based for the winter at Bayonne and at Pau were impressed by what they saw of these places. In the event, the French were soundly beaten, and the British withdrew. One of the unlikely consequences was that the pleasures of these cities became more widely known in Britain. Biarritz (next to Bayonne) and Pau became highly fashionable 19th-century winter resorts for the British, which further reinforced the historic links between Aquitaine and England.

Toulousains reading this will be indignant to see so much about Bordeaux and so little about their own city. Between Toulouse and Bordeaux there is an intense rivalry, a mutual respect combined with a mutual disdain. For Toulouse has had, in the main, a quite separate history from that of Bordeaux; yet both are now regarded as great cities of the South West. The mighty Garonne river unites them, and both are dynamic centres of industry and commerce vital to the economy of this quarter of France. Toulouse has a more southern atmosphere, and would claim to be a more lively city, with more *joie de vivre*, and maybe the Bordelais would not dispute this (although no doubt some would!). The real long-standing difference between the two is that the wealth and power of Toulouse came from land, from the feudal structure, from the native aristocracy, whereas

Bordeaux gained its wealth and power from trade and commerce, and from its colonial rulers.

In a rather insincere gesture towards the historic regional feeling of some parts of the country, in 1972 the French government created a number of regions with a measure of autonomy on certain issues. Administratively, the South West was divided ineptly into two, with Bordeaux and Toulouse as provincial capitals.

Since then, for modern administrative purposes, Aquitaine has been the name given to an area broadly overlapping northern and western Gascony. It includes three coastal départements of the South West, and two inland départements, one of which (Dordogne) is outside our region. Bordeaux is the capital of this new Aquitaine. The rest of South West France is nowadays administered under the name Midi-Pyrénées, an artificial concept with no historical identity. The capital of the Midi-Pyrénées is Toulouse, which used to be the capital of the Mediterranean county which subsequently became Languedoc.

Many in Toulouse see the creation of the Midi-Pyrénées region as yet another attempt by Paris, the latest in a series going back for centuries, to conquer the separatist feeling of Languedoc: one more attempt by Paris to 'divide and rule' the provinces of the South. The original county of Toulouse extended in the 13th century from the Rhône in the east to Gascony in the west and almost to Le Puy in the Auvergne. It was a land which nominally owed allegiance to the King of France but which in practice was entirely independent of French rule. The *langue d'oc*, or Provençal

language, was spoken here, and the feudal structure operated on different, more libertarian lines. The county of Toulouse, as a potential ally of the kingdom of Aragón, was seen (correctly, one must guess) as a threat to France. The wave of Cathar heresy which engulfed the county at that time made the region equally a threat to the power of the Catholic church in southern France. Joining forces, ostensibly to overcome the Cathars, the pope and the French king launched the war which was intended finally to conquer Languedoc, destroy its identity, and bring it under French rule. This was fought as a religious war, the Albigensian Crusade, so-called because Cathars were at first largely concentrated in the diocese of Albi and were known to their enemies as Albigenses.

The crusade lasted from 1209 to 1229, and at the end of it the county of Toulouse submitted to the sovereignty of the French king. Nevertheless Languedoc remained recalcitrant and rebellious, and always longed for freedom from France. It has showed this defiant character over and over again through the years, most notably during the religious wars of the 16th and 17th centuries. Napoleon succeeded in wiping out regional feeling in most of France, and managed to weld the country into the single nation that we see today. Yet in Languedoc the restless yearning for some identity which would set it apart from the rest of France has continued right up to the present day.

To emphasise its attitude to these new divisions, Midi-Pyrénées has chosen the distinctive twelve-pointed Languedoc cross as its symbol. This crest still emblazons the town hall in Toulouse.

Getting There

The most direct ferry and road access from Britain to the South West is via the Channel ports of St. Malo and Caen. Motorail services from Calais to Bordeaux, Biarritz and Toulouse provide a fast direct link with the Channel. Other direct motorail services run from Lille to Bordeaux and Biarritz. The airports of Bordeaux, Toulouse and Lourdes/ Tarbes have frequent direct flights from several British airports.

Driving and Maps

Remember that the basic rule in France is still *priorité à droite* — give way to traffic coming from the right — unless signposts indicate to the contrary. Signs which show you are on a road *with* priority (i.e. others must give way to you) include: a diagonal cross on a triangular sign if it has the words *Passage Protégé* below; a yellow lozenge-shaped sign. Signs showing that you must give way include: all 'Stop' signs; a yellow lozenge crossed out; a triangular sign at roundabouts with the words *Vous n'avez pas la Priorité*. On D roads in the country, there are white posts at all junctions: if there are red lines on your posts, you do not have priority. In towns, *priorité à droite* still applies almost without exception.

Use Michelin regional maps Aquitaine (234) and Midi-Pyrénées (235), with a scale of 1cm=2km, or IGN *Serie Rouge* regional maps Bordelais-Périgord (110), Pyrénées-Occidentales (113), and Pyrénées-Languedoc (114), which have a scale of 1cm=2½km. More localised are the Michelin yellow maps (same scale as regional maps, but on smaller sheets), or IGN *Serie Verte* with a scale of 1cm=1km. For touring, the Michelin motoring atlas of France (containing the yellow maps in book form) is invaluable. For even more detailed maps suitable for walking, use IGN *Cartes de Randonnées*, with a scale of 1cm=½km.

Museums and Galleries

Note that opening times of museums and galleries etc. are liable to frequent alteration. Many buildings, including churches, are closed between 12 noon and 2pm; churches should never be visited during services except to take part in the service.

Hotel and Restaurant Closed Periods

Most French hotels and restaurants close for 1 or 1½ days a week (hotels remaining open only for guests already booked in), and also may have a closed period of a week or a month. These dates may vary from one year to the next.

Some French Words used in the Text

Appellation or *Appellation Contrôlée*	highest official quality-control wine category
autoroute	motorway (usually with toll)
avenue, av	avenue
bastide	fortified medieval town on grid pattern
boules	French-style bowls, played on any open space
boulevard, bd	boulevard, avenue
carte	bill of fare, a menu
Cave, Cave Coopérative	winery owned communally by local wine-growers
CDT (Comité Départemental de Tourisme)	tourist office for the département
chai(s)	cellar(s) where wine is made
commune	administrative area like a ward or parish
corniches	high steep-sided bays descending to the sea
CRT (Comité Régional de Tourisme)	regional tourist office
département	administrative area similar to a county
esplanade	outdoor promenade, esplanade or terraces
Établissement Thermal	bath house or pump room at a spa
étang	shallow lagoon
GR	Grande Randonnée — long-distance waymarked footpath
j.f.	*jours feriés*, holidays
Logis, Logis de France	federation of family-run country hotels
menu	a set meal
OTSI	Office du Tourisme-Syndicat d'Initiative (see SI below)
pays	a country, a district, a locality
paysan	local country person, usually a peasant farmer
place, pl	square
platanes	plane trees
préfecture	local administrative headquarters
quai	paved river embankment, often part of public highway
Relais et Châteaux	federation of independent luxury hotels of character
route de, rte de . . .	the road to . . .
route nationale	classification for a main road
rue	street, road
seigneur	lord, nobleman, possessor of a local fief, a feudal landowner
seigneurial	belonging to a *seigneur*
SI	Syndicat d'Initiative (local information office)
VDQS, Vin Délimité de Qualité Supérieur	official second-rank wine category
vieille ville	'old town', the historic quarter of a town
vignoble	vineyard region
Vin de Pays	'locality wine', lowest official wine category

Conversion Tables

km	miles	km	miles	km	miles
1	0.62	8	4.97	40	24.86
2	1.24	9	5.59	50	31.07
3	1.86	10	6.21	60	37.28
4	2.48	15	9.32	70	43.50
5	3.11	20	12.43	80	49.71
6	3.73	25	15.53	90	55.93
7	4.35	30	18.64	100	62.14

m	ft	m	ft	m	ft
100	328	600	1,968	1,500	4,921
200	656	700	2,296	2,000	6,562
300	984	800	2,625	2,500	8,202
400	1,313	900	2,953	3,000	9,842
500	1,640	1,000	3,281	3,500	11,483

ha	acres	ha	acres	ha	acres
1	2.5	10	25	100	247
2	5	25	62	150	370
5	12	50	124	200	494

kg	lbs	kg	lbs
1	2.2	6	13.2
2	4.4	7	15.4
3	6.6	8	17.6
4	8.8	9	19.8
5	11.0		

°C	°F	°C	°F	°C	°F
0	32	12	54	24	75
2	36	14	57	26	79
4	39	16	61	28	82
6	43	18	64	30	86
8	46	20	68	32	90
10	50	22	72	34	93

2
Food and Wine

The rich, succulent, highly flavoured cooking of South West France takes its inspiration first and foremost from the rustic traditional cuisine of the Armagnac region, that peaceful and productive farm country at the heart of old Gascony, and the green slopes of Béarn to its south. An expansive people with panache and flair, unstinting in both generosity and appetite, Gascons like hearty food served in full measure. It doesn't do to hang back at a Gascon table. The region offers exceptionally fine quality ingredients and good traditional styles of preparation. Even Gascony's keenest proponents of the flimsy *nouvelle cuisine* have tended to admit that portions must be filling enough that diners may leave the table well satisfied.

This is a land which fairly lives on the goose and the duck and everything which can be made from them. Above all, although for some dishes pork fat or butter are preferred, the fat of the goose is the basic cooking medium; it reaches a very high temperature, and gives the food a distinctive mouthwatering aroma and flavour.

The highly prized (and highly priced) *foie gras* — literally fat liver — of these two farmyard fowl is produced by forcefeeding the birds with the local maize. The process of force-feeding geese and ducks is known as *le gavage*. Various methods are used to force maize down the funnel: common on farms is a simple round-ended stick to push the maize far enough into the throat to activate the bird's swallowing reflex. This quickly causes the metabolism to become unhealthy and the liver to enlarge. Incidentally, the question whether or not it is right to inflict this on the geese is exclusively a British preoccupation. The French are so far from having any qualms about it that a guided tour of a goose farm to watch the *gavage* is considered one of the treats of a Gascon holiday, and shopkeepers in the towns cash in by selling postcards showing geese being force-fed. Restaurants pride themselves on being able to serve an *hors d'oeuvre* of high quality *foie gras* of goose, which the knowing will eat with a glass of the best sweet wine — Sauternes or Jurançon. It is often served with the season's fresh fruit: grapes in September, apples in winter, melon or strawberries in summer. There are literally scores of recipes which call for *foie gras* to be prepared in various ways, often with truffles (another astronomically expensive delicacy). Especially liked is *foie gras* lightly cooked in butter, accompanied by a little sauce made of muscat grapes which have been heated through in the same pan with a drop of Armagnac, and served with fresh grapes.

Such refined meats are the essence of many a Gascon dish. Confit, seen on menus and in markets all over the region, is the potted meat (essentially the wings, legs and offal) of duck or goose cooked and preserved in its own fat. (Any poultry can be preserved as confit, as can pork.) It is much used in cooking, especially as an addition to enrich the region's many stews and casseroles. In an area which is also fond of charcuterie and all manner of sausages, the most refined example is surely cou farci, a goose's neck stuffed with its own meat. Along similar lines, pâtés too are extremely well liked here, especially pâté de foie gras of either goose or duck.

Of course pâté can mean several different things in France, all derived from the same idea of the basic ingredients being made into a paste (which is what pâté means). A pâté en terrine is finely ground meats, seasoned, and baked in an earthenware terrine lined with pork fat. But pâté also refers to a sort of pie, in which the meat is baked in a pastry case, even if it is made in a mould rather than a pie dish. Pâté en croûte is also under a pastry crust. The original pâté de foie gras, as invented by the 19th-century chef Jean Joseph Close, was cooked with truffles en croûte — it was more or less what is now called pâté de foie gras aux truffes. Nowadays though, pâté de foie gras normally refers to the terrine preparation. The regulations state that pâtés, galantines, purées and mousses of foie gras must contain at least 50 per cent foie gras. Anything less can only be called pâté de foie, liver paste. A pâté with 75 per cent foie gras can be called a parfait.

Apart from affecting the liver, the intensified nourishment of the maize-fed goose and duck makes the rest of the meat exceptionally tender and tasty (although curiously lean). Magret (breast) of canard (duck) or oie (goose) are available all over South West France. They are only lightly cooked — sometimes almost raw — and can be prepared in almost any way that comes to mind — fresh, smoked, dry, fried, grilled or in sauce. The chicken, which also thrives to gorgeous plumpness on the nutritious maize diet, provides a more 'everyday' dish. Needless to say, none of these birds are churned out by factories, as they would be in Britain, but live wholesomely in sunlit muddy farmyards. Along the country lanes they scatter into the farm gate at the approach of the occasional car.

Henri IV, brought up in the Pyrenees, asked nothing more than that he and his subjects could be sure of their 'chicken in the pot'. Poule au Pot (literally, chicken in the pot) has become a favourite dish in the South West; no doubt it is somewhat grander than the good king anticipated: the chicken is stuffed with ham or veal and egg-yolk, garlic and herbs and casseroled for three or four hours with leeks and potatoes in a pot seasoned with wine.

Turkeys too are raised here and benefit as much as the others from the good quality corn and the outdoor life. In fact the corn forms the basis of some substantial foods for people as well as their poultry. Cruchades are small savoury biscuits made of corn flour. Broyo and miques are cornbreads or savoury puddings made by boiling the maize flour in vegetable bouillon until stiff enough to cut. They go perfectly with the numerous hearty stews and soups which form the backbone of the region's cookery — as if they were not already sufficiently filling!

13

Poule au pot is only one example. The great favourite is *garbure*, as substantial a stew as ever man invented. Made of large quantities of boiled potatoes and fresh vegetables, cooked together with ham and other meats, and poured onto slices of bread, *garbure* should be thick enough for the ladle to stand upright in the pot. Eat it not just with a spoon, but with knife and fork as well, and when — towards the bottom of the bowl — the heavy mixture seems to want liquid, it is permissible to pour in a glass of robust red wine (this is called *faire chabrot* or *goudale*). *A chaque saison sa garbure* is the saying, because the recipe, infinitely flexible, varies according to what vegetables are in season. Among the commonest of the other thick soups are *alicuit* (or *alicot*), literally cooked birds, a stew of vegetables and the giblets of chicken or turkey; and *estouffat*, a highly seasoned stew of vegetables and two or three kinds of meat (usually beef and bacon) cooked long and slow. *Daubes* and *civets* — both slow-cooked stews or casseroles of meat with red wine — will quite often be seen on country menus. Common in Béarn, *ouliat* is an onion soup (in the Bigorre Pyrenees it's called *toulia*); with garlic and tomatoes added it becomes a *tourin*; now add leeks and cheese and it becomes a *soupe de bergère*.

Wild birds, especially the pretty wood pigeon, are a particular target for Sunday afternoon sportsmen in this part of France. The wood pigeon — *palombe* — usually ends up in a *salmis*; it is first roasted then cooked in a sauce of red wine, onions, ham, and wild mushrooms. Quail (*caille*), partridge (*perdreau*) and woodcock (*bécasse*), roasted and stuffed, are much liked too. Although they are now protected by law even thrushes (*grives*) and larks (*alouettes*) are considered fair game — in the opinion of the local people, no bird is too small to be caught and cooked.

Cookery varies from one district to another; considerable topographical and cultural differences within South West France have inevitably led to different food specialities developing. The Pyreneans, for example, like stronger flavours than the people of the lowlands and the area contributes highly spiced charcuterie and piquant cheeses (both cow and sheep), as well as preserved hams. The Landes is also noted for its hams, although the Landes and the Bordeaux districts, closer to the Atlantic, favour fish dishes as much as meat. The Bassin d'Arcachon, the curious shallow inlet on the Landes coast, provides the perfect breeding ground for oysters — *huîtres d'Arcachon* have a considerable reputation not just in the South West, but all over France. In these maritime districts, lamb raised on the salty pastures near the sea or along the Gironde estuary (especially at Pauillac in the Médoc) makes a frequent appearance. Bordeaux, while perhaps not the most distinguished contributor to French cuisine, has devised at least one item of renown: the winey vegetable-based *sauce bordelaise* which makes a good companion for red meats. Apart from a bottle of good red wine poured into the pot, its other essential ingredients are shallots and bone-marrow. Local working people sometimes make a *sauce bordelaise* so thick, and with so much in it, that it can be eaten on its own or with bread.

Wine sauces, perhaps not surprisingly, feature strongly in the Bordelais. Crayfish *à la bordelaise* are cooked in a meat and vegetable base and served with a sauce made of local white wine. Lampreys, those strange creatures with such delicate flesh, are caught in the Gironde and served à la bordelaise in a thick sauce of red wine and their own blood. The cèpe mushroom (much used throughout the South West) can also be served in bordelaise style, but in this case the sauce does not include wine — though fresh grape juice can be used.

The desserts of the South West, like the main courses, mainly derive from the ideas of inland Gascony. Pastis gascon (or lou pastis) is a filling fruit pastry traditionally made with goose fat, though now butter is often used. More common, croustade is another sweet, cakey pastry with slices of apple. Cornmeal made from local maize is used for some traditional un-French puddings, which make only a rare appearance: millas (or milhassou), for example, is made by boiling the grain in milk with eggs, butter, and sugar. It will usually be flavoured with lemon juice or lemon peel or combined with some kind of fruit.

Fruit tends to be used quite liberally in this part of France. Very often it has been deliciously marinated in Armagnac before finding its way into the cakes and pastries. Productive fruit orchards along the Garonne mark the Armagnac's northern limits. Around Agen, for example, pruneaux (prunes) are a great speciality. Dozens of confiseurs in the town sell them stuffed (fourrée) and candied — an expensive delicacy. But prunes can be used equally well in savoury dishes, such as Oie farcie aux pruneaux, goose stuffed with prunes.

Gastronomically, as in other ways, two parts of South West France do not quite fit in with the rest, although there's a considerable overlap. The Toulousain, on the eastern boundaries of the region, looks as much to Languedoc as to Gascony for its gastronomic ideas. In and around Toulouse, Languedoc specialities such as cassoulet are widely available. Cassoulet is a tremendously substantial casserole, based on beans with plenty of pork, pork fat, confit d'oie, and sausage. Another unexpected speciality of Toulouse is made of violet flowers: these are crystallised and turned into a confectionery. Equally astonishing is that the roots of the violet can then be used to make a liqueur. Toulouse has numerous excellent restaurants, and is something of a focus for the cookery of both Gascony and Languedoc.

The Basque country, a land unto itself, follows its own traditions in cooking. Basques eat spicier food than either the Spanish or the French, making use of the delicately piquant piment d'Espelette pepper. A favourite local sauce, succulent and tasty, is made of peppers mixed with tomatoes; this can be cooked (sometimes with ham) in scrambled egg to make a popular starter — the sauce and the egg dish are both known by the same name, pipèrade. Like other South-Westerners, Basques are fond of soups and stews, and have their own specialities, especially Elzeckaria (vegetables) and Ttoro (fish). Food which is caught, gathered or hunted in the wild features even more strongly in Basque cuisine than in Gascon, especially cèpes mushrooms, pigeon, such game as wild boar, and of course, fish from the numerous inland rivers. But the preparation involves more complex seasoning. There are several varieties of strong spicy charcuterie — Loukinkos, Tripoxa, Xingara — and hams. Best known is the jambon de

Bayonne, so-called although it often originates in the Ossau valley in Béarn and is cured at Orthez. This fine salted ham can be eaten raw, in paper-thin slices; cooks make good use of it too in many a Basque dish. Goose products such as *confits* — often known as *lou trebuc* in the Basque country and Béarn — are certainly popular here, but much of the Basque cooking is done in butter and duck fat rather than goose fat. Ewes' milk cheeses made in the hills form a larger part of the diet, while for dessert, uncomplicated cakey desserts and flans (sometimes with fruit added) are traditional: *gâteau basque* is the obvious example. Excellent handmade chocolates and *touron*, a soft almond-paste confectionery with nuts, are particular specialities of the Basque coast, especially Bayonne, which for a long time was the only place in France where chocolate was made.

Wine

When one thinks of South West France, it is not only food which comes at once to mind, but also wine. To the English, the area around Bordeaux has been famous for centuries — since the days when Aquitaine was ruled by the Plantagenets — for excellent red wines, although it is also the greatest region in the world for sweet white wines, and produces some first-class dry whites too. Whole encyclopaedias have been written on the wines of Bordeaux, for the subject is a vast one. Indeed, many large volumes have been devoted just to small areas within the Bordeaux *vignoble* — Médoc, for example, and even the tiny neighbourhood around the village of Sauternes. In addition, the South

West has several other small but distinguished districts producing some outstanding wines ranging from the elegantly sweet white Jurançon to dark subtle reds such as Madiran.

BORDEAUX: All the *crus* and *Appellations* of the Bordeaux regions are explained in more detail in Chapter 3.

The Bordeaux wine region comprises the whole Gironde *département*; any wine produced within its borders is entitled to at least one of the general Bordeaux *Appellations* (Bordeaux, Bordeaux Supérieur, Bordeaux Rosé or Bordeaux Clairet), but there are some 35 other *Appellations* denoting that the wine has the notable qualities of a smaller district within the *département*. These vary considerably in size from extensive areas like Graves to tiny village-sized *Appellations* like Margaux. Within the Médoc and to a lesser extent some of the other districts, the relative merits of the châteaux (in the Bordeaux, a 'château' is any wine-making farm, whether grand or humble) are measured by a fairly complex — and arguably outdated — hierarchy of *crus* (page 41).

Inevitably, not every drop from such a hugely productive wine region reaches the standard that gives Bordeaux its reputation. On the other hand, the majority of Bordeaux red wines do indeed attain a worthy quality, and a startling number of the world's most sought-after and expensive red wines are made here. Using combinations of Merlot, Malbec, Cabernet Franc, and, especially important for its distinctive flavour, Cabernet Sauvignon grapes, the better reds possess a finesse and an extraordinary depth and complexity quite evident to even the most unaccustomed palate. They are well known for their ability to improve and mellow with age, often benefiting from being kept for well over twenty years.

The principal red wine districts are along both banks of the Gironde (Médoc and Haute-Médoc on the left, Côtes de Bourg and Premiers Côtes de Blaye on the right) and on the right bank of the river Dordogne (the St. Émilion, Fronsac and Pomerol districts, which include several small *Appellations*). Some other outstanding reds come from a few châteaux just south of Bordeaux, within the Graves *Appellation*, even though outside France this is often thought of as primarily a white wine district.

Dry white wines are not what Bordeaux is best at, although most are reasonable and a few are exceptional. Three grape varieties are combined — Sauvignon, Muscat and Semillon. The two main dry white districts are most of the triangle of land between the Garonne and Dordogne rivers (Entre-Deux-Mers) and, better, the left bank of the Garonne (Graves). However, for sweet white wines few other places can reach the standard set by Bordeaux. 80 per cent Semillon grapes are combined with 20 per cent Sauvignon Blanc; the sweetness results from the effects of a fungus, the all-important *pourriture noble* (noble rot) on the skins of ripe Semillon grapes, which dries out the juice and concentrates the sugar content. The main sweet white wine district is a small area on both sides of the Garonne, downriver from the town of Langon. Two of the little *Appellation* districts on the left bank (Barsac and Sauternes) have achieved an unparalleled reputation for their clean-tasting, elegant but extremely sweet 'dessert' wines, which are nowadays more likely

Checking the wine in a Médoc chai

to be taken as an aperitif, or with cheese or *foie gras*, than with dessert.

For centuries the entire wine production of the Bordeaux region was shipped to England in a vast fleet of specially adapted ships. A keen French desire to regain these vineyards was no insignificant factor in the course of the Hundred Years War. In these early days, and going back to the Roman period, all the wine was of the type known as Clairet — a light red — hence the English name for Bordeaux red wines, claret. Clairet, this original Bordeaux wine, is still made using the traditional *saignée* method — light pressing and short maceration. Because of its light colour Clairet is now sometimes regarded as a rosé. A glass of Clairet demonstrates forcibly how wines have improved over the years, for on the whole this is now one of the very

17

poorest in the Bordeaux area. It is not, however, unpleasant. Fruity, not bone dry, but fairly thin and acid, it is easy to drink and is one of those light, fresh wines, best served cool, which are sometimes described as 'perfect for summer drinking'. Certainly it is hard to imagine anyone fighting wars over it!

ARMAGNAC: Most of Armagnac produces surprisingly undistinguished white wines which, when distilled, become transmuted into the great brandy which bears the name of this old county (see page 164). And as well as making a fine *digéstif*, Armagnac is used in combination with grape juice to make two interesting aperitifs, Floc and Pousse-Rapière, which are much liked on their home ground, though rarely seen elsewhere. For brandy purposes, Armagnac has been divided into Haut-Armagnac (capital Auch), Ténarèze (capital Condom), and Bas-Armagnac (capital Eauze). Within these borders some of the grapes are made into a variety of ordinary *Vins de Pays* table wines; by far the best of them, crisp and slightly *pétillant* whites made from the Sauvignon grape, carry the label Côtes de Gascogne. The ancient Côtes de St. Mont vineyards east of Aire-sur-l'Adour produce drinkable *VDQS* reds, rosés and whites.

Beyond the brandy area, on Armagnac's northern and southern fringes, several other reasonable and some outstanding wines are produced. *Appellation* Côtes de Buzet, on the northern side (based around Nérac and Buzet), are good and relatively inexpensive reds and dry whites. In the same area *VDQS* wines carry the Côtes de Brulhois label. On the north-east edge of Armagnac, local wines include the St. Sardos *Vin de Pays*. On the southern

side, also very good and still little known outside the region are the wines of the Madiran *Appellation* (a rural area on the left bank of the Adour). The dark strong Madiran reds, using the unusual Tannat grape, age magnificently. They are almost too robust in their early years, and are not sold at all until nearly two years old, but after some eight or ten years they become deeply mellow and enjoyable. They improve further with the passing of a few more years, and some say that even 50 years is not too long for a Madiran. They are a boon for visitors to the South West, allowing an opportunity to enjoy rich, mature red wines which perfectly accompany the Gascon cuisine at remarkably low cost. Among the best producers in Madiran are Peyros, Barréjat, and Laplace.

From a small corner of the Madiran comes a little-known sweet white wine called Pacherenc-de-Vic-Bilh. Pacherenc, it seems, is the name of the grape, while Vic-Bilh, locals explain, means something like 'old villages'. The wine is of a high quality, heady and strong, with a curious flavour.

THE PYRENEES: One of the most interesting wines of the South West comes from the Jurançon district, along the left bank of the Gave, just south of Pau at the foot of the Pyrenees. With a distinctive, pronounced but agreeable taste, Jurançon is a delicately sweet white wine (which many consider an ideal accompaniment to *foie gras*). Gros Manseng grapes are the main ingredient for a medium-sweet Jurançon, while the grander and even sweeter wine is made with Petit Manseng. Jurançon producers seem almost too conscious of the vagaries of the Béarn climate and of the fluctuating and generally declining market for 'dessert' wines. As well as making small quantities of their best sweet vintages, which call for late harvesting (with the risk of the crop being ruined by snow), they have come up with various ideas that give something to fall back on when either the harvest or the market is difficult. For example, at the growers' *Cave Coopérative* at Gan, some vintages are blended under the label Viguerie Royale and aged about five years; while the fanciful label Apéritif de Henri-IV denotes a Jurançon made of very ripe Gros Manseng grapes, to be drunk within the year. But Prestige d'Automne, from late-gathered Petit Manseng which have been subject to *pourriture noble*, is a 'real' Jurançon Rich and full, this benefits from aging for some 15 years, and does not really need to be served chilled.

There are dry white Jurançons as well, which can be harvested relatively early. Nowadays Jurançon growers turn more and more of their annual harvest into the dry wine — the Grain Sauvage from the *Cave Coopérative* is popular — and although some of these are perfectly acceptable they are on the whole much less remarkable than the area's traditional sweet and semi-sweet wines.

Most of the other vineyards farther west or south are producing the reds, whites, and especially the light rosés of the Vins de Béarn *Appellation*.

PAYS BASQUE AND LANDES: The Basque hills are in general not devoted to growing grapes, with the exception of the Irouléguy district spreading from Bidarray to St. Jean-Pied-de-Port. Here inexpensive rosés and (a more recent development) reds and whites are made, almost entirely for local consumption. They vary in quality, and some are refreshing and highly drinkable, though on the whole Irouléguy wines do not climb much above the standard of drinkable *ordinaire*. The Pays Basque avails itself too of the odd Vin de Sable from the Landes, so-named because it is indeed grown in soil which consists almost completely of sand. Among the better Landes wines are the reds, rosés, and dry whites of Tursan, an inexpensive *VDQS* from near the little town of Geaune close to the border with Armagnac.

THE COUNTY OF TOULOUSE: For drinkable, unpretentious table wines Toulouse looks not so much west towards Armagnac as east towards the red *Vin de Pays* of the Côtes du Tarn and, better, the reds and whites of the Gaillac *Appellation*. Gaillac's best, the bright, white, slightly *pétillant* Perlé, is refreshing and palatable. The other local wine of Toulouse comes from a smaller *Appellation* district just north of the city, Côtes de Fronton, producing an enjoyable and bargain-priced red. Farther north, on the banks of the Garonne and the Tarn, there are some enjoyable if unremarkable local *Vins de Pays* and a *VDQS*, Vin de Lavilledieu.

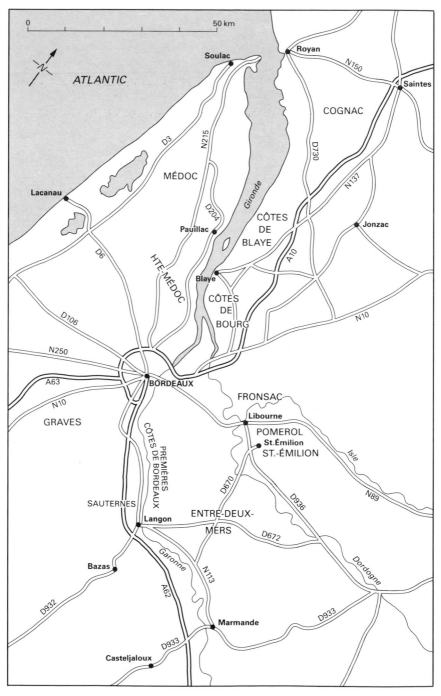

3
Bordeaux & the Great Vineyards

The heart of medieval English France, the pivot around which the rest of Aquitaine has always turned, is Bordeaux and the navigable stretches of river which converge upon it. Along the banks of these great waterways — the Garonne, Dordogne and Gironde — prestigious vineyards thrive as they have done for nearly 2,000 years. Today the very name of Bordeaux brings fine wines to mind. The vineyards which enclose the city, which even penetrate into the streets of its suburbs, produce the largest quantities and some of the best-known names of the French wine industry (see page 33).

The region still has a certain indefinable affinity with England. Many great châteaux are owned by English (and Irish) families who settled here centuries ago. Local people know enough of their own history to remember that the English proved relatively tolerant and easy masters, and that Bordeaux's wines have always been highly respected by their neighbours across the Channel. (Britain is still the world's largest importer of Bordeaux wines.) It is curious too that the Bordelais — the people of Bordeaux and its region — have a reputation for being more phlegmatic and reserved than other Frenchmen: the same characteristics which are attributed to the English themselves.

Bordeaux (pop: 211,000; including suburbs: 624,300), the great city at the 'edge of the waters' (as its name implies), has a tremendous atmosphere of history, solidity and prosperity. It fairly radiates an awareness of its ancient importance. The old heart of the city stands impressively along the south bank of the wide Garonne, which curves handsomely here to form a magnificent harbour known because of its shape as Port de la Lune ('moon port'). Bordeaux's city crest has long shown the harbour in heraldic form, as a silver crescent with blue waves. The waterfront — river and quays — still presents a stirring spectacle, a broad view of which can be enjoyed from the Pont de Pierre, the superb 19th-century bridge which spans the river in 17 arches.

Its accessibility by river and sea has made Bordeaux a vital trading centre since the distant Gallic past. It was natural that the Romans should enlarge the town, then called Burdigala, and make it a local administrative capital. Under their rule, the city thrived on its trade with Rome, Britain and the rest of the empire.

Overleaf: *Elaborate fountains of the Monument des Girondins in Bordeaux*

21

Tens of thousands of *amphorae* filled with local wine travelled in big trading vessels along the Garumna (Garonne) from Burdigala. None of this importance was lost under the Visigothic and Frankish dominion, and when Aquitaine was united with England under the Plantagenet crown, Bordeaux became the major point of contact between the monarch's English and French territories. Once again, wine ships made up a large proportion of the huge merchant fleet operating from the city's docks, with some 300 vessels departing from Bordeaux fully laden with the new vintage each autumn. Some English people preferred to live in this southern, balmier part of the kingdom, and there was a good deal of settlement from across the Channel.

During the Hundred Years War, when France tried to conquer the English territories while England tried to expand them, the Black Prince, son of Edward III made his court here (1356–71). Although he was so-called only because of the colour of his armour, his reputation was black indeed outside the English domains. He terrorised large areas of southern and western France, destroying and pillaging. His premature death from illness was a severe setback to the English side in the war.

Bordeaux and its village neighbours were the last corner of Aquitaine to be retaken by the French, in 1453 as the Hundred Years War came to its end. Returned to the control of the French king, the city suffered a certain depression, and the merchant class lost many of the civil rights they had enjoyed under the English. Dealing with their discontent and rebelliousness posed a problem for several generations of French kings. Louis XI introduced the Parlement de Guyenne which enabled Bordeaux to have a certain measure of self-rule, but resentment of the French monarch flared up from time to time. The *gabelle*, or salt tax, not popular anywhere in France, led to furious rioting when it was introduced here in 1548. One of the many important reforms instituted by Cardinal Richelieu was the system of Intendants — local governors — appointed by the crown, which restrained the Bordeaux Parlement's tendency towards complete autonomy. This was perhaps why the city keenly supported the Fronde Insurrection (1648–52) against the rule of Cardinal Mazarin during the minority of the King, Louis XIV.

Although Bordeaux was clearly anti-Royalist, its liberalism and moderation did not go down at all well with the dictatorial leaders of the 1789 Revolution. At the Revolutionary parliament, the National Assembly, Bordeaux's representatives were 'moderate revolutionaries' who supported the original more humanitarian and anti-authoritarian ideals of the Revolution. This 'party' within the Assembly were called Girondins, and had support from representatives of other regions too. Of course in the end the Girondins lost the day, the 22 leaders being executed by the more fanatical Jacobin forces which were in the ascendant. During the period of the Terror which followed (1793–4), a further 300 people considered insufficiently in accord with the authoritarian, centralist Jacobins were executed in one of Bordeaux's main squares (but this was only a small number compared with those guillotined during the Terror in some other French cities).

Ironically, it is to the despised period of the French monarchy that Bordeaux owes most for its present appearance and atmosphere. During the 18th cen-

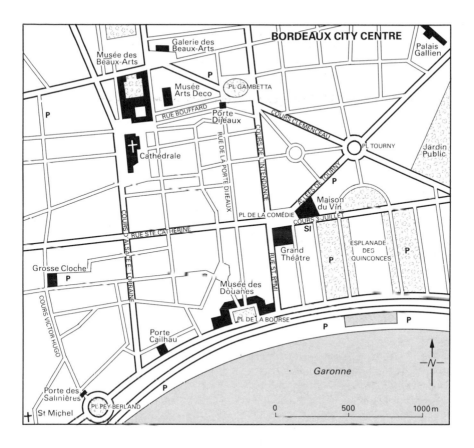

tury before the Revolution, under the government of its royal Intendants, much of the city had been grandly reconstructed, and at the same time had benefited enormously from growing transatlantic and far-eastern trade, as well as a rapid increase in the production and consumption of Bordeaux wines. 19th- and 20th-century Bordeaux continued the expansion, and for brief periods during the Franco-Prussian War (1870–1) and at the beginning of the First World War the city was considered important — and safe — enough for the seat of the government of France to be transferred here from Paris. After the Second World War the city made another advance with the election of Jacques Chaban-Delmas as its mayor. Dynamic, youthful, radical, he met opposition at first from the local establishment of wealthy vine-growers; overcoming this resistance he was able to bring about an enlargement of the port, so drawing new industries to the town, and creating a more general prosperity for its citizens. Bordeaux has since grown further to become a large provincial university city with extensive industrial suburbs. Yet it retains at its heart, and carefully protects, a magnificent old quarter where the town had its origins.

Almost the whole of the *vieille ville*

25

and city centre consists today of substantial and imposing 18th-century stone buildings. It is worthwhile taking the time to go amongst them on foot, strolling along the town's chic main boulevards and historic narrow back streets, several of which are traffic-free.

There are many good places to start a walk round the old quarter; since car parking in Bordeaux can be difficult, one possibility would be to begin from the big parking area which extends along both sides of the tree-lined esplanade (or place) des Quinconces, which is dominated by its fabulous, amazingly elaborate Monuments des Girondins, a memorial erected in 1894 in honour of the executed Girondins. Other statues in the square recall two distinguished citizens: Montaigne (1533–92), the influential political philosopher whose liberal ideas were spelled out in his *Essais,* who became the city's mayor, and Montesquieu (1689–1755), another important liberal political thinker (he argued that the legislature, the executive, and the judiciary should each be independent of the others — a cornerstone of modern democratic ideas), who was elected president of its Parlement. As a starting point for a look at the city centre, the esplanade has the advantage that the main Office du Tourisme is very close by, on the corner of allées d'Orléans (the road running along the south side of the esplanade) and busy cours 30-Juillet.

Opposite the Office du Tourisme is the Maison du Vin, with information for understanding or buying local wines and visiting vineyards. The short cours 30-Juillet opens into spacious place de la Comédie, which has always been one of the focal points of the centre of Bordeaux. During the Roman period, the city's forum stood here, and the temple. All along one side rise the Corinthian columns and imposing frontage of the Grand Théâtre which gives the square its name. Built in 1773 by Victor Louis on the site of the old Roman temple (cleared away as recently as 1680 on the orders of Louis XIV), the theatre is one of the best examples of this classically-inspired style; the Muses and goddesses, standing on a balustrade above the columns, are really astonishing. The sumptuous interior is no less impressive.

Cross the square to reach rue Ste. Cathérine, which soon intersects rue de la Porte Dijeaux. These two straight and narrow pedestrian thoroughfares are the principal axes of the *vieille ville.* The Porte Dijeaux itself, in the busy place Gambetta, is one of a number of gateways and triumphal arches which can be seen around the town. Some are remains of the original city gates into the town through the city walls, although the ramparts themselves have since disappeared, but Porte Dijeaux, like the fine *place* in which it stands, was erected as part of the great 18th-century reconstruction.

Take rue Bouffard to Bordeaux's city-centre landmark, the Cathédrale St. André, in the centre of place Pey-Berland. This could almost be called Bordeaux's 'museum quarter'. On the way down rue Bouffard you will see, in the 18th-century mansion Hôtel de Lalande, the Musée des Arts Décoratifs (Decorative Arts). Among other museums close at hand are the Musée Beaux-Arts (Fine Arts), the entrance to which is in cours d'Albret; Musée Jean

Bordeaux: the Grand Théâtre, pl de la Comédie

Moulin (interesting collections relating to the Resistance, deportation, and the Nazi occupation), in place Jean Moulin just off place Pey-Berland; and the Musée d'Aquitaine (regional history and important archaeological finds), in cours Pasteur.

Facing the cathedral, Bordeaux's Hôtel de Ville is housed in the grandeur of the 18th-century episcopal palace (it can be visited). The cathedral itself, with its slender elaborate Gothic spires, is quite interesting, if uncared for. Started in the 11th century, the building was added to over the centuries and underwent many changes during the Gothic period. In the 19th century it suffered tragically at the hands of the architect Paul Abadie, whose 'restoration' ruined a number of fine French cathedrals. Here his improvements included the demolition and removal of the cloisters. The most notable feature now is the Porte Royale (royal door) on the north side, with its 13th-century statuary. Inside, there is a striking contrast between the original wide, aisleless nave and the immense Gothic choir which took over 100 years to build (the whole of the 14th century). Standing separate from the cathedral is a highly decorated mid-15th-century belfry, the Tour Pey-Berland.

From the belfry, turn down rue des Trois Conils, which meets rue Ste. Cathérine at place St. Projet. Turn right along rue Ste. Cathérine, one of the old quarter's main pedestrian streets. It takes a straight course to another of the proud gateways built in the 1750s, the Porte d'Aquitaine in place de la Victoire. About midway between place St. Projet and Porte d'Aquitaine, turn into the imposing cours Victor Hugo, soon reaching the Grosse Cloche (great bell) which stands astride rue St. James on

The Grosse Cloche at Bordeaux, one of the city's distinctive landmarks since the Middle Ages

the left. The Grosse Cloche, a belfry over a gateway, was originally the site of one of the 13th-century city gates and was later incorporated into Bordeaux's 15th-century English town hall. In those days its bell was the bringer of all good and bad tidings to the local people, and was rung to announce the start of the all-important annual *vendanges*, grape harvest. It is still viewed as something of a symbol of the city by many of its natives. A little farther down cours Victor Hugo, rue des Faures on the right leads to Tour St. Michel. This is the belltower of the spacious 14th- and 15th-century Basilique St. Michel, though it stands separate from it. (There do seem to be a lot of belfries in Bordeaux.) The modern stained glass inside the church is the work of Max Ingrand. The hexagonal Tour, including the spire, soars to 114 metres, making it, so locals claim, the 'highest tower in the Midi'.

Return to cours Victor Hugo along rue de la Fusterie. This comes to Porte de Salinières, which faces the old stone bridge across the Garonne, the pont de Pierre. Formerly called Porte de Bourgogne ('Burgundy Gate'), Porte de Salinières was built in 1775 as part of the city's ambitious 18th-century building programme. Follow the quais — that is, the main road beside the Garonne — passing Porte Cailhau, set back down a side road on the left. The name means (in *langue d'oc*) Stone Gate, and this remarkable-looking structure has a more interesting history than most of the other gateways. It started life in 1309 as the entrance into the palace of the dukes of Aquitaine. Obviously, the palace later became a prized possession of the Plantagenet kings, so when Bordeaux had been retaken by the French, Porte Cailhau was rebuilt (1495) as a triumphal arch in honour of Charles VIII.

A few paces farther along quai de la Douane one arrives at place de la Bourse, which is the highlight of this old waterfront area. The curved place forms a magnificent ensemble of attractive and dignified 18th-century architecture looking out across the river. The architects were Jacque-Ange Gabriel and his son, and the place was designed and constructed slowly, one building at a time, over a period of some 17 years. The first to be completed, in 1738, was the Douane (Customs House), clearly an important office in that period of flourishing sea trade. The Bourse (Exchange), perhaps equally vital to the town's prosperity, was completed in 1749. The Musée des Douanes (Museum of Customs and Excise) in the place has a curious collection of material relating to customs duties and customs officers throughout the ages.

Walk away from the river along rue Philippart, at once reaching the small paved square place de Parlement, which looks delightful and inviting with its restaurant tables laid with their linen and wine glasses.

From this point it is easy to wander out of the old quarter and back to place de la Comédie. This is one of the focal points of the busier, broader streets of the present-day town centre, bounded by what Bordeaux residents call *Le Triangle*. The other corners of the triangle are place Tourny and place Gambetta, and the streets which connect them are cours de l'Intendance, cours Clémenceau, and allées de Tourny — all have a good deal more traffic, more crowds, more money, and more chic than the humbler back alleys of the *vieille ville*. They have no less charm either, in their way, with plenty of ornate style in a grand 18th-century way. The artist Goya lived at 57 cours de l'Intendance, where he died in 1828. Place Gambetta was where the guillotine stood and was kept busy at its gruesome work during the Terror; the square is just a public garden now. Allées de Tourny is named after the man who was largely responsible, during his term of office (1743–57) as Intendant, for the extensive rebuilding of Bordeaux at that time. A statue of him can be seen in place Tourny.

Ideal for a quiet sit down or a picnic away from the crowd, the pleasant Jardin Public (public gardens) lies back from cours de Verdun, a few minutes' walk from place Tourny. At the far end of the gardens there's a natural history museum. Beyond the gardens, the ruins of the amphitheatre of Roman Burdigala stand ignored just off rue Fondaudège. Known as the Palais Gallien, this remnant — just a section of wall and a few arches remain of the 3rd-century arena which could once seat 15,000 spectators — shows something of the extent of Roman Burdigala. Also worth seeing in streets a little outside the central area are the church of St. Seurin (in place des Martyrs de la Résistance), mainly 12th, 14th, and 16th centuries, standing at the site of a paleo-Christian settlement; the interesting and effective new development of Mériadeck (along rue Claude Bonnier); and (north of place André Meunier, near the river) the Romanesque 12th-century church of Ste. Croix, once part of a prosperous abbey, which unfortunately, like the cathedral, was absurdly 'restored' by Abadie.

There's nearly always something interesting going on in Bordeaux, with daily markets and 15 café-theatres. Throughout the summer months there are exhibitions at the Galérie des Beaux-Arts. Above all, in May the city holds its annual Music and Dance Festival, two weeks of first-class entertainment. Perhaps because of the juxtaposition of Bordeaux's awesome industry and docks with its equally awesome vineyards, one cannot help but view the Bordelais (the word means both the people and the district of Bordeaux) as knowing both how to work and how to play. Drinking good wine and selling it have been local customs at least since Roman times: many of the great vineyards were planted in that era. However it was not until the 17th and 18th centuries, with the development of techniques permitting the mass production of bottles and corks, that wines from the Bordelais achieved the high reputation which they hold today.

The city of Bordeaux remains as always the commercial centre of what has become, in effect, France's most successful wine region, covering an area of some 135,000 hectares (a third of a million acres). Altogether there are about 8,000 wine châteaux in the Gironde département, where the name 'château' means any farm where grapes are grown for making into Appellation Contrôlée wine; some are indeed châteaux — castles or mansions — but many are ordinary family houses surrounded by their vines. Another feature of the Bordelais terminology is that despite the value and high quality of the wines, the Appellation Contrôlée classification is awarded to areas (encompassing several châteaux, producing wines of differing standards), rather than to individual growers. Individual châteaux may in places be better distinguished by their cru classification, especially in the Médoc districts, where the cru categorisation is comprehensive, although an old cru classification may not reflect the present standing of a château. These idiosyncrasies of the Bordeaux region make it a little harder than in some other areas to learn which wines are the very best — a great deal of experimentation is required! One further remarkable feature of the Bordeaux vignoble is that it excels at all three types of French wine: crisp dry whites, rich sweet whites, and hearty full-bodied reds.

The best of the Graves Appellation is surprisingly close to the centre of Bordeaux, with the distinguished Château Haut-Brion standing in the south-western suburbs. Important near-neighbours of Haut-Brion are Château La Mission Haut Brion, Château Les Carmes Haut Brion, Château La Tour

Haut Brion, and Château Pape-Clément. There are several famous producers around the village of **Léognan** (on the D651, about 14km from the city centre), notably Domaine de Chevalier, Château Haut-Bailly, Château Larrivet-Haut-Brion, Château de la Louvière and Château Fieuzal. At **Martillac**, where there are other good wine châteaux. **Labrède** is best known for something other than wine: Montesquieu (1689–1755) was born here at Château de la Brède (open for visits). The town's church has a good Romanesque facade. At **Portets**, Château Cheret-Pitres makes rich red wines and only small quantities of white; nearby Château Rahoul, although for some a little too modern and scientific in its approach to wine, produces outstanding results. On the way back, pause at **Cadaujac** for the interesting (if variable) wines of Château Bouscaut, on the left of the main road, and very shortly after, at Château Couhins, one of the best of the classic dry white wines of Graves. Although most Graves wines are good dry whites, richer and with more character than those of Entre-Deux-Mers, some of these better-known châteaux may with justice be even prouder of their reds than their white wines.

The prettiest of the Bordeaux wine country lies all to the city's east. To explore it in leisurely fashion, leave Bordeaux by crossing the brown waters of the Garonne over the pont de Pierre. Turn right at once (onto the D113) to follow the north bank of the river; the rushing water can be glimpsed through roadside trees. Although no one would claim that the Garonne, at this stage in its journey, is clean and pure, the water is not as polluted as its murky colour might suggest; the bottom is sandy, and this stretch of river is tidal and dis-

turbed. On the other side of this quiet, shady road are grand houses. Many are 18th-century bungalows, known as *chartreuses*. At Latresne, join the D10, turning right to continue upriver through a succession of vineyards and wine villages.

Although they are 'between the two seas' of the Garonne and the Dordogne, these belong to the Premières Côtes de Bordeaux district and produce mainly good reds and a few medium-sweet white wines. This countryside along the Garonne banks used once to be marshland, but during the Middle Ages the English brought in Flemish (i.e. Dutch) experts to drain and cultivate the land. Now it is delightful country. Each village has its small Romanesque church.

At the small town of **Cadillac** can be seen the Bordeaux area's only true Renaissance château (that is, a château of the 'Loire valley' type). The dry moat which surrounds it always was dry. Built in the early 17th century, the château was long ago partly destroyed, its stone being sold to build the local mansions. It was, in addition, a women's prison for over a hundred years; a few cells remain. Nevertheless it has some good features inside, including lovely painted ceilings, which were preserved in good condition by having been covered over, and vast, beautiful marble fireplaces. Lately it has benefited from restoration. Cadillac was originally an English *bastide*, built in the 13th century; River Gate and Clock Gate survive of its old fortifications. Today the little town is a charming local agricultural centre, and peasant farmers come every Saturday to its covered market square to sell their produce.

At **Loupiac** sweet white wines are made, for which the village constitutes a small *Appellation* in its own right. A 3rd-century Roman villa, around which Loupiac grew, has been excavated in one of the vine fields here. Mosaics in the villa indicate that it was occupied by the noted poet Ausonius, although it is not clear at what period in his life. Farther on, **Ste. Croix-du-Mont**, another sweet white wine village with its own *Appellation*, is a pretty place on a hill (hence the name) with good views. The church, together with a former fortress which now houses the Mairie (town hall) and school, stand on a lofty terrace. From this point the famous wine château d'Yquem can be seen on a crest on the far side of the Garonne. To its left, the immense forest of the Landes stretches into the far distance. On close inspection, the 'Mont' of Ste. Croix is somewhat strange; its many caves and grottoes show that the hill was created by prehistoric crustaceans; it is made entirely of their shells.

The History of Bordeaux Wines

When the Romans conquered what is now Aquitaine in the middle of the 1st century BC, one of their first acts was to plant grape vines on the right bank of the Dordogne (around St. Émilion) and along the left bank of the Garonne (the present-day Graves area). Cultivation was extended and refined along both rivers throughout the Roman era, which continued until the 5th century ad. After the Roman withdrawal, vineyard ownership was largely taken over by the land-owning monastic communities. During all this long period, the Bordeaux region produced only light red wine (*clairet*) using a short maceration period. It is recorded that flavour and digestibility were exceptionally good, but that the wine had to be very young and had no keeping quality. (In any case, all wines were drunk young by modern standards as suitable airtight containers did not yet exist in which they could be aged and matured.) This assessment seems remarkable now; to modern tastes *clairet* — though light, crisp, and easy to drink — is the least distinguished of Bordeaux wines.

The period of English rule, from the 13th to the 15th centuries, saw vineyards being acquired by English merchants and there was a further expansion of the wine industry to satisfy the huge demand from England for Bordeaux *clairets*. During the 17th and 18th centuries a rising 'new rich' class caused yet more land to be purchased for vine cultivation, mainly along the banks of the Gironde. Even at that time, Bordeaux wines were typically *clairets*, with highest prices being paid for wines from areas some of which are today considered the most inferior parts of the Bordeaux region.

A transformation took place in the 18th century, when large-scale manufacture of bottles and corks permitted the ageing of wines, which greatly enhanced some of them, especially in the Médoc. Matured wines varied considerably in quality, so in 1855 a hierarchy of *crus* was formalised at the request of Napoleon III. Early this century, *cru* gradings were introduced for the other top Bordeaux wine districts. In the 1930s the system of *Appellation d'Origine Contrôlée* established the different characteristics of each district. Since then Bordeaux has gone on to become the most productive quality wine region in the world.

The Bordeaux *Appellations*

(Note that in all *Appellation* districts there are producers who do not make the local traditional wine. For example, there are châteaux in the Sauternais making dry white wines.)

Along the left bank of the Gironde and the Garonne

MÉDOC (all red): Médoc, Haut-Médoc, St. Éstephe, Pauillac. St. Julien, Listrac, Moulis, Margaux
GRAVES (some red, mostly dry white): Graves, Graves Supérieur
SAUTERNAIS (sweet white): Cérons, Barsac, Sauternes

Between the Dordogne and the Garonne, and along the left bank of the Dordogne

Dry white: Entre-Deux-Mers, Graves-de-Vayres
Sweet white: Ste. Foy-Bordeaux

Along the right bank of the Garonne

Red: Premières Côtes de Bordeaux
Sweet white: Premières Côtes de Bordeaux, Cadillac, Loupiac, St. Croix-du-Mont, Côtes de Bordeaux-St. Macaire

Along the right bank of the Gironde and the Dordogne

BOURG AND BLAYE: Côtes de Blaye (dry white), Premières Côtes de Blaye (red), Côtes de Bourg (red, dry white)
FRONSAC, POMEROL, AND LE ST. ÉMILION (all red): Fronsac, Canon-Fronsac, Pomerol, Lalande-de-Pomerol, St. Émilion, Lussac-St. Émilion, Montagne-St. Émilion, Puisseguin-St. Émilion, St. Georges-St. Émilion, Bordeaux-Côtes de Castillon, Bordeaux-Côtes de Francs

---

All other wines produced in the Bordeaux wine region are entitled to one of the general *Appellations*: Bordeaux (red, dry white), Bordeaux Supérieur (red, sweet white), Bordeaux Rosé (rosé), Bordeaux Clairet (light red, sometimes described as rosé).

St. Macaire, another few kilometres upriver, is an old village which was rebuilt as a *bastide*. Its walls survive, and the central square, place du Mercadier (which is Gascon for market), is still beautifully arcaded. The church, originally Romanesque, was 'modernised' in the Gothic period. With everything made of attractive honey-coloured stone, giving a mellow reflection of the bright sunlight, on a fine day it is blissful to wander within the tranquil central area. The newer, livelier part of the village is along the N113, which skirts the old centre and crosses the Garonne. St. Macaire produces sweet white wines with their own *Appellation*, Côtes de Bordeaux St. Macaire.

33

St. Macaire wines are not bad, but take the N113 to the other side of the river to make a short tour of the greatest sweet white wine districts in the world. At first, on reaching the Garonne's south shore, the road runs into **Langon**, which itself is in the area (rather a sprawling one) covered by the Graves *Appellation*. The Graves wine district extends right back from Langon to Bordeaux, the vineyards heavily interspersed in places with the Landes *pignadas* (pine woods), and produces good quality red and dry white wines. Langon is a prosperous little local commercial centre, with a notable restaurant (the chef is a member of the gastronomic Darroze clan) and although not an especially interesting town it makes a very good base for exploring both banks of the Garonne.

The N113 continues north from Langon along the Garonne's left bank, immediately finding itself passing through the vineyards of the Sauternais. The village of Sauternes itself lies to the south west, while the road heads towards the almost equally illustrious neighbouring village **Barsac**, close to the river, which has its own *Appellation* quite separate from Sauternes. Beyond, the N113 continues 3km further to arrive at **Cérons**, another Sauternais sweet wine village with its own *Appellation*, although a little less distinguished than the other two.

From Barsac, turn back on country roads towards Sauternes, or, if coming from Langon, leave town on the D8, signposted Villandraut, at once entering the Sauternais *vignoble*. After 7km turn right where signposted for Château d'Yquem.

Standing in idyllic rural calm surrounded by vines, the château is medieval with many later additions, and has not been lived in for some time. The building itself is not the point though — and it is fitting that the châteaux's owner, the Count of Lurs-Saluces, is mayor of the five villages of the Sauternes commune, since Yquem is the very essence of the name Sauternes, and is, besides, the crown to the whole art of making sweet (or dessert) wine. Anyone may stop and park at the château and stroll around the vine fields and the courtyard, but to have a peep inside the *chais* where the wine is made is nearly impossible. There are good views back across the valley to Mont Ste. Croix, on which we stood earlier admiring the Sauternais in the distance.

The Yquem vineyard covers about 100 hectares (250 acres), and produces only about 60,000 bottles per year: say one glass of wine from a square metre of vineyard. Sauternes is made from approximately 80 per cent Semillon and 20 per cent Sauvignon grapes, with just a few Muscat. The *pourriture noble* sucks away the liquid from inside each grape, shrivelling it, and leaving a condensed residue of fruit sugar inside. The resulting wine is devastatingly sweet — the popular adjective is 'luscious'.

Conditions are right for *pourriture noble* in a number of small areas on both banks of the Garonne. The rot finds its paradise in the fields of the Sauternais. The land here is warm for much of the year; its slopes overlook the confluence of the little river Ciron and the broad Garonne. As it happens, the waters of the Ciron are much cooler than those of the Garonne, and during the chill nights of autumn this causes a dense mist which hangs over the meeting point of the valleys. In autumn, as the grapes reach ripeness, the moist air, slowly warmed by the southern sun as the day progresses, clings to the grapes until as late as noon. In this warm

Château d'Yquem, at Sauternes, which produces one of the most celebrated sweet wines in the world

humidity the fungus thrives on the grape skins, making each of the little fruits precious — so precious, indeed, that during the harvest each grape is cut individually, instead of, as is normal elsewhere, being clipped off in bunches. The harvest can therefore last a long time in the Sauternes district, often as long as two months, from 20 September until 20 November. For harvesting, the ideal conditions are said to be mist until lunchtime, then the grapes can be gathered after lunch when the air is warm and dry. The preferred workers for the grape harvest are old women, who are reputed to be slower, more patient, less forceful than men or younger women, and so less likely to damage the tender rotten grapes or to pick them before they are completely ready.

Travelling partly out of vines and into tobacco fields, country roads lead to **Bazas**, an important little Roman town which was a bishopric from the 5th century onwards, and in the Middle Ages became a *bastide*. It remains protected by ramparts, and at its centre has a lovely main square, spacious and arcaded, overlooked by the richly decorated Romanesque portals of a grand cathedral, St. Jean Baptiste. Originally 13th-century, it was reconstructed from 1576 to 1635 after being damaged by Protestants. It lost its cathedral status in 1790, and is now more correctly known as a basilica. The interior startles by its proportions, unexpectedly large for such a small town (pop: 2,000). There is excellent red and blue stained glass, and the ambulatory is very fine, with impressive chapels. The early Gothic stonework is quite simple, but elegant, and on a big scale. At night the cathedral is illuminated to good effect. Whether by day or by night, the square looks attractive, with several 16th- and 17th-century mansions. The Alchemist's House is particularly striking, and now houses the town's tourist office. On Saturdays an important cattle market makes the square even more picturesque.

Turn back west along the D3 and north on the D932 or the D223 towards the Château de Roquetaillade. Outwardly this is a handsome little medieval fortress combining two structures, one dating from the 12th century, the other built in 1306 by another nephew of Pope Clement V. It has six splendid round towers and a square keep. The palatial interior is mainly of later date, with magnificently vaulted rooms, restored frescoes and vast fireplaces. The castle was furnished in an excessively ornate style by its 19th-century restorer Viollet-le-Duc.

Return on the D222 through Langon and across to St. Macaire and the north bank of the Garonne. Continue eastwards beside the river along the N113 through the *Appellation* district Côtes de Bordeaux St. Macaire and into the more distinguished dry white wine area, Entre-Deux-Mers. Pause at **La Réole**, a strategically situated old market and wine town with some picturesque corners and many interesting buildings. At the summit of the town, see the extraordinary Romanesque 12th-century Hôtel de Ville with its ground-floor market (this is one of the few civic buildings which survive from that era); and the ancient Benedictine abbey, with its impressive staircases and 13th-century abbey church of St.

Pierre. It has clear views over the Garonne to the vines on the other side. The N113 continues across the Gironde border, out of the Bordeaux wine country and into the Armagnac region (now usually known as Gascony). To see more of the great Bordeaux vineyards, turn away north from the Garonne. The Garonne is tidal as far inland as La Réole, but the tide rarely reaches any farther upriver, and the Entre-Deux-Mers region reaches its limit shortly after the town. The D670 takes a direct route through the heart of the Entre-Deux-Mers *Appellation* district, allowing a view of many places of interest in the area. For a more meandering route, left and right turns off the through road allow you to make discoveries among the vine-covered countryside.

The Entre-Deux-Mers region, France's largest *Appellation* district, is entirely devoted to white grapes (mostly Sauvignon, Semillon, and Muscat varieties), which are used to produce clear, pale white wines with a crisp, bone-dry but delicately fruity character. They do not attain the highest levels of quality, and are mainly made in village *Caves Coopératives*. Their lightness and brightness feels characteristic of the whole area; even the vine bushes appear to have a pale colour. They are planted farther apart than in other wine districts, and grown a little taller, specifically to allow a greater exposure to sunlight. And the tidal waters of the rivers Garonne and Dordogne, between which the region is enclosed, seem almost to carry some of the freshness of the sea air into these rolling inland hills. As well as the large fields of neatly tended vines, this gently undulating peaceful countryside is made attractive by other agriculture and by the many little woods and copses, and there are villages well worth a pause.

Sauveterre-de-Guyenne, a small *bastide* built in 1281, still has all four gateways, substantial and arched, and a spacious market square enclosed by pavements beneath stone arcades.

Westwards across the Entre-Deux-Mers hills, the pleasant small town of **Créon**, an old *bastide* which does not preserve much of its original appearance, has a remarkable abbey church known as La Sauve-Majeur. Constructed between 1079 and 1231, now partly ruined, this building retains an imposing octagonal tower and several fine capitals. To the north, the shallow, gravelly river Dordogne marks the northern boundary of the Entre-Deux-Mers region.

Across the river is an altogether different wine region, producing some of the most distinguished and powerful rich reds of the Bordelais. This is the area loosely known as Le St. Émilion, encompassing several notable *Appellations*. During the English rule, St. Émilion wines were awarded the title *vin honorifique* (honourable), signifying that they were of suitably high quality to be offered to the king himself. The vineyards are superbly well kept, many with red roses growing at the end of each row of bushes. Around the villages or towns the châteaux stand proudly alone within their valuable fields; if they are not real châteaux, many are dignified mansions, rich country houses, with beautifully manicured walled gardens.

After crossing the Dordogne, the D670 turns sharply left to follow the river's right bank; almost at once a right turn is signposted for St. Émilion. This road passes through the vineyards of Château Ausone, one of the greatest names

of St. Émilion wines, to approach the town from the south.

St. Émilion (pop: 3,000) is a good deal more than just an important wine village. It is a remarkable-looking small town, and a historic one. For centuries it was in effect a strategic frontier city on the border between England and France, or at least between English and French territories, and was defensively designed and well fortified. Its frontier position even predates the English presence in Aquitaine; for the river Barbanne just north of the town was the traditional dividing line between the southern *langue d'oc* and the northern *langue d'oil* (which became the French language). From a military point of view, the town's position is ideal, climbing steeply to a high hilltop terrace with a commanding view. Down below, a considerable extent of the once-moated medieval ramparts have survived. There are parking areas at several places around the outside of the walls, and for a simple visit it is best to leave the car here. Within the walls, there's a lot to see, but it is not easy to describe a sensible step-by-step route around the town's confusing lanes. Perhaps a good starting point would be the parking area — a market-place on Sundays — at place Bouqueyre, on the south side (that is, the river Dordogne side) of town.

From here walk up, for example, rue de la Porte Bouqueyre and rue de la Grande Fontaine to rue de l'Hermitage, where you can turn right past the Chapelle de la Trinité (see below) for place de Marché. Most of the buildings in St. Émilion are built of an attractive golden pale stone, although the oldest houses — some of which date back to the middle of the 12th century — are also heavily timbered. The fine building

stone was too soft for paving, so many of the narrow old streets in the heart of the town are cobbled with Cornish stone; it was cheaper and simpler to bring this stone by sea from England than try to obtain suitable cobblestone from some part of hostile France.

The relaxing and pleasant place du Marché (or place de l'Église Monolithe) is one of the town's two principal squares; in the middle of it, an august acacia tree planted in 1798 still thrives. The other square, place de Clocher or place des Créneaux, looks down on place du Marché from the top of a sheer escarpment right beside it. A door and windows cut into this escarpment or cliff-face lead into St. Émilion's greatest curiosity, the so-called Église Monolithe. The word monolithic is being used here in its literal sense of a 'single stone', for the church is entirely carved out of the interior of the hill, and consists therefore only of the single natural rock which the hill comprises. No building stone or building materials were used in its construction. Yet it follows the Romanesque design which was imposed on builders and architects over the centuries by the use of stone blocks, as if the 8th-century monks who carved it believed that churches must of necessity have this design and shape. Even as we see it now their underground church, of cathedral proportions, is eerily impressive, dank and dark, with a mysterious atmosphere. How much more so originally, when — one has to stand and imagine it — the windowless walls were all covered with frescoes. This odd 'building' acquired a strange later addition:

Vineyards at St. Émilion. The roses are a traditional barometer of the vine's health — no longer necessary, but a pretty custom

St. Émilion: inside the Église Monolithe

the 12th-century belltower, which stands above it, in the open air of place du Clocher. No longer a church, the Église Monolithe has good acoustics and is the setting for concerts during the month of May.

A labyrinth of natural passages and caves leads away from the church into the surrounding rock. The whole of St. Émilion stands on underground galleries like these, an estimated 240km of them altogether. The monks who carved the Église Monolithe were the followers of St. Émilion (or Aemilianus), an ascetic, originally from Brittany, who lived almost 40 years in an adjacent cave and died here in about AD767. He carved primitive 'furniture' out of the rock, and there was a source of clean water. Benedictine monks dug out the catacombs to use them, and built (above ground) the Chapelle de la

Trinité over Émilion's hermitage. The Knights Templar, who had commanderies (fortified garrison-temples) throughout the Entre-Deux-Mers region and on the banks of the Dordogne, also established a commandery in St. Émilion's catacombs. The water which flows in certain passages is a new phenomenon; it first appeared only about five years ago. St. Émilion's catacombs can be visited on guided tours (enquire at the Office de Tourisme).

Re-emerge into place du Marché, and turn up rue de la Cadène, passing beneath the arch of the splendid porte de la Cadène (from the Occitan cadena, a chain). Follow the direction upwards, turning along rue des Girondins and rue du Clocher, to reach the upper square, place du Clocher, where clustered café and restaurant tables offer repose and refreshment. The south side of the square is effectively a terrace giving a splendid view down onto St. Émilion's picturesque jumble of tiled rooftops and tangled lanes and green countryside beyond. In the foreground, to the right, the grim sturdy walls and tower of the Château du Roy rise above the houses. The château was built in about 1225 as the seat of the English monarch's power, and remained the base for local administrative offices until the 18th century.

Soaring high from place du Clocher, or des Créneaux, is the bizarre 13th-century belltower (with 15th-century spire) of the subterranean church below the square. The tower stands close to a quite separate collegiate church — a puzzling arrangement! Adjacent to the huge and attractive upper church (with domes, good interior stonecarving, traces of frescoes, fine north-west portal), which was built in the 12th century to replace the Église Monolithe and is still in use, are beautiful Gothic cloisters. Beside the belltower is St. Émilion's most luxurious hotel-restaurant, the Hostellerie de Plaisance.

The town's busy tourist office occupies the Collegiate Church's attractive deanery, and opens onto the place. By this time you will already have noticed that St. Émilion suffers from a great number of visitors, many of them day-trippers, who meander in groups about the steep cobbled streets and crowd at the outdoor café tables. Many have been brought by coach and seem not quite sure where they are or what they are looking at. St. Émilion is certainly aware of its tourism potential, although as yet there are mercifully only a handful of hotels actually in the town itself: those which there are maintain a high standard and are in suitably grand old hôtels. Scores of unlikely shops, whose proprietors are anxious not to miss out on the tourist cash, sell smart souvenir boxes of macarons, the humble local confectionery which used only to be available on special occasions. St. Émilion wines, of course, can also be bought in presentation boxes from numerous shops.

Staff at the Office de Tourisme have to be able to speak English, German, Spanish and Italian all day long ... and consequently are, I find, a little jaundiced in their attitude to visitors. They do however have much useful information about the town, the region, vineyards which can be visited, wine tastings, guided tours, and so on. Inside the office a wall map shows local wine châteaux, and there's an 18th-century wine press on display.

Turn left out of the tourist office and go back down rue du Clocher to meet rue Guadet, which runs, albeit ever so windingly, on a north–south axis through the town. It was at a house in this street that the last of the Girondins, seven of them, remained in hiding until discovered and executed in 1794. Just south (right) as you reach rue Guadet is a fork in that road, with rue de la Porte Brunet leading off to the left; at the junction are Templar ruins known as the Logis de la Commanderie, as well as the enticing old inn Auberge de la Commanderie. A few paces beyond the Auberge are the delightful cloisters of the ruined 15th-century Franciscan monastery, Le Cloître des Cordeliers (because of the cord which they wore around their habit, Franciscans were known as *cordeliers* in France until the

Revolution). Rue de la Porte Brunet continues to the fortified porte Brunet gateway.

Going the other way (northwards) up rue Guadet, the street passes through the lovely old town to porte Bourgeoise, the upper gateway. To its east are remnants of the 13th-century Palais Cardinal; while just west of the gate is a surprising fragment of 13th-century wall, the remains of a Dominican priory church, standing surreally in the open fields.

St. Émilion has a keen sense of tradition and ceremonial, and during the year a number of picturesque *fêtes* take place. These mostly stem from the vine-

Crus

In 1855 Napoleon III ordered that the best wine-producing châteaux of the Médoc peninsula be graded by quality. They were categorised with *Prémier Cru Classé* at the top, followed by four lower grades of *Cru Classé*, followed by *Cru Bourgeois Exceptionnel, Cru Bourgeois Supérieur*, and finally *Cru Bourgeois*. Subsequently, two lower grades were named, *Cru Artisan* and *Cru Paysan*. Initially only four châteaux were designated as *Prémier Cru Classé*: Lafite, Latour, Margaux, and one Graves wine château, Haut-Brion. Château Mouton-Rothschild was added to the list in 1973, but there have been few other changes made to the original *cru* classifications. Over the years the *cru* grading has meant less than it did, as some second- and third-rank *Cru Classé* have moved up to become among the finest of all Médoc wines.

In other Bordeaux wine districts, slightly different *cru* classifications were brought in. In St. Émilion, the top category *Prémier Grand Cru Classé* takes in a wider spectrum of quality than the Médoc top rank. In the Graves area, all the best châteaux are simply designated as *Cru Classé* — there is no second category. The Sauternais has three grades, with only one château, d'Yquem, in the top class. The Entre-Deux-Mers and Pomerol districts have no *cru* grading system.

The word *cru* comes from the verb *croître*, to grow (it has a different root from *cru*, raw), and since the 19th century has been translated into English as a noun, 'growth'. However the word encompasses a wide meaning, including the soil in which the grapes are grown, and the wine-making tradition of the château. *Cru* would be more accurately expressed in English as 'vineyard'.

grower's preoccupation with the quality of his wine and, like any other farmer's, with the weather and the seasons. The most important custom is the Ban des Vendages, when the opening of the grape harvest is officially declared from the top of the Tour du Roy at the Château. The announcement is made with a fanfare by the President of the Jurade of St. Émilion. The fanfare can be heard in the surrounding fields and is still taken as the signal to begin harvesting the grapes. The members of the Jurade (St. Émilion's traditional ruling council, founded in 1199 by King John), wearing the traditional red robes and flat hats of their office, then lead a procession down to the Église Monolithe for a traditional ritual and blessing. Another important occasion is the movable Fête de la Fleur, when the first flowers appear on the grape bushes in spring — the most crucial moment in the vines' development.

The illustrious St. Émilion *vignoble*, threaded with tiny backroads, is tranquil and pretty country, with roses decorating the edges of vine fields, and signs proclaiming the name of the châteaux to which the fields belong. The D17 goes into the little town of **Castillon**, which prefers to be called Castillon-la-Bataille in honour of the fact that the last battle of the Hundred Years War was fought here. At the start of the 1450s English power in Aquitaine, or Guyenne, was crumbling beneath a powerful and sustained French attack. Bordeaux itself fell in 1451, although it was temporarily recaptured by hastily despatched English reinforcements under John Talbot, Earl of Shrewsbury, in 1452. Shakespeare has immortalised Talbot as the fearsome Old John Talbot in *Henry VI (Part I)*. John Talbot's hold

on Bordeaux was insecure, and the vine-rich countryside around it was brimming with French soldiery. Later in the same year, the English outpost of Castillon came under fierce assault. John Talbot had little choice but to desert Bordeaux, briefly he hoped, to fight off this new threat.

On the battlefield of Castillon, English rule in Aquitaine was brought to an end: John Talbot was killed in the fighting, and his men trounced, while other French troops took Bordeaux. Those of the English soldiers who survived escaped in disarray to their ships in the Gironde. A good many Gascons, loyal to the English crown and unwilling to live in a French Aquitaine, fled with them. Castillon today seems happy enough under French rule though; built on a high ridge with fine views, the village commemorates its past in typical French style — with a spectacular *son et lumière* display on summer evenings. The rest of the time it gets on with producing good, drinkable reds of the Bordeaux Côtes de Castillon *Appellation*. In the other direction, the village of **Pomerol** consists of little more than its church, its Bureau de Poste, and a Monument des Morts, all in a tiny area tightly enclosed by its famous vines. The prestigious Pomerol *Appellation* area circles tightly round the village. Pomerol's rich, tasty, full-bodied reds generally range from good to excellent. The *Appellation's* most respected, and most expensive producer is Château Petrus (just south of the village on a minor country lane, the D245), which actually makes remarkably little of its sought-after wine. During my visit the

Church and fortifications beside the water at Talmont-sur-Gironde

chais had only 50 barrels in store; back in 1924, I was told, the château made just one barrel of wine.

Pomerol is right on the edge of **Libourne**, the big, busy and industrialised town well placed on the riverbank at the confluence of the Dordogne and its tributary the Isle. Not a lovely place now, Libourne nevertheless retains its impressive old fortified 14th-century waterside gateway, porte de l'Horloge, with its pointed towers. The layout of the town centre still shows clearly that it was originally a *bastide*, and the main square, Grande Place, has kept its arcaded pavements. The town was built in 1270 by Edward I (before he acceded to the throne, as can be seen from the date). At the same time the seneschal of Gascony, Roger de Leybourne, made the new town his base and had a castle built here; the town's name is derived from his. The Black Prince resided here at times, and his son Richard II was born at Libourne. During the English rule the town had considerable trading and administrative importance, but nowadays it has little charm or interest. A couple of kilometres down river from Libourne is **Fronsac**, a simple village backed by delightful hilly wine country with its own Côtes de Fronsac and Canon-Fronsac *Appellations*, making excellent, reliable strong reds. Fronsac *Appellation* vines continue for several kilometres along the D670, or along the prettier back-country roads like the D246 and the D138[E3].

North from Bordeaux, world-famous vineyards dignify the otherwise rather characterless countryside on either side of the great Gironde waterway.

The left bank of the Gironde is duller country perhaps, than around St. Émilion, but produces even greater wines.

For this strip, extending almost from Bordeaux to Pointe de Grave, wedged between the Landes forest and the Gironde, is the Médoc. The whole region has for centuries maintained a position of the highest eminence for its complex, dignified red wines, above all some of the full-bodied and full-flavoured vintages of the Haut-Médoc region (the southern half). In the Médoc there are two principal *Appellations*, Médoc and Haut-Médoc, and six smaller, more distinguished *Appellations* based around the villages of St. Estèphe, Pauillac, St. Julien, Moulis, Listrac, and Margaux. There is an atmosphere of calm prosperity in the villages, most of which have a number of wine châteaux; some are indeed enviably grand country houses. Some are household names, and produce the wines which one has tasted only on special, celebratory occasions. It is exciting to visit them, like meeting a famous actor. The great vineyards grow roses along the edges of their fields, and they look for all the world like bouquets grown to honour the grapes. The Médoc is not entirely devoted to winemaking however; there is mixed farming, and there are stretches of countryside with not a grape bush in sight.

Approaching from Bordeaux, the Médoc wine road, the D2, passes through the neat vineyards and modest little wine villages of the Haut-Médoc. On the edge of tiny **Issan**, Château Palmer, one of the best Margaux producers, is a truly imposing little mansion with flags flying, including the Union Jack. **Margaux** itself is a larger village. The great Château Margaux is a grand neo-classical mansion locked away within its gates and flanked by its famous vines on the southern outskirts of the village. A Maison du Vin on the

Main Festivals in the Bordelais

May

BORDEAUX — Mai Musicale: two-week season of music and dance of international standard.

June

St. ÉMILION — Fête du Printemps, de la Fleur and de la Jurade: colourful, traditional fairs with 'proclamation' of the new wines by the Jurade (2nd or 3rd Sunday in the month).

July

ROYAN — Fêtes de la Mer: traditional local sea festivals.

August

LIBOURNE — Fest'arts: shows and entertainment in the streets of the town (several days at the end of the month).

September

ST. ÉMILION — Ban (or Jurade) des Vendanges: ceremonial procession and declaration by the Jurade to open the year's grape harvest (3rd Sunday, or Sunday nearest 20th September).

October

MARCILLAC — every year the traditional Fête des Vendanges marks the end of the grape harvest.

---

northern edge has information about châteaux, visits, and the wines.

Farther on, little **Lamarque** has a miniature river port (3km from the village) connected by car ferry to Blaye on the right bank of the Gironde (see page 47). Just a few hundred metres farther along the D2 from Lamarque, turn right at **Cussac-le-Vieux** to see Vauban's Fort Médoc (1689) one of three fortresses protecting the Gironde river. Impressively conceived, sturdy, enclosed by earthworks and waterways, Fort Médoc stands stern and indomitable beside the flowing current. Within its walls (you have to pay to enter), the fort is now grassy and empty.

A few kilometres farther along the D2, gorgeous flowers flourish in front of Château Beychevelle, an 18th-century

chartreuse just outside its tiny village. From here to Pauillac great wine châteaux are clustered closely together. Around **St. Julien**, the renowned names of the St. Julien *Appellation*, the three châteaux of the Léoville estate (Les Cases, Barton and Poyferré), Château Talbot, and one of the best of the Pauillac, Château Latour, all lie near to the road. It is startling, after this rural journey, to arrive at **Pauillac**. No pretty wine village this, but quite a large town, and dominated by oil refineries. Nevertheless, the black fumes presumably do no harm to the grapes, for some of the world's most prestigious châteaux are within sight of them. A useful Maison du Vin et du Tourisme explains which vineyards can be visited.

Go straight through town to find

45

Château Mouton-Rothschild on the other side. This most illustrious of wine châteaux is geared up for a constant stream of visitors, who are taken on guided tours (by appointment). The well cared-for grounds and wine-making premises have a modern, productive appearance. The wealthy proprietor Baron Philippe de Rothschild, who died in 1988, gave Mouton-Rothschild a style and flair for which it is noted. The wine label, for example, is a beautiful work of art, and a new one is commissioned for every year, while the premises house a remarkable collection of art relating to wine. Nearby, next to the road, Château Lafite-Rothschild (known usually as Château Lafite and owned by a different branch of the family) produces wine almost as good, though arguably more variable. This too is a magnificent residence, with a splendid vegetable garden as well as vineyards.

As the D2 veers round to the left, the astonishingly flamboyant Château Cos des Tournels stands on the corner. Turn right immediately after the château to travel along a minor country lane into **St. Estèphe** (badly signposted), the most northerly of the great Haut-Médoc villages. It is satisfyingly quiet and rustic, and absolutely uncommercialised except for a Maison du Vin by the church in the sleepy central square.

All the vine country west and north of this point is in the Médoc *Appellation*, slightly inferior in quality to the Haut-Médoc district. There's more to see in this countryside though. Well worth a pause is the ancient church at **Vertheuil**, a peaceful, basking village on the D20, 5km from St. Estèphe. The church, a delightful building although terribly damp inside, was formerly the abbey church of an Augustinian monastery. Its lovely 12th-century Romanesque doorway, a little spoiled by later additions, depicts peasants gathering the grape harvest.

This is the border of the Landes forest. Already the countryside is patched with *pignada*, pine woods. Continue just a few kilometres farther west, and the forest engulfs the whole landscape. One could continue north, on the main road or on narrow country lanes, towards Pointe de Grave. The most northerly Bordeaux vineyard is Château Noillac, a *Cru Bourgeois* near the village of Loirac. Turning south instead, it is simple to connect with the N215 (and then the D1) for a fast journey through the western parts of the Haut-Médoc *Appellation* back into the city of Bordeaux.

To see the right bank of the Gironde, one could cross directly from the Médoc at Lamarque to the harbour at Blaye. However, if coming from Bordeaux or St. Émilion and Fronsac, you could travel on the tranquil D669, following the signs to Bourg and Blaye. The road passes close to the grand, if curious, Château du Bouilh, construction of which was left uncompleted after being interrupted by the Revolution. Six km farther along the caves of the Grottes de Pair-non-Pair, during the Aurignacian period of the Stone Age (ie 27,000–30,000 BC) were lived in by men and women who etched and painted numerous beautiful animal sketches on the walls.

The *ville haute*, or upper town, of **Bourg** (pronounced Bourk) stands on top of a limestone cliff high above the Dordogne close to its confluence with the Garonne, the two rivers joining to form the immense, sandy Gironde.

Well within the lifetime of this old fortified town this site was actually beside the Gironde rather than the Dordogne, but continuing alluvial sedimentation between the two great streams has extended the Dordogne river north of the town. The view over the water from Bourg's handsome Terrace du District (as it is called), while impressive, is not a pretty one: oil refineries are its main feature. The upper town keeps remnants of its 13th-century fortifications and a number of fine medieval dwellings. The 17th-century Château de la Citadelle, twice rebuilt (in the 18th century and then again after the Second World War), was the summer residence of the archbishops of Bordeaux. It has an attractive park of lovely trees and a terrace with magnificent river views. The cliff on which Bourg stands is a maze of underground galleries and corridors, many of them used as cellars. The upper town is joined by picturesque lanes and steps to Bourg's *ville basse*, or lower town, with its river port. At the bottom of steep, winding rue Cahoreau, the main street between the two districts, stands the old Porte de la Mer, the 'sea gate', locally known as the Batailleyre.

From Bourg to Blaye it is enjoyable to stay on the shore road, which makes its way through a succession of small river ports. Most of the Côtes de Bourg *Appellation* area lies north of the town. The wines of this district are mixed in quality, the best of them being superb reds, rich and full and benefiting from long maturation, and can be bought for surprisingly low prices. Indeed, top-quality Bourgs arguably represent the best bargain available in Bordeaux wines. About halfway between Bourg and Blaye one crosses into the area covered by the Côtes de Blaye (dry whites) and Premières Côtes de Blaye (red) *Appellations*, a productive region whose good drinkable wines are generally within easier reach of the average pocket than most Bordeaux. Blaye wines are widely available in Britain; for many supermarkets and bargain-priced foodstores they form a large proportion of the 'château bottled' Bordeaux wines on offer.

Blaye, like Bourg, comprises an old fortified section on high ground, and a more recent lower town and port. The difference is that Blaye's huge hilltop Citadelle has more ancient origins, and is now surprisingly little-visited and virtually deserted, containing few habitations or other buildings currently in use, even though it is in superb condition and has its own little streets and squares. Lower Blaye's somewhat shabby and unappealing town centre consists of little more than a single busy main street which curves round the Citadelle. This, called at various points cours de la République, cours Vauban and cours du Port, is part of the Gironde coast road.

Blaye was from Roman times onward, and perhaps before, an obvious location for a fortress: with a dominating view clear across the tidal waters, it is the first point, or rather the last, at which the Gironde is narrow enough to defend. The massively fortified citadel one can see today dates from 1689, and is mainly the work of Vauban, who destroyed almost all of the walled medieval town which previously stood here: 260 houses were knocked down in one operation. In their place he created this purpose-built military base. To complete the defences of the Gironde, he built Fort Médoc on the opposite bank of the river, and Fort Pâté on an island midway between the two.

A number of fortified gateways penetrate the Citadel's sturdy ramparts: one allows cars to enter (Porte Royale); another is for pedestrians only (Porte Dauphine); the other entrances are now disused — one of these leads into a tranquil vineyard between the Citadel's inner and outer walls. Inside the Citadelle, the ruins of a small triangular medieval fortress, the Château des Rudel, are a relic of the town which originally stood here. The castle was the birthplace and home of one of the most influential 12th-century troubadours, Jaufré Rudel, who developed the classic troubadour theme of *amor de lonja*, love from afar, after falling in love with Princess Melissende of Tripoli; eventually he sailed to join her, but fell ill on the way and on his arrival, so it is said, died in her arms.

The Château des Rudel itself replaced an earlier castle-basilica in which Roland, the nephew of Charlemagne, was buried after being killed in AD778 at the momentous battle against the Moslems at Roncevaux (or Ronceval), although the exact location of the grave is not known. Previous to that, the Roman *castrum* Blavia stood on this site. Although there are some fascinating buildings inside the Citadel, there is practically nothing in the way of everyday facilities like cafés or shops. There is, however, an incongruous campsite, a small museum, and, in the main square (place d'Armes), a slightly pretentious restaurant and hotel (unexpectedly affordable). Next to the hotel is the Ancien Couvent des Minimes (a former convent), an attractive 17th-century building recently restored. From the west side of the Citadel walls, particularly from the Tour de l'Aiguillette, there is a marvellous view of the Gironde and beyond.

Blaye is one of two places on the Gironde's right bank from which small car ferries cross to the other side of the vast swirling river. With about half a dozen crossings daily, the Blaye ferry connects with Lamarque (see page 45) in the Médoc, on the way skirting close to Vauban's Fort Pâté on the mid-river Isle de Pâté. The other crossing is across the mouth of the Gironde, from Royan to Pointe de Grave. The Royan route is much longer and more expensive, so if a trip over to the Médoc is planned, it may be better to cross from Blaye.

The D937 is the main road from Blaye to Royan (it joins the N137 at Le Pontet, and turns left onto the D730 at Mirambeau). The coast road (numbered D255 at first) leaves Blaye on the north side of town, and makes its way through some bustling agricultural villages: Braud-et-St. Louis, St. Ciers, St. Bonnet, St. Thomas and others, each with a fine central church. Shortly after St. Ciers, the road leaves the Gironde département, so also leaving the Bordeaux wine region. It passes at once into the Charente-Maritime département, which is cognac country. All the way from the Gironde border to Royan, the signs beckon with 'Cognac — Pineau'. Curiously enough, cognac, that most elegant of *digéstifs*, is distilled from very inferior white wines, thin and sharp. While Blaye wines are, of course, not the best which the Bordeaux region has to offer, it seems odd that along this road one vine field in the Gironde département can make its produce into very drinkable red and white Bordeaux wines, while its neighbour produces poor-quality Charente wine for making into cognac.

The farm-made cognac is inexpensive if nothing else; and indeed some is reasonably good. The other drink, Pineau de Charente, is something of an acquired taste — I must admit I have acquired it! — and is a favourite apéritif in western France, especially here in the cognac country. It is made by maturing a mixture of cognac and grape-pressings. The taste is bittersweet, and it is served cool.

Fishing cabins on the Gironde waterside

The Gironde riverport at **Mortagne-sur-Gironde** lies below the main village; serious fishing goes on here. Not far from the fishing harbour is Mortagne's strange little attraction, sign-posted as the 'Église Monolithe' or as the 'Ermitage St. Martial'. Set back from the shore road (the D245), this consists of a cave-house with several rooms (supposed to be a former monastery), and a terribly steep flight of steps which passes through a fissure in the cliff-face to give access from top to bottom. The bottom formerly was the bank of the Gironde, and it is said, plausibly, that Compostela pilgrims made their descent to the riverside down these steps.

Talmont, the next of the waterside villages, is remarkable, memorable, almost dreamlike. The setting is striking enough: jutting into the immense river, a rocky promontory protected by high ramparts. But it is even more pleasing to take a look within the impressive fortifications: all the village streets are lined with masses of tall flowers, especially hollyhocks. Everywhere, flowers. A superb little Romanesque church of pale sandstone, with its small graveyard, crowns the seaward walls. The church, 12th-century (earlier at one end than the other), has lovely stone carvings, especially over the main entrance; it fairly emanates peace and simplicity, and the interior is satisfyingly uncluttered. The only flaw in Talmont is that it is dedicated almost totally to tourism; yet perhaps one cannot object to that, for this place is in any case more like a work of art than a real village. In truth it is not utterly given over to tourists, for there are still a few fishing families here, and an exquisite miniature Mairie (town hall) to run their affairs.

The D145 continues north beside a long dyke, beyond which stretch vast mud-flats. The road soon reaches **Meschers-sur-Gironde**, a secret little place on the estuary shore. The village has an impressive old church of pale stone blocks, with a rather austere interior. Like many churches on the Atlantic coast, it has a model of a ship hanging inside.

What worlds away that ancient relationship with the ocean and its tides feels from the atmosphere of modern seaside resorts like **St. Georges-de-Didonne**, barely 5km farther up the coast. Here one is on the fringes of the Royan holiday area, but St. Georges is an altogether smaller, quieter place, with good food shops and a contented air. It has huge sandy beaches, not at all

49

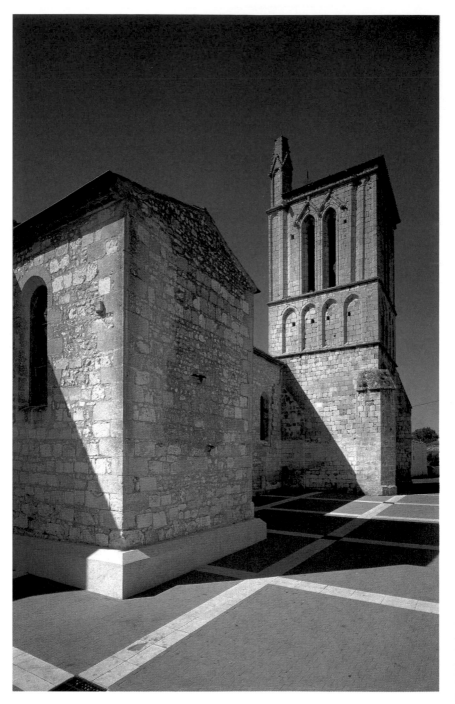

crowded, with occasional beachside restaurants. The seafront road runs right beside the Grande Conche, a huge gently curved bay with an immensely long sandy beach: a beautiful sight. This is effectively part of **Royan**, and the northern end of this impressive beach is in the centre of town.

One might expect Royan to be soulless and charmless, since it was entirely rebuilt after the Second World War, largely using reinforced concrete. Stylish pre-War Royan was totally destroyed in just twenty minutes on 5 January 1945 by Allied bombs; until the war it had been one of the leading watering places in France, and nearly as popular as Biarritz. In fact, while the architecture of the new town does leave something to be desired, it is a congenial and pleasant resort. Outside the French holiday season (mid-July to the end of August), the town is quiet. The promenades are always agreeable, and benefit from the light and air of the Atlantic, together with the moderating shelter offered by the Gironde. Its waterfront is arranged around a series of sandy bays, called conches, at the mouth of the Gironde. Along the front cheap seafood restaurants vie for trade. There is a pleasure harbour packed with small vessels, and a little dock from which ferries leave for the Pointe de Grave on the other side of the estuary, and pleasure boats set off for tours of the Cordouan lighthouse. The lighthouse (Phare de Cordouan), a remarkable Renaissance construction 66m high, standing in splendid isolation on an underwater rock, does deserve a visit. Over the centuries it has served double duty as a guide to peaceful shipping and

The church at Meschers on the Gironde's north bank

a first outpost of defence against any hostile vessel. First erected in 1371, the lighthouse was in a dangerous condition by the 16th century. The ornate base of the present structure dates from the end of that century, and a new tower was added in 1788.

Rising from the centre of Royan is the curious angular tower of its cathedral, built in 1955–8. Like the other buildings in town, it is made entirely of concrete, and has acquired, as concrete will, a tatty and unprepossessing appearance. Nonetheless, this building, designed by Guillaume Gillet, has a great following, and has been widely acclaimed as one of the most magnificent pieces of modern architecture, showing the versatility and elegance of concrete. Yet aesthetically it is frankly *not* a great success; made vaguely in the shape of a ship (the main entrance being beneath the prow) and looking also like organ pipes, the whole effect leaves one singularly unmoved. The interior is of a surprising and original shape, at once angular and elliptical, but gaunt and stark, and again revealing all too clearly the shortcomings of the material from which it is built.

North-west of the town, the coast road passes through several unappealing little resort areas, eventually reaching the fine Coubre lighthouse, from the top of which there are marvellous coastal views. Inland, the Forêt de la Coubre has attractive pine, holm oak and acacia, with a dense, almost exotic undergrowth. As in the Landes, beneath a thin layer of humus, the soil is just sand. Long footpaths make their way through the generally deserted forest.

To see the real Landes, or to return to Bordeaux via the Médoc, take the car ferry across the Gironde from Royan to Pointe de Grave.

Hotels and Restaurants

BLAYE: Citadelle (57.42.17.10), modern characterless, pretentious hotel-restaurant within old building at the quiet heart of Blaye's Citadel. Impressive Gironde views.

BORDEAUX: There are many outstanding **restaurants** in the city. Prices tend to be on the high side sometimes, although standards are also high. The very best of Bordeaux's restaurants are: **Le Chapon Fin**, 5 rue Montesquieu (56.79.10.10); **Pavillon des Boulevards**, 120 rue Croix de Seguey (56.81.51.02); **Jean Ramet** place Jean Jaurès (56.44.12.51); **Le Rouzic**, 34 cours du Chapeau Rouge (56.44.39.11); **La Chamade**, 20 rue des Piliers-de-Tutelle (56.48.13.74).

Other excellent restaurants, offering good value, are: **Clavel St. Jean**, 44 rue Charles-Domercq (56.92.91.52); **La Tupina**, 6 rue Porte de la Monnaie (56.91.56.37); **L'Alhambra**, 111bis rue Judaïque (56.96.06.91); **Le Buhan**, 28 rue Buhan (56.52.80.86); **Le Cailhau**, 3 pl du Palais (56.81.79.91); **Le Loup**, 66 rue du Loup (56.48.20.21); **Le Vieux Bordeaux**, 27 rue Buhan (56.52.94.36).

Reasonable hotels include:

Hôtel de Bayonne, 4 rue Martignac (56.48.00.88), well modernised, comfortable old hotel in heart of city, moderately priced.

Hôtel Majestic, 2 rue du Condé (56.52.60.44), traditional old city hotel of charm and comfort, well placed, not expensive.

Hôtel de la Réserve, 74 av du Bourgailh in the suburb of Pessac (56.07.13.28), a peaceful old Relais et Château in attractive grounds, with excellent restaurant.

BOULIAC (on the D10, 9km from Bordeaux): **Amat**, 3 pl Camille-Hostein (56.20.52.19), beautifully located by river, moderately priced top-class restaurant, and expensive rooms.

Auberge du Marais, 22 rte de la Tresne (56.20.52.17), excellent unpretentious restaurant specialising in regional dishes.

LANGON: Hôtel Restaurant Claude Darroze, 95 cours Gén. Leclerc (56.63.00.48), superb accommodation, quite moderately priced. Excellent but expensive restaurant with good selection of Armagnacs.

MARGAU: Relais de Margaux (56.88.38.30), luxurious hotel-restaurant in attractive setting, expensive.

ROYAN: Family Golf Hôtel, 28 bd Garnier (46.05.14.66), pleasant little waterfront hotel, beside the main beach.

Hôtel des Bleuets, 21 façade Fonçillon (46.38.51.79), reasonably comfortable, modestly priced 2-star Logis at Fonçillon, quite central, quiet, some distance from the main beach.

ST. ÉMILION: Auberge de la Commanderie, rue Cordeliers (57.24.70.19), appealing traditional hotel-restaurant, well modernised, surprisingly inexpensive.

Hostellerie Plaisance, place du Clocher (57./24.72.32), excellent hotel and restaurant in magnificent building at top of town, rather pricey.

Logis de la Cadène, pl du Marché-au-Bois (57.24.71.40), good cheap restaurant in little *place*.

SAUTERNES: Le Saprien (56.76.60.87), imaginative, accomplished restaurant, welcoming atmosphere, fairly expensive; **Les Vignes** (56.76.60.06), good, sensible village restaurant with excellent local wines, moderate prices.

Museums and Châteaux

BLAYE: Pavillon de la Place (Musée d'Histoire et d'Art du Pays Blayais) (57.42.13.70) *Jun–Sep, Sat, Sun, and j.f. (jours fériés — public holidays), pm only.*

BORDEAUX: Musée d'Aquitaine, 20 cours Pasteur (56.10.17.58). Colourful historical displays. *10–6. Closed Tues and Wed.*

Musée d'Art Contemporain (C.A.P.C.), rue Foy and rue Ferrière (56.44.16.35). Ambitious permanent and temporary exhibitions on the latest developments of modern art, housed in an imposing 19th century warehouse, the Entrepôt Lainé. *11–7 daily (until 8 on Fri), closed Mon.*

Musée des Arts Décoratifs, Hôtel de Lalande, rue Bouffard (56.90.91.60). Local works, housed in 18th-century mansion. *2–6. Closed Tue.*

Musée des Beaux-Arts, cours d'Albret (56.10.16.93). Collections from 15th–20th centuries. *10–12, 2–6. Closed Tue.*

Musée des Douanes, 1 pl de la Bourse (56.52.45.47). Historical museum of Customs and Excise. *Summer: 11–6; Winter: 11–5. Closed Mon.*

Musée Militaire, Caserne Boudet, 192 rue de Pessac (56.86.19.45). Collections of weapons, uniforms etc. spanning two hundred years. *Sat, 2–5, or by arrangement.*

Muséum d'Histoire Naturelle, Jardin Public (56.48.29.86). *2–5.30. Closed Tue.*

Casa de Goya 57 cours de l'Intendance (56.52.79.37). House where Goya lived and died. Memorial centre — not an art gallery. *2–6.30. Closed Sat and Sun.*

Centre National Jean Moulin, pl Jean Joulin (56.10.15.80). Important museum of the Resistance. *2–6. Closed Sat, Sun, j.f.*

Conservatoire International de la Plaisance, bd Alfred Daney (56.11.11.50). Unusual multi-faceted navigation 'museum' and entertainment inside former German wartime submarine base, believed to be a unique example. *10–7 daily, closed Mon.*

Le Croiseur Colbert, quai des Chartrons (opposite cours de la Martinique) (56.44.96.11), intriguing museum inside a 10,600-ton warship moored close to the city centre. *Open daily from 10. Apr–Oct: last entry at 5.15. Nov–Mar: last entry at 4.15, closed Mon and Tue.*

Grand Théâtre, pl de la Comédie. Magnificent 18th-century interiors. *Guided visits (1 hr). Early Jul: Tue–Sat, at 10.30, 3, 4.30; mid-Jul–end Aug: Mon–Fri, at same times; rest of year: Sat at 3. Closed j.f.*

Paleo-Christian site at St. Seurin. *Guided visits (¾ hr). Apr–Oct, Tue and Sat pms only.*

LE BOUILH (near St. André-de-Cubzac): **Château** *Guided visits (½ hr). Jul–Aug. Thur, Sat, Sun, j.f.*

BOURG: Château de la Citadelle. *Guided visits (20 min). Closed Mon.*

LA BRÈDE: Château. Montesquieu's palatial home. *Easter–end Jun, and 1–11 Nov: Sat, Sun, j.f., 2.30–5.30; Jul–Sep: 9.30–11.30, 2.30–5.30 exc Tue; Oct: Wed, Sat, Sun, j.f. Rest of year closed.*

CADILLAC: Château. *Guided visits (1 hr), am and pm. Free tasting. Closed Mon.*

FORT MÉDOC: Fort. *10–6.30. Jun–Sep: daily; rest of year: Sun and j.f., only.*

LIBOURNE: Musée Archéologique et des Beaux-Arts, pl. Abel Surchamp (57.55.33.44). Fine art from the 16th to the 20th century, and local history.

MALLE (near Sauternes): **Château.** Beautiful early 17th-century mansion and gardens. Interior has good paintings and furniture. *Mar–Oct: 3–7. Closed Wed.*

MALROMÉ (near St. André-du-Bois): **Château** (56.63.74.92). The château where Toulouse-Lautrec spent his last days. *Open daily mid-Jun–mid-Sep.*

PAIR-NON-PAIR, GROTTE DE: Caves. Prehistoric artwork. *Guided visits (½ hr), am and pm. Closed Tue, some j.f. and all Oct.*

LA REOLE: Ancienne Abbaye (56.61.10.11). Museum in former abbey. *Guided visits (1 hr), Sat and Sun, pm only. Closed j.f.*

ROYAN: Musée, in town hall. *Summer: Wed and Fri, 10–11.30, 1.30–5. Mon pm only. Winter: Mon, Wed, and Fri, pm only.*
Musée du Phare de Cordouan (56.09.61.78). Museum in Renaissance lighthouse accessible by ferry from Royan. *Ferry: usually two daily unless bad weather (46.50.55.54); approx 5-hr return trip including visit to lighthouse. Lighthouse: Mid-June–mid-Sep: Guided visits (½ hr), am and pm.*

ST ÉMILION: All the following can be visited on an organised guided tour arranged at tourist office — **Église Monolithe, Chapelle de la Trinité, Cloître de la Collegiale (cloisters of Collegiate Church), Musée d'Archéologie (Archaeology Museum).** (Some can be visited individually).
Cloître des Cordeliers. *Easter–11 Nov: 10–12, 2–6.30.*
La Tour du Roy. *9.30–12, 2.30–6.45.*

ST MACAIRI: Musée des PTT d'Aquitaine, in main square of walled old town (56.63.08.81). Unusual little museum of the post office. *Apr–Oct. am and pm. Closed Tue.*

VAYRES: Château. *Guided visits (1 hr), Jul–Aug: 3, 4, and 5; rest of year: 3 and 4 on Sun and j.f.*

Tourist Offices

CRT offices (regional information for the whole of Aquitaine): 10 rue René Cassin, Bordeaux 33049 (56.39.88.88; fax 56.43.07.63). For Royan and environs see CDT for Charente-Maritime below.

CDT offices (information on the département): GIRONDE — 21 cours de l'Intendance, Bordeaux 33000 (56.52.61.40; fax 56.81.09.99); CHARENTE-MARITIME— 11bis rue des Augustines, La Rochelle 17008 (46.41.43.33; fax 46.41.34.15).

OTSI offices (local information): BAZAS — pl de la Cathédrale (56.25.25.84); BLAYE — allées Marines (57.42.12.09); BORDEAUX — 12 cours du 30-juillet (56.44.28.41; fax 56.81.89.21); CASTILLON — in Mairie (57.40.00.06); LANGON — allées Jean Jaurès (56.62.34.00); LIBOURNE — Pl A. Surchamp (57.51.15.04); MESCHERS — pl de Verdun (46.02.70.39), high season only; PAUILLAC — La Verrerie, quai Léon Perrier (56.59.03.08); LA RÉOLE — pl de la Libération (56.61.13.55), high season only; ROYAN — in the Palais de Congrès (46.38.65.11; fax 46.38.52.01); ST. ÉMILION — pl du Clocher or des Créneaux (57.24.72.03; fax 57.74.47.15); ST. GEORGES-DE-DIDONNE — bd Michelet (46.05.09.73), closed Sep–Feb; TALMONT — in Mairie (46.90.80.97). Where there is no tourist office, apply to the Town Hall (Mairie or Hôtel de Ville) for information.

Loisirs-Acceuil (hotel booking service): at CDT office in Bordeaux.

Sports and Leisure

CYCLING AND RIDING: there is a wide range of cycling and riding routes which pass places of interest throughout the region. Contact the Comité Sportif d'Aquitaine, 5 cours de Verdun, 33000 Bordeaux (56.52.80.90).

SWIMMING: many towns have free (or inexpensive) municipal swimming pools, and Bordeaux has several.

VINEYARD VISITS: apply to local tourist offices and Maisons du Vin for details of Châteaux offering visits and/or tastings. Château Mouton-Rothschild — phone (56.59.22.22) two days ahead to take part in guided visit. Château Lafite-Rothschild — phone (1.42.56.33.50) to arrange visit; very few requests granted. Château Margaux — phone (56.88.70.28) two weeks ahead to arrange visit.

Maisons du Vin

Offer information about local wines and vineyards, usually opportunities for tasting, and often wine for sale.
BARSAC — 56.27.15.44; BLAYE — 11 cours Vauban (57.42.91.19; fax 57.42.85.28); BORDEAUX — 1 cours du 30-juillet (General information 56.00.22.66, fax 56.00.22.77; Médoc wines 56.48.18.62, fax 56.79.11.05; Entre-deux-Mers wines 56.81.66.42); CADILLAC — 56.27.11.38; CASTILLON — 6 allées de la République, 57.40.00.88; FRONSAC — 56.84.30.06; ST. ÉMILION — several in area, variable opening times, usually no tasting, apply to tourist office; MARGAUX — on main through-road (56.88.70.82); MONTAGNE (summer) — 57.84.00.13; PAUILLAC — (signposted) La Verrerie, quai Léon Perrier (56.59.03.08; fax 56.59.23.38); ST. CROIX-DU-MONT — 56.62.01.39; ST. ESTÈPHE — pl de l'Église (56.59.30.59), no tasting. General information on all Médoc châteaux: 56.48.18.62.

Gironde Ferries

ROYAN–POINTE DE GRAVE: several daily each way. Single fares — car approx. 120F, passenger/pedestrian 15F. Enquiries 56.09.60.84.
BLAYE-LAMARQUE: about 6 daily. Single fares — car approx. 120F, passenger/pedestrian 15F. Enquiries 46.38.59.91.

4
The Landes

The 175-kilometre journey from Bordeaux to the Basque Country astounds the unprepared: the whole distance, with rare clearings, is spent passing through a single pine plantation. This is the strange, sparsely populated Landes de Gascogne, now completely covered by the largest forest in Europe.

It begins with remarkable suddenness. There appears to be no transitional zone. Certainly there are many fields of corn, tobacco or pasture which lie inside the forest, yet along most of its periphery, most strikingly on the eastern side, the pines give way abruptly to rich and fertile farmland. On the margins, the forest does tend to consist of a more picturesque natural woodland mixing pine with other trees; penetrating farther, it gives way to relentless long straight lines of tall dark planted trees. This too has its haunting appeal: many times, driving through these strange woods, I have yielded to the temptation to stop the car and walk among these calm giants and breathe their cool, scented breath.

Most people who visit the region have but a slight encounter with the pine forest, for the Landes possesses another extraordinary phenomenon. Along its 200km of Atlantic shore stretches Europe's largest beach, and probably one of the straightest, now known as the Côte d'Argent — silver coast — a magnificent sight of dazzling brilliance and awesome dimensions. Powerful waves fan into huge curves along the smooth sand, throwing pearly clouds of salt mist high into the air. Superb pale sands, intense Atlantic light, towering surf-white breakers dwarfed by the monumental proportions of the beach, fill the eye. From the top of ocean-side dunes, beach and forest can be surveyed in a single spectacular sweep.

In recent years a government-funded plan of coastal development has led to the building of a few new resorts as well as the expansion of older, more established seaside settlements. Like most newly constructed, purpose-built towns, these on the whole lack much character; however, facilities tend to be good, and not expensive. Large distances separate these holiday areas, with great tracts of open beach between them. And always nearby, just behind the coast, the Landes forest provides the great escape into greenery and tranquillity.

A hundred years ago this immense forest did not exist. At that time, and for centuries before, the Aquitaine coast was an inhospitable wilderness of howling winds and shifting sands. The

57

Landes had always been a large sandy zone of low fertility, dotted with scrub and clusters of coastal pine, and broken up by unhealthy marshes — the very word *landes* means bleak and barren open country. At its northern fringes the Landes gave way to *pignada*, pine forest, but to the east the sands constantly encroached farther inland, and not slowly either: they were eating their way into the Gascon countryside at the rate of ten or twenty metres per year.

Despite the poor prospects of living on such terrain, the Landes had its native population, speaking their own *patois*, dwelling in isolated cottages or small hamlets, and keeping flocks of undernourished sheep and goats. The local people managed to make these limited resources go a long way, eating the animals' meat, drinking their milk, and wearing their coats. To get about in the difficult terrain, they wore stilts. Stilt-walking has become a local sport.

Louis XVI, interested in the feasibility of constructing a naval base on the Landes coast in the Bassin d'Arcachon, asked engineer Charlevoix de Villers to study the problem. In 1779 he issued a report suggesting windbreaks and plantations as ways to control the Landes coastal environment. Louis's plans came to nothing, but they sparked renewed interest in the problem of the Landes, and in the late 1780s an ambitious programme was launched to 'rehabilitate' the region and halt the expansion of the sands. At first, under the management of civil engineer Nicolas Brémontier (1738–1809), this programme concentrated on bringing the coastal strip under control. It is surprising to learn that most of the huge coastal dunes now so characteristic of the Landes, were created artificially at that time to protect the hinterland. They acted as an essential windbreak and a barrier against blowing sand. The dunes themselves were held in place by planting *gourbet*, also known hereabouts as the *roseau des sables*, a low-growing plant with long spreading roots which fixed the sandy soil. To this day the dune vegetation has to be constantly maintained by the Office National des Forêts. The low-lying terrain inland, which held stagnant water, was drained, and the shallow marshy lagoons close to the coast dredged and turned into proper *étangs* (lakes connected to the sea). In the 1850s the programme, taken over by François Chambrelent, turned its attention away from the seashore towards the arid interior. The essence of the scheme as it progressed in the 19th century was the planting of economically viable pine forests, pines having proved themselves one of the few plants which could survive here. One also comes across some smaller plantations of cork oak, which continue to make a contribution to the local economy.

The whole programme was to take more than half a century to complete, and while it went on the populace accustomed themselves to the idea of living enclosed by 14,000 square kilometres (1,400,000 hectares — some 3¹/₂ million acres) of forest.

Today the pine forest of the Landes takes three distinct forms. First, around the edges, and at places in the interior, there are attractive naturally occurring woods, consisting largely of Atlantic pine mixed with acacia and other trees and a dense bracken undergrowth. Secondly, there are the large areas which are maintained by the Government as natural reserves, and notably the Parc Régional. These offer a chance to penetrate and understand the affor-

A typical farm in a Landes forest clearing

ested region and its wildlife. Thirdly, the bulk of the forest is the neat parallel rows of pine grown as a crop, which are cut down, cleared and quickly replanted. In addition, throughout the forest there are clearings, or even areas which were never afforested, in which other crops are grown, principally maize as animal fodder.

The Landes back country is astonishingly rustic. Life remains simple in the small villages. Although in reality quite accessible, they are unvisited and so feel very remote. Some are still not even on paved roads. Traditional old houses are generally low and shuttered, made with narrow bricks and heavy timbers, and give the forest villages an unexpected charm.

The Médoc peninsula, that slender triangle of flat sandy land bordered by the waters of the Gironde on one side and the Atlantic breakers on the other, consists far more of *landes* than of vineyards. The great wine country of the Médoc and Haut-Médoc *Appellations* runs along the eastern side of the triangle, while the remainder is marsh, sand-flats, and *pignada*. There is no Atlantic coast road, but the D101 runs through the hinterland forest, with a succession of minor access roads leading down to small beach resorts. The Médoc Landes, with its easy access to beach, forest and wine country, has earned a certain popularity and makes a good holiday base.

The northermost point of the peninsula is Pointe de Grave, where a memorial monument records the landing of

59

American troops in 1917. The Pointe has tremendous sea views, somewhat marred, unless you like that sort of thing, by petrol refineries down the Gironde coast. Offshore the old wave-beaten Cordouan lighthouse can be seen beyond the opening of the Gironde estuary. A car ferry connects Pointe de Grave with Royan (see page 51) on the other side of the estuary.

Adjacent to the Pointe, and sheltered by it, **Le Verdon-sur-Mer** is an important harbour town at the mouth of the Gironde. Previously a quiet seaside (or properly, riverside) resort, it has seen a steady industrial expansion since the last war. Only 5km separate this Gironde beach from the grander Atlantic shore at **Soulac-sur-Mer**, which progress has taken in the opposite direction. Formerly a major port, it is now a holiday resort with a fine beach and good facilities. When the Romans founded this harbour town, which they called Noviomagus, it fronted onto the Gironde. Sand deposits have changed the lie of the land considerably at this northern corner of the peninsula. The original harbour of Noviomagus became unusable after the 6th century, but Soulac's east side managed to continue as a river port during the Middle Ages and it was much used by Compostela pilgrims. When troops arrived from England in a last-ditch effort to save Bordeaux from being taken by the French at the end of the Hundred Years War, they landed at Soulac. The town's highlight today is the lovely Romanesque basilica Notre-Dame-de-la-Fin-des-Terres, a 12th-century Benedictine abbey church which was gradually threatened and then finally submerged by the drifting sands, and had to be abandoned in 1757. During the Landes reclamation, it was uncovered and cleaned, to excel-

lent effect. Its name — Our Lady at the Ends of the Earth — seems to say something about the character of this coast during the early Middle Ages.

Starting from Soulac, the D101 progresses southwards through the Médoc peninsula. A right turn leads to the seashore at **Montalivet-les-Bains**, noted for its extensive naturist holiday area. Continuing south, another turn skirts the northern end of Lac d'Hourtin-Carcans and leads to the small beach resort at Hourtin-Plage, while the through-road runs into **Hourtin** village. Hourtin marks one end of a popular drive known as the Route des Lacs. This route, with certain deviations, is effectively the same journey from Hourtin to Hossegor as will be described in this chapter. Half the distance, as far Mimizan, can be travelled along waterways which link the lakes. Most of the Route des Lacs is not itself within sight of the lakes, but several turnings connect the road to lakeside 'ports'. These lake beaches have much to recommend them. Quite apart from their refreshing position amidst pine woods, the large lakes provide a gentler environment than the ocean shore, and they have good sandy beaches which are safer for children than the wave-beaten Atlantic coast. On the lakeshore close to Hourtin, the new resort of **Hourtin-Port** has made a special effort to provide facilities for families and children, and its motto is '*les enfants d'abord!*' — children first!

At Hourtin, the D101 meets the D31, the main inshore road south from here. Where the road reaches **Carcans**, a right turn (the D207) skims the southern edge of the Lac d'Hourtin-Carcans at the popular lakeside resort **Maubuisson**, where canal cruisers pause on their travels from one Landes lake to another,

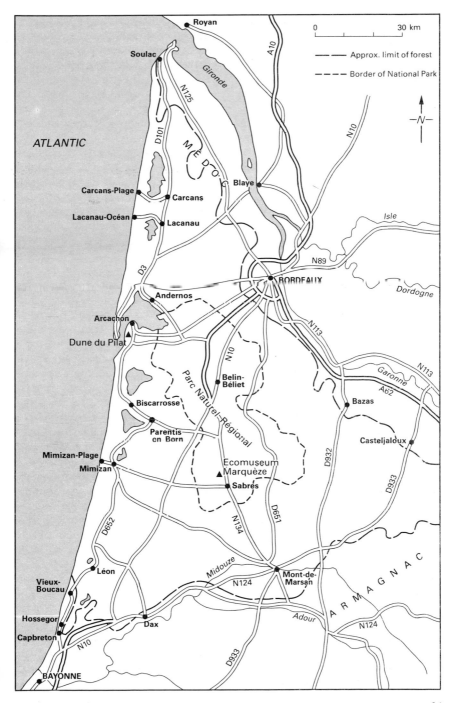

ATLANTIC

Royan

Soulac

Gironde

N125

D101

M É D O C

Carcans-Plage
Carcans

Lacanau-Océan
Lacanau

Blaye

Isle

D3

N89

BORDEAUX

Dordogne

Andernos

Arcachon

Dune du Pilat

N113

Belin-
Béliet

N10

Parc Naturel Régional

Garonne

N113

A62

Biscarrosse

Bazas

Parentis
en Born

Casteljaloux

Mimizan-Plage
Mimizan

Ecomuseum
Marquèze

Sabrès

D932

D933

N134

D651

D652

Léon

Midouze

A R M A G N A C

Vieux-
Boucau

N124

Mont-de-
Marsan

Adour

N124

Hossegor

Dax

Capbreton

N10

D933

BAYONNE

0   30 km

— — —   Approx. limit of forest

- - - - -   Border of National Park

—N—

and reaches the sea at **Carcans-Plage**, a tiny resort with the usual magnificent sandy beach. Self-catering accommodation predominates here, and there are minimal facilities for tourists. Nearby, on the western shore of Lac d'Hourtin-Carcans, Bombannes is a large open-air sports and leisure centre. The whole area west of the lake, and its southern neighbour Lac de Lacanau as well, is a protected region of the forest. Drive through it from Carcans-Plage to **Lacanau-Océan**, a large and well-equipped resort town. It is modern, but not entirely new: along the waterfront and in the town's centre there is a lot of turn-of-the-century architecture. The whole place is geared to holidays and relaxation, and has plentiful sports facilities. The beach, of course, is superb. The long colourful main street has an agreeably indolent holiday atmosphere, with many restaurants, snack bars, and souvenir shops. Lacanau-Océan is still expanding, and building work continues on the outskirts. The tourist office is in place de l'Europe, on the main road out of town towards inland Lacanau.

The D3 runs south through Le Porge towards **Lège**, which consists mainly of holiday villas. 8km west from Lège, reached through densely wooded country, **Crohot** — though barely noticeable on a map — is quite a popular beach access, with several campsites hidden among the trees. On the Michelin map it is called Grand Crohot Océan, and other names for the same little place includes Le Grand Crohot and Plage de Grand Crohot. A long walk over the crest of a hugh dune brings you to the vast and beautiful sandy beach with its awesome waves. The dune summit gives a marvellous inland view too, of the pines rolling away into the distance like a second ocean, the treetops billowing like waves as they echo the contours of the land. Crohot has no beach facilities, but the bathing is *surveillé*.

The D106 continues beyond Lège all the way down the narrowing spit of land, the Presqu'île which nearly encloses the Bassin d'Arcachon on the seaward side. The road goes through a succession of small, unremarkable waterfront holiday areas and oyster harbours — Claouey, Les Jacquets, Petit Piquey, Grand Piquey, Piraillan, Le Canon (where there stands a cannon which locals like to claim was used against the English during the Napoleonic wars), L'Herbe, La Vigne — until it reaches **Cap Ferret** at the southern tip of the Presqu'île. All these small resort villages are part of the single *commune* of Lège-Cap Ferret. Cap Ferret itself consists mainly of fine holiday villas scattered among the trees, and is a pleasant place to stay for a quiet week or two although it is, to be frank, not particularly rewarding for the day visitor. Its small-scale *centre ville* has a large sandy beach, not crowded, which turns into mud-flats as it reaches away from the shore into the Bassin waters. The main attraction of Cap Ferret is its sailing, with the Bassin d'Arcachon and the open sea both nearby.

The sea opening of the large Bassin d'Arcachon, marking the southern edge of the Médoc peninsula, is the only interruption in the smooth line of sandy beach which reaches from the Gironde to the foothills of the Basque Pyrenees. There is no proper coast road around the Bassin, although the D106 from Cap Ferret to Lège, the D3 from Lège to Facture, and the D650 from Facture to Arcachon, make a circuit of it. For much of the distance the road forces its way through built-up areas, and is sometimes congested with local traffic in summer. Residential turnings off the road lead down to the Bassin's waterfront. For the most part, the Bassin d'Arcachon has no sand beach, except in a few small patches, but considerable distances of its perimeter can be followed on enjoyable walkways. At low tide, when the Bassin seems to empty like a bath, vast mud-flats are suddenly exposed. These are the favourite haunts of huge populations of seabirds and water fowl. In the midst of the Bassin, the Île aux Oiseaux is a protected sanctuary for wildfowl, and there is another bird sanctuary at Le Teich on the water's edge. Large areas of the shallow Bassin are devoted to the cultivation of shellfish, especially oysters, in immense *parcs à huîtres* (literally, oyster parks). The wooden cultivation frames can be seen sticking from the flats, or emerging from the water when the tide is in. Arcachon's oysters have long been renowned in France, and indeed among gourmets in other countries.

Among the Bassin's holiday attractions are sailing and waterway cruising to the Landes' other inshore lakes; the Bassin has numerous little harbours and creeks in which to pull up. Just as along the Cap Ferret peninsula, the main resort districts between Lège and Arcachon can hardly be called towns at all; they consist mostly of oyster harbours surrounded by holiday houses either in the woodland or looking out over the Bassin, although each has its centre with shops and facilities. Approaching from Cap Ferret or from Lège, the D3 passes through them in rapid succession: Arès; **Andernos**, the oldest and most agreeable of the resorts on this side of the Bassin — note its Église St. Eloi with vestiges of 4th- and 12th-century structures; Taussat; Cassy, Lanton; Audenge; Facture and Biganos (these last two are unpleasant, industrial places); **Le Teich**, which has the important 120-hectare *parc ornithologique*, bird sanctuary, mainly for water fowl; **Gujan-Mestras**, a busy, picturesque fishing port and major oyster-farming centre; **La Hume** which has a 'medieval village' with craft workshops; and

Oyster 'farmers' in the Bassin d'Arcachon

finally La Teste, which was an established village and small resort before Arcachon, but has now become something of a suburb to the later town. Properly called La Teste-de-Buch, it was the capital of Buch, a Landais region of old Gascony. Its medieval rulers, bearing the title Captals, were staunch supporters of the English.

On a ridge of land which penetrates into the Bassin from the south, and standing at its opening to the Atlantic, **Arcachon** dates back only to the middle of the 19th century. Even that short past makes it one of the few Landais coastal towns with any history at all. It came into being in quick response to the new improvements in the Landes. In fact Arcachon owns its existence partly to La Teste, an oyster harbour which in the 1840s was connected by railway to Bordeaux, and attracted a few summer visitors who enjoyed walking by the water or bathing in it, ostensibly to improve their health (the concept of sea bathing had not yet fully detached itself from the idea of the spa). The village of La Teste lay inland from its harbour, while some of these early holidaymakers, generally well-to-do people, preferred more secluded accommodation closer to the water. Many of them built substantial chalets and summer houses on the stretch of waterfront which was to become present-day Arcachon.

The site was not entirely wild even then; a few fishing families already lived there, and their little chapel housing an alabaster statue of the Virgin and Child had long been a minor place of pilgrimage for the devout. In 1852, Adalbert Deganne had a small château constructed by the present Plage d'Eyrac. A new resort sprang up here with amazing rapidity. In 1857 it was inaugurated as a town, and in the same year

the railway from Bordeaux, formerly terminating at La Teste, was extended to Arcachon. In 1859, Napoleon III paid a visit, which in those days was all that was needed to ensure the future prosperity of a town. And so it proved: hitherto the railway line had been operated only in summer, but during the 1860s, the railway company and the bankers Péreire got together to create Arcachon's Ville d'Hiver (Winter Town), a stylish residential and winter holiday area on higher, wooded land set well back from the waterfront, which was intended to make profitable the operation of a year-round railway link with Bordeaux. One of its first buildings was the palatial Casino Mauresque, now called the Casino de la Forêt. In view of the comment of the English traveller Augustus Hare that 'Arcachon has nothing to enjoy and nothing to admire', it is astonishing to read some of the names of Arcachon's regular winter visitors during the subsequent years: Alfonso XII, and then Alfonso XIII, of Spain, Queen Victoria's daughter Princess Louise, and, among commoner folk, author Alexandre Dumas for example, and the composer Debussy, and later, the poet Gabriele d'Annunzio.

With the building of the Ville d'Hiver, the original beachside development became known as the Ville d'Été (Summer Town). In 1903, Deganne's château became the Casino de la Plage, and Arcachon continued to grow in popularity. Later expansion to the east of the Ville d'Été was known as the Ville d'Automne (Autumn Town), and even more recent development to the Ville d'Été's west has, inevitably, taken the name Ville de Printemps (Spring Town). Arcachon's Ville d'Hiver today is a peaceful and prosperous residential quarter, now sometimes called the Ville Forestière, centred on the Parc Mauresque. It is set back and uphill from the busier waterfront Ville d'Été, which has become Arcachon's town centre and the focus of its tourism. The tourist office occupies modern premises in the attractive circular place Roosevelt. The main shopping street is avenue Gambetta, which connects place Roosevelt with the beach and the main pier, Jetée Thiers. Several other shopping streets, some with pedestrianised sections, lead off avenue Gambetta. Although very geared towards tourism, Arcachon has an enjoyable, civilised, almost elegant atmosphere.

Following its waterfront around from east (the Bassin) to west (the ocean), start with the town's port, used by fishing vessels, holiday craft, pleasure boats, and the small ferry (pedestrians only) which on summer days frequently connects Arcachon with Cap Ferret. The adjacent Plage d'Eyrac, terminating at the Jetée d'Eyrac pier, was the original Arcachon resort of the 1850s. Close to the Jetée d'Eyrac a famous, and excellent, museum and aquarium has fascinating displays of all the animal, bird, reptile and aquatic life of the Bassin, with a special section on oysters. Beyond lies the sandy Plage d'Arcachon, backed by an agreeable boulevard and promenade centred on the Jetée Thiers. This plage reaches as far as the Jetée Legallais, beyond which another pier, the Jetée Croix des Marins, is close to the site where the mysterious Virgin and Child statue was discovered by Franciscan monk Thomas Ylliricus. It is now known that the statue, for centuries considered by the naïvely devout to be of literally divine origin, is made of Nottingham alabaster and probably came from a shipwrecked trading ship. A succession of simple

Arcachon's Vierge à l'Enfant, humble originator of the town

chapels housed the statue until in 1858, with the expansion of the town, a larger basilica was built entirely containing the smaller Chapelle des Marins (Sailors' Chapel), as it was known. The basilica lies just a few minutes inland from the Jetée Croix des Marins in place Notre Dame. Unfortunately the original chapel was destroyed by fire in 1986, but it has been reconstructed.

65

Beyond this point a coastal highway, called by a succession of watery names (boulevard de l'Océan, de la Mer, des Goëlands) leads round the headland through the ocean-facing suburbs of Les Abatilles and Le Moulleau and the separate little resort of Pyla. These are quiet, well-manicured districts, quite chic and attractive, still with a few very grand old private houses. Between the road and the sea stretches a good beach rising to wooded dunes. South of **Pilat-Plage** is the dune to beat all dunes, a great hill of sand 114m high and nearly 3km long. Called the Dune du Pilat, this extraordinary man-made phenomenon is still growing as wind-borne sand accumulates. The dune has become one of the major attractions of the Aquitaine coast. There are shops, cafés, and a huge car-park (fee payable) at the base of the hill, and while many prefer to make the tiring scramble up the sand itself there are makeshift steps to the summit. From the top there's a magnificent view of coast and forest.

A coast road, the D218, continues south through the pines. Inland, generally not visible from the road, clusters of oil derricks stand in clearings to the north of the attractive Étang de Cazaux et de Sanguinet. This is the first of the several productive Landes oil-drilling areas, which form an important part of the region's economy but which are not at all noticeable to the traveller because of the screen of trees. At **Biscarrosse-Plage**, reached after some 20km, it is comfortable villas which hide behind the pines, while more exposed to view, near a superb beach, the town has a casino and good facilities for visitors. The D146 turns inland to the growing town of **Biscarrosse** and the Étang de Biscarrosse et de Parentis. The Biscarrosse-Parentis area has long been a

centre for hydraviation ('flying boats'), and Biscarrosse has an interesting museum on the subject. On a similar, but more modern theme, there is now also a base for aerospace testing. Though largely 20th-century, Biscarrosse reminds visitors (and itself) of an unexpectedly long past with a conspicuous 15th-century church spire and a 16th-century château. The D652 heads past the *étang* to **Parentis-en-Born** (Born was another of the old districts of the Gascon Landes). Oil derricks spread across the southern part of the *étang* and across the country around Parentis, and there are other industrial establishments near the town. Although most of this development is concealed by the curtain of pines, a certain industrial acridity hangs in the air. That's a pity, because Parentis, a small town built around the massive squat tower of its church (with a short slender spire on top), would otherwise be quite a likeable little place. The town has a museum about the Landes oil production.

Although much of the distance from Parentis to the next little town, Mimizan, is through unappealing country, there are many genuine old Landais timbered houses in this district. By contrast, **Mimizan** consists mainly of recent building, with villas extending into the woods away from the unimpressive town centre around its church. The highlight of the town is the attractive Étang d'Aureilhan just north (signposted as Le Lac). Beside the water a lovely Promenade Fleurie (floral walk) makes a delightful stroll. On the western side of town the brick tower which survives of an 11th–13th-century abbey stands beside the road; there is a small museum opposite. On the seashore 5km away, the charmless new resort **Mimizan-Plage** has a dreary half-built look

The Landes interior has oak woods as well as pine, and there are many quiet, idyllic corners like this riverside at Uza

and a selection of disappointing accommodation. Between Mimizan 'town' and 'beach' the principal landmark is a large paper mill which has generated a mountain of wood chips to rival the Dune du Pilat and a smell which cannot be rivalled at all. It wafts over Ville or Plage according to the wind.

Beyond Mimizan, the D652 heads out of the Born district and into neighbouring Marensin, country with more character and more of the traditional low, shuttered Landais dwellings constructed of heavy timbers and thin bricks. Occasional side roads and tracks on the right give access, through pinewoods, to the beach, while turnings to the left off the main road lead inland through the trees to some fascinating rustic villages. In many places

the woodland is less dominated by pine, and there are some pretty areas of oak and acacia. It is worth exploring on these back roads: one rewarding drive (just an example) would be from **St. Julien-en-Born** to the interesting and picturesque villages of **Uza** and **Lévignac** (simple hotel), through **Linxe** (pronounced Lainks; restaurants, two reasonable hotels), and rejoining the main D652 perhaps at Léon.

Léon, an attractive village beside the Étang de Léon, has a lot of charm. Attractive timbered houses stand around the old market square next to the church. In the square, two good little traditional hotels offer inexpensive board and lodging. The lake and the beautiful Courant d'Huchet which links it to the sea are banked by remarkable and lush vegetation. Enjoyable boat excursions — marvellous on a summer morning — can be taken along the Courant, which reaches the sea at the tiny isolated village of Huchet.

The Marensin district gives way in the south to the Maremne, in which the Basque influence begins to be strongly marked. As one drives from Léon to Bayonne this increases, and the region has more visitors and more holiday development than the rest of the Landes. Specially constructed holiday villages tucked away among the trees offer inexpensive accommodation and ample leisure facilities.

Boucau means a harbour entrance or river estuary (from the Gascon *bouco*, mouth) and **Vieux-Boucau**, or Vieux-Boucau-les-Bains, was once — incredibly — at the mouth of the river Adour. Since being artificially deviated in 1578, the river now twists down much farther south towards Bayonne. The 16th-century harbour built at the new mouth of the Adour in Bayonne was called Boucau-Neuf. Even that dramatic shift was by no means the first to be made by the Adour, which originally flowed out to sea at Capbreton (see below). In 1164 it suddenly sprouted a new arm which ran to Bayonne, although Capbreton remained its principal estuary until the 14th century. Then shifting sands caused the river suddenly to find a different course, to Vieux-Boucau. During the two centuries that Vieux-Boucau was on the Adour, an important port, known as the Port d'Albret, grew up around the estuary. Of course when the river was moved again the town went into a rapid decline. But tourism has revitalised it, and today Vieux-Boucau, standing astride the Canal de Moïsan, consists mainly of modern precincts and is a popular resort with several *villages de vacances* and plenty of sports and leisure facilities. The central area is rather attractively paved and largely pedestrianised. Vieux-Boucau lies on the north bank of the Lac d'Albret and the old harbour, which is now fed by a canalised *courant* flowing from an inland *étang*. On the other side of the *courant*, adjacent to Vieux-Boucau, a new Port d'Albret, still coming into being, will be developed into a resort and leisure area between the lake and the ocean.

The D652 follows the *courant* inland to the busy commercial town of Soustons and its *étang*, while the D79 stays with the coast, soon arriving at the saltwater Lac de Hossegor. Signs give drivers a choice of routes into **Hossegor**. The most scenic is the waterside road on the west of the lake. Hossegor is a pleasant little town, a more stylish resort than most, historic in parts but thoroughly modernised. It has good leisure facilities and a beautiful Atlantic beach, as well as its 'White Beach' on the shore of the lake. Most of Hossegor lies on a sort of peninsula almost entirely enclosed by water — Atlantic on the west, lake on the east, and, connected to the lake by canal, the extensive old harbour to the south. The harbour is the ancient Port de Capbreton, a major port at the mouth of the capricious Adour until the Middle Ages when a blockage by sands caused the river suddenly to change its course (see Vieux-Boucau above). One might assume that the equally likeable town of **Capbreton**, on the south side of the harbour, must practically have merged with Hossegor by now, but nothing could be farther from the truth. The two *communes* seem eager to keep at arm's length, eyeing each other distrustfully across the harbour water, and you may find that the tourist office of one affects to know nothing of the other. For visitors though, Hossegor and Capbreton can be regarded almost as two towns in one.

Like Hossegor, Capbreton offers visitors a fine beach and good facilities, and from its *jetée* there are superb views. Capbreton has by far the longer history, having grown up with the trade of its Adour harbour, but little survives to show its great age, other than the lighthouse on top of the Église St. Nicholas, which through the centuries lit the way for the brave local whalers and sailors. The church and tower were largely rebuilt in the 19th century, but it deserves a visit nonetheless. Its interior walls have unusual stations of the cross and remarkable frescoes. All around the bottom of the walls are inscribed the names of a thousand citizens who were buried in the church up to 1533. The church was then extensively rebuilt, only to be badly damaged again by Huguenots in 1577 (although some other names inscribed on the walls are those of sailors who died at sea in the years 1672–1724). Then during the Terror (1794) the building was once more attacked, the present structure being erected as soon as the revolutionary fervour had quieted. Throughout these misadventures, the 15th-century *pietà* statue in the porch survived as an object of great veneration for the town's sailors.

The river Adour, at the southern edge of the Landes forest, marks the border of the Basque homeland. The great old Basque capital Bayonne stands right on this frontier, and in the last few kilometres south from Capbreton the forest breaks up increasingly to reveal cultivated fields. Many of the

---

Course Landaise

Bullfighting is popular in the Landes, especially in the region around Dax and Mont-de-Marsan. Not only the cruel but dignified Spanish *corrida* is performed (and the crueller, less dignified *novillada*, using young bulls and young men), but also the *course portugaise*, which does not involve the final *mise à mort*, killing, and sometimes the *course à la cocarde* from Languedoc, which inflicts no injury on the bull at all (although it is usually slaughtered afterwards).

However, the main type of 'bullfighting' in the region is the local form known as *course landaise*, which does not use bulls at all, but cows. This has little resemblance to traditional bullfighting, and is perhaps best translated simply as 'cow-baiting'. Originating in the Landes in the 15th century, it is derived from the cow-running and bull-running which still takes place in the streets of some Spanish towns, but here it is contained within an arena and has more discipline. The animal is deliberately provoked and angered by a team of acrobatic *sauteurs* (jumpers) and *écarteurs* (dodgers) whose skill consists in the precise way in which body and arms are turned to avoid the cow's charges. The points of its horns are covered to ensure that the men sustain no injuries. Much of the effect is intentionally comic, with the audience cheering the men's efforts and taunting the animal's frustration and bewilderment.

farms are growing vines for the Landes wine aptly known as *vin de sable* ('sand wine'). Travellers heading for Biarritz should note that only the name Bayonne appears on road signs. For Bayonne and Biarritz see Chapter 5.

Whether approaching from Hossegor and Capbreton or from Biarritz and Bayonne, the main roads, the N10, then the N124, cut through the overlapping fringes of the green Basque country, and the Landes forest to **Dax**. As the main road arrives in St. Paul-lès-Dax, part of the northern suburbs of the town, it passes the Église St. Paul, mainly 14th-century, but remarkable for the 11th-century carved frieze of the Last Supper which has survived on its Romanesque apse. Today the old spa town of Dax has grown large and hectic and sprawls on both sides of the Adour. Its ancient centre, though, is contained within a very small, walkable area on the south bank of the river. This original heart of Dax, consisting mainly of narrow historic streets and a few squares, is bordered by busy boulevards which run slightly outside the course of the town's former ramparts. The two bridges over the Adour from the north are the main D947, and the older and busier avenue de St. Vincent de Paul which goes directly into the main square, place Thiers (where the Syndicat d'Initiative is). The square is attractive with its trees and café tables. Everything of interest in Dax can be reached within a few minutes on foot from place Thiers. Beside it, a pleasant park borders the Adour on one side and has relics of the 14th-century town walls on the other. Close to the park (on its north side), there's a *fronton* (a wall for playing pelota) and a big modern circular *arènes* (arena) for staging bullfights, *course landaise* and other outdoor entertainments.

By far the most important 'sight' of Dax is the Roman hot bath (signposted as the Fontaine Chaude), behind place Thiers. This of course gives the town its name, which like Ax and Aix, was originally known simply as Aquae (more properly, Aquae Augustae); by the Middle Ages the name had become Acqs or d'Acqs. The hot baths are, in effect, a large open-air rectangular pool of hot water, enclosed within white arcaded walls. The water bubbles up naturally into the pool, while overflow outlets pour constantly — and have done for an extraordinarily long time: in 1933, Dax held its bimillenary celebrations. Put your hand into the running overflow to discover just how warm the bathing water is; it emerges from an underground source at 64°C. While this original pool has taken on the role of a curiosity, modern *établissements thermals*, using the same waters, function in the town, in particular near the river. They attract many *curistes*. Mud-pack treatments play an important part in the cure, the mud being known as *peloïde de Dax*. Esplanade Charles de Gaulle, extending away from the bath, was the centre of the Roman town.

La Fontaine-Chaude, the steaming Roman bath at Dax

Main Festivals in the Landes

May

MIMIZAN-PLAGE — Fête de la Mer: sea festival, floral parades (on the 1st)

July

MONT-DE-MARSAN — Fête de la Madeleine: colourful summer festivities with parades, bullfights and *course landaise* (mid-July).

August

SOUSTONS — annual festival with pelota games and *course landaise* (beginning of the month).
DAX — big annual festival with fireworks, entertainments, games, bullfights, *course landaise* (mid-August).
ARCACHON — Fête de la Mer: lively, colourful fair, fireworks, oysters, Bassin crowded with boats (on the 15th).
Several smaller Fêtes de la Mer at coastal towns on the 15th.

Several towns have music festivals during July or August: Andernos, Dax, Mugron, Hossegor, Soustons, and others.

MONT-DE-MARSAN — Racing events throughout the year, especially in February, March, May, June and September.

Turn right beyond the bath up rue Cazade. Pass rue du Palais on the left, in which Louis XIV and his new bride Marie-Thérèse stayed briefly in 1660 after their wedding at St. Jean-de-Luz. In rue Cazade, the Crypte Archéologique is a museum of Dax's Gallo-Roman period, and on the other side of the road, the Musée et Bibliothèque de Borda, housed in the Hôtel St. Martin d'Ages, contains displays on local history and culture. The name honours J-C Borda, the distinguished 18th-century astronomer who was born at Dax. The road rises to reach a rather massive and unlovely cathedral in classical style, built at the turn of the 18th century. It stands on the site of the Gothic church erected by the English in the 14th cen-

tury. During the Plantagenet and English period, Dax strongly supported the English rule, and was repaid with many civil privileges. The main street, rue des Carmes, returns to place Thiers, or one could walk to place Salines, a few paces east of the cathedral, to find a vestige of the town's Roman walls.

Compared with most other French spas, Dax has few pretensions to any elegance or style. It is worth mentioning that while hotels in Dax seem cheap, for the most part prices are matched by a correspondingly low standard.

Dax makes much of its proximity to the birthplace of St. Vincent de Paul (not to be confused with the 3rd-century St. Vincent de Xaintes, the town's first bishop). Roadsigns point the way to the supposed birthplace or, as it is known more poetically hereabouts, the *berceau* (cradle) of Vincent de Paul (1581–1660), who founded the missionary order known as the Lazarists and a number of respected religious charitable orders, notably the Filles de la Charité. Child of a poor peasant family himself, Vincent rose to great heights as a result of his intelligence, energy and concern for the suffering of others. Louis XIII held him in the greatest esteem. Vincent's real home or birthplace disappeared long ago, and on its approximate site (on the D27, just off the main Mont-de-Marsan road, the N124) stands a curious oriental-looking basilica. Next to it, a recreated Landais farmhouse is intended to give some impression of the sort of place in which Vincent would have been born and raised; opposite the house is a huge oak tree, said to be 800 years old. Originally called Pouy, the local hamlet renamed itself St. Vincent de Paul in his honour. Even considering the excellent work he did in alleviating the spiritual and material poverty of his age, the adulation he receives seems excessive. Vincent de Paul was canonised in 1737.

The main road from Dax to Mont-de-Marsan, the N124, makes its way through a number of agreeable villages on the margins of the forest, more or less following the course of the Adour river. At Tartas, the road crosses over the Midouze, a tributary of the Adour, and heads away from the river into **Mont-de-Marsan** (pop: 28,300), préfecture of the Landes. Although it is the capital of the département, Mont-de-Marsan stands on the very edge of the wooded area. The town is quite extensive, but its centre remains small and easily explored on foot. The focus of Mont-de-

Marsan, and the ancient heart of the town, is the peninsula at the confluence of the rivers Douze and Midou. United, the two streams become the Midouze. This central area has a number of interesting and pleasing old buildings. Most of the rest of the town, whether north or south of the rivers, is modern.

South of the town centre are the *fronton* and the *arènes*, the arena at Mont-de-Marsan being particularly well known throughout the region for its bullfights, both *corrida* and *course landaise*. Rue Gambetta crosses from the south bank of the Midou onto the 'island', while another bridge, a few metres downstream, crosses the Midouze, giving a delightful view of the two rivers joining over weirs. Picturesque old mill buildings stand at the confluence, while on the left bank beside the bridge there is an extremely interesting and unusual semicircular *lavoir* still in perfect condition. Rue Gambetta is the main street through the middle of the area south of the river; having crossed the Midou it becomes place Charles de Gaulle, overlooked by the modernised former theatre. Mont-de-Marsan has attractive little markets on Saturday mornings, one in the old market-place off place St. Roch (south of the Midou), but more especially inside, and in front of, this old theatre, which has been remade and retitled as Les Halles (covered market). The theatre is, or was, a fine classical structure standing on the 'island' between the two rivers. The conversion from theatre into market has been well done, and may perhaps be forgiven since Mont-de-Marsan is hardly large enough to support a full-time theatre.

The meandering rue des Musées runs from the theatre to a group of fine 14th-century buildings of gorgeous

honey-coloured stone. The two principal buildings both now house museums of mainly local interest: the Musée Dubalen, with collections on the district's prehistory and natural history, and, in a sturdy square castellated keep called Donjon Lacataye (relic of a castle of Gaston Phoebus, Count of Béarn), a fine arts museum named after the local sculptors Charles Despiau (1874–1946) and Robert Wiérick (1882–1944), and showing their work among others. Rue des Musées turns away from the museums to join rue Victor Hugo. Turn left and walk along this main street to see some interesting architecture old and

new. The Préfecture is a simple, very unpretentious modern building with classical echoes. A few paces farther, the church too is neo-classical, and looks more like a civil building than an ecclesiastical one. On the other side of the road again, the Old Prison is an intriguing variation on the classical theme — it has few windows, and a magnificent archway entrance.

From here, rue du 8-mai 1945 crosses the lush valley of the Douze to the wooded Parc Jean Rameau on the north side of town. Beyond are the town's industrial area, its important military aircraft testing station, and the

Wood and Resin

The rows of pine trees in the Landes are, no less than the wheatfields or vineyards of other regions, an agricultural crop. The farmers, constantly seeking to discover varieties which reach maturity faster, sell the timber for use in building or, more frequently, for processing into paper and other products. Although less common than it used to be, still a distinctive feature of the Landes pine forest is the sight of trees being tapped for resin, another part of the 'tree-farmers'' crop. Pine resin, despite the strong competition from petrol-based synthetics, continues to have valuable industrial applications, generally being made into turpentine or used in plastics. Pine resin is known as *gemme*, tapping as *gemmage*, and the tappers as *gemmeurs* or *résiniers*. Various methods are used to draw resin from the tree. All require incisions to be made into its trunk. The principal tool used is a special hatchet-like blade called a *hapchot*. Traditionally, long deep cuts were made, and were allowed to 'heal' naturally. Nowadays, using a smaller and lighter *hapchot* (known as a *bridon*), short cuts on the trunk are kept open for a number of years. Once the trunk is cut, resin simply flows out. Originally it was allowed to run down into containers at the base of the tree, but subsequently it became the custom to secure purpose-designed pots with nails and hooks onto the trunk itself to enable better collection of the resin. Since the 1970s, plastic bags, stapled onto the trunk immediately below the incision, have been replacing pots. Also growing in popularity is the technique in which dilute sulphuric acid — sprayed every twelve days into a much shallower cut made with a *rainette* — causes the tree to 'bleed' resin more profusely. It is this method which leaves the purple trace seen on tapped trunks. The drawing off of resin makes the timber drier and easier to season when a tree is eventually felled.

large race-track — Mont-de-Marsan's horseraces are as famous as its bullfights and *courses landaises*.

East of the town, reached within a few kilometres on minor roads, opens the rich farm country of Armagnac. South too, towards the Basque country and the Pyrenees, the pine forest is soon left behind. But the D933 runs for many kilometres north-east through the easternmost rural regions of the Landes, woodland broken up by fields, eventually reaching Casteljaloux (see page 171) on the frontiers of the Landes, Armagnac, and the Bordeaux vineyards. The D932 follows another wooded, rural course northwards from Mont-de-Marsan to Bazas (see page 35), the Sauternais and the Garonne river. A minor road the D651, heads due north through the pine forest from Mont-de-Marsan all the way into Bordeaux, some 120km away, partly spent crossing the Landes' Parc Naturel.

The busier N134 travels north-west from Mont-de-Marsan across the Landes passing through **Garein** with its pine processing factory, and soon enters the Parc Naturel. Side roads give access through the trees to a number of environmental exhibition centres, *villages de vacances*, riding centres, and demonstration workshops where visitors can see traditional Landes industry and crafts. Around the village of **Sabres** there are *gîtes* to rent and other self-catering accommodation. In the village, note the good Renaissance features of the parish church. A little train travels 5km through forest from Sabres to the Marquèze Ecomusée de la

Resin-tapping in the Landes forest is still an important part of the local economy

Parc Naturel Régional des Landes de Gascogne

Created in 1970, the Regional Natural Park of the Landes de Gascogne is a conservation and recreation area at the heart of Europe's largest forest. It extends approximately from Sabres in the south to the Bassin d'Arcachon in the north, and is divided about equally between the départements of Landes and Gironde. The 206,000-hectare Parc encloses the whole length of the river valleys of the Grande and Petite Leyre which, united as the river Leyre, flow into the Bassin. Within the borders of the Parc there is an abundance of opportunities for peaceful leisure activity not damaging to the dense pine woodland: marked footpaths, a 330-kilometre circular cycle track, bridleways for riders, waterways suitable for canoeing, and other sports facilities as well as picnic areas, inexpensive *gîte* accommodation, traditional Landais craft workshops open to the public, museums (notably the Ecomusée de Marquèze which preserves a 19th-century Landes farmstead, and the former pine resin processing factory at Luxey), and the Le Teich bird sanctuary on the Bassin d'Arcachon. The work and the way of life of the Parc residents — it contains 22 *communes* — is regarded as part of what is being conserved: village architecture consists mainly of traditional timbered and shuttered Landais dwellings, while several parish churches have been attractively restored. There are information offices at the Parc's principal entry points: Pissos, Sore, Sabres, and on the N10. The main administration and information centre of the Parc Naturel Régional des Landes de Gascogne is at Sabres (58.07.52.70; fax 58.07.56.85).

Grande Lande (there is no road access). This interesting open-air 'eco-museum' recreates a large 19th-century Landaise *airial*, a homestead and its dependencies in a cultivated clearing within the pine forest. Marquèze is in the fertile Leyre valley, always an island of relative prosperity in the Landes.

From Sabres, the D44 and the D626 go west towards Mimizan on the coast through forest and maize-field clearings. The D44 passes **Solférino**, which in 1857 was 'presented' to Napoleon III as a model example of the new type of Landes village following the afforestation. The former Mairie houses a museum of that era.

To continue north from Sabres through the Parc Naturel, take back roads or the main N124 to **Pissos**. This village has a Maison des Artisans (on the route de Sore, the D43) where furniture and pine products are sold, together with other traditional local produce. At Saugnac-et-Muret the N134 eventually meets the N10, the major highway which plunges across the Landes from Bordeaux to the Basque Country. Taking the Bordeaux direction, within 10km it reaches the modest village of **Belin-Béliet**, birthplace of Eleanor of Aquitaine (1123). The N10 carries on with little deviation into the heart of Bordeaux, about 40km away, while right turns through the woods quickly emerge into the vineyards of the Graves *Appellation* on the left bank of the Garonne.

Hotels and Restaurants

ARCACHON: Arc Hôtel, 89 bd de la Plage (56.83.06.85), solid comfortable well-equipped waterfront hotel in modern building, reasonably priced.
Hôtel Point France, 1 rue Grenier (56.83.46.74), good modern hotel geared towards family holidays, well placed, not expensive.
Grand Hôtel Richelieu, 185 bd de la Plage (56.83.16.50), pleasant, comfortable hotel near beach, more expensive than some, own restaurant.
Hôtel Gascogne and **Restaurant l'Ombrière**, 79 cours Héricart de Thury (56.83.42.52), moderately priced accommodation in neat, clean rooms 200m from the sea. The restaurant, only a little more expensive than average, is one of the best in town. Its flowery terrace is more agreeable than the charmless modern interior.

DAX: Hôtel-Restaurant Le Parc, pl Thiers (58.75.86.17), comfortable, pleasant 3-star Logis with good restaurant, well placed beside river and park next to pl Thiers, acceptable prices.
Restaurant du Bois de Boulogne, allée du Bois de Boulogne (58.74.23.32), very good and astonishingly inexpensive.
Splendid Hôtel, 2 cours de Verdun (56.56.70.70), grand building (former palace), adjacent to pl Thiers, remarkably moderate prices, own restaurant.

HOSSEGOR: Hôtel-Restaurant Beauséjour, av du Tour-du-Lac (58.43.51.07), well equipped, comfortable, reasonable prices.
Hôtel-Restaurant Huîtrieres du Lac, 1187 av du Touring-Club (58.43.51.48), likeable 2-star Logis with excellent seafood restaurant by the lake and canal.

LÉON: Hôtel-Restaurant du Centre, in main square (58.48.74.09), simple hotel in attractive old building, with amazingly cheap and generous *menus*.
Hôtel-Restaurant du Lac, at lakeside (58.48.73.11), quiet inexpensive simple hotel with good view.

MIMIZAN: Au Bon Coin du Lac, 34 av du Lac (58.09.01.55), rather unusual and good hotel with first-class restaurant, beside the attractive lake at Mimizan town.
Hôtel du Parc, 6 rue de la Papeterie (58.09.13.88). This road runs 2km from the paper mill to Mimizan-Plage. Fortunately the hotel is almost at the Plage end and usually out of range of the mill's smells. Clean, comfortable, friendly, with (for its price) a remarkably generous breakfast.

MONT-DE-MARSAN: Hôtel-Restaurant Le Midou, 12 pl Porte-Campet (58.75.24.26), popular traditional local restaurant *avec chambres*, inexpensive.

SABRES: Auberge des Pins, rte de la Piscine (58.07.50.47), excellent traditional Landais 2-star Logis with restaurant, in the Parc Régional, inexpensive.

SOUSTONS: Hôtel de la Bergerie, av du Lac (58.41.11.43), good, appealing hotel, peacefully situated in attractive old building, modest prices, own restaurant.
Pavillon Landais, av du Lac (58.41.14.49), an excellent restaurant *avec chambres*, tranquil attractive location by the lake, reasonable prices.

Other accommodation: Most of the coastal resort areas have plenty of camping, caravan and self-catering accommodation at low rates. In addition there are a number of resort hotels or holiday camps, including naturist resorts, near the seashore or beside lakes. Contact CRT or CDT (see below) for details of all the accommodation in their region.

Tourist Offices

CRT offices (regional information for whole of Aquitaine): 10 rue René Cassin, Bordeaux 33049 (56.39.88.88; fax 56.43.07.63).

CDT offices (information on the département): GIRONDE — 21 cours de l'Intendance, Bordeaux 33000 (56.52.61.40; fax 56.81.09.99); LANDES — 22 rue Victor Hugo, Mont-de-Marsan 40011 (58.06.89.89; fax 58.06.90.90).

Main Maisons du Tourisme and OTSI offices (local information): ANDERNOS — 33 av Gén. de Gaulle (56.82.02.95); ARCACHON — esplanade G. Pompidou (56.83.01.69; fax 57.52.22.10); ARÈS — pl du Port (56.60.18.07); AUDENGE — allées de Boissière (56.26.85.17); BIGANOS — Hôtel de Ville (56.82.63.69); BISCARROSSE and BISCARROSSE-PLAGE — 19 av de la Plage, Biscarrosse-Plage (58.78.20.96); CAPBRETON — av du Prés. Pompidou (58.72.12.11); CAP FERRET — 12 av de l'Ocean (56.60.63.26) summer only; see also Lège; CARCANS-MAUBUISSON — bd du Lac, Maubuisson (56.03.34.94); CAZAUX — pl Gén. de Gaulle (56.22.91.75); DAX – pl Thiers (58.90.20.00); GUJAN-MESTRAS — 41 av de Lattre-de-Tassigny, La Hume (56.66.12.65) summer only; HOSSEGOR — pl Louis Pasteur, part of av Paul Lahary (58.43.72.35); HOURTIN and HOURTIN-PLAGE — pl de l'Église (56.41.65.57), and for resort information and bookings, Maison de la Station (56.09.19.00); LACANAU-OCÉAN — pl de l'Europe (56.03.21.01); LANTON — Port de Cassy (56.82.94.46); LÈGE-CAP FERRET (the Presqu'île from Lège to Cap Ferret is under a combined administration, and this is its main tourist office) — 214 rte du Cap Ferret, Le Canon (56.60.86.43); LÉON — at the Mairie (58.48.76.03, July–August only); MAUBUISSON — see Carcans; MIMIZAN and MIMIZAN-PLAGE — 34 av M. Martin, Mimizan-Plage (58.09.11.20); MONT-DE-MARSAN — 2 pl Gén. Leclerc (58.75.22.23); PARENTIS-EN-BORN — pl Gén de Gaulle (58.78.43.60); PYLA-S-MER — Maison du Tourisme, Mairie Annexe, Rond-Point du Figuier (56.22.02.22); SOULAC-SUR-MER — rue Plage pl Marché (56.09.86.61); LE TEICH — Hôtel de Ville (56.22.88.09); LA TESTE — pl Jean Hameau (56.66.45.59); VIEUX-BOUCAU — Le Mail, Port d'Albret (58.48.13.47).

Where there is no tourist office, apply to the Town Hall (Mairie or Hôtel de Ville) or Loisirs-Acceuil (hotel booking service) at CDT office in Bordeaux.

Places of Interest

ARCACHON: Aquarium et Musée, 2 rue Jolyet (56.83.33.82). Excellent museum of the wildlife of sea, land and air in the Bassin d'Arcachon, with section on oyster cultivation *Apr, May and Sept: 10–12, 2–5; Jun, July, Aug: 9.30–8.*

BISCARROSSE: Musée de Hydraviation (58.78.00.65). History of seaplanes etc. *Summer only, open daily.*
Naturama (Musée de la Nature). (58.78.72.01). Lakeside museum of animals and insects around the world. *Easter–15 Sep, daily.*

DAX: Musée Borda, 27 rue Cazade (58.74.12.91). Local arts, crafts, history, archaeology. Interesting summer exhibitions. *May–Oct; 2–6 daily. Nov–Apr; 2–6, closed Sat, Sun.*
Biblioteque Borda, same address. Important regional archives. *Wed and Fri, 2–5.*
Musée de l'Alat (58.74.66.19). Unusual collection of military light aircraft, including prototype helicopters. *Enquire at tourist office for current opening times.*

MIMIZAN: Musée du Vieux Bourg (58.09.00.61 or 58.09.22.22), opposite remnants of medieval abbey. Museum of local history. *15 Jun–15 Sep. 10–12, 2.30–6.30. Closed Sat pm and Sun.*

MONT-DE-MARSAN: Musée de Despiau-Wlérick in the Donjon Lacataye (58.75.00.45). Fine arts, mainly sculpture, housed in 14th-century keep *9–12, 2–7 (closed Tue).*
Musée Dubalen, in the Chapelle Romane (58.75.00.45). Natural History *9–12, 2–7 (closed Tue).*
Musée de Plein Air, between the other two museums (58.75.00.45). *9–12, 2–7 (closed Tue).*
Centre d'Art Contemporain, 11 rue St. Vincent de Paul (58.75.55.84). Shows of modern painting and sculpture.

PARENTIS-EN-BORN: Musée du Pétrol (58.78.41.03). Concerning the discovery and exploitation of oil in the Landes. *Easter–Oct, 9–12, 2–6. Closed Tue.*

Near SABRES: Musée de Plein Air de Marquèze or Ecomusée de la Grande Lande. In the Marquèze clearing in the Parc Naturel Régional, access by rail only (58.07.52.70). *1 Jun—15 Sep: daily, Apr–May and 15 Sep–Oct; Sat pm, Sun, and j.f. only.*

SOLFÉRINO: Musée Napoléon III (58.07.24.92). Museum of the Napoleonic 'model village' of the Landes. *By appointment, all year.*

Near LA TEICH: Parc Ornithologique (56.22.84.89). Extensive bird sanctuary at the delta of the Leyre river where it reaches the Bassin d'Arcachon, an important migration route and home of many species of resident birds. Over 260 species sighted annually. *Mar–Sep: 10–6, Oct–Feb: Sat, Sun, j.f. only 10–6.*

Sports and Leisure

CYCLING: The Comité Départmental du Tourisme of the Gironde issues a map showing the département's principal long-distance *pistes cyclables*, cycle routes. There is a 330-kilometre circular cycle route within the Parc Naturel Régional des Landes (see Nature Park below). Many towns have cycle hire and marked cycle routes. Enquire at local SI.

GOLF: The area is now a favourite with golfers, and there are many golf links open to the public. The Aquitaine Comité Regional du Tourisme (CRT) publishes a brochure, *Golf Aquitaine*, listing all the clubs, their addresses, and facilities. Notable golf locations in the Landes include: Arcachon — 35 bd d'Arcachon (56.54.44.00) with a large 'international' 18-hole course; Hossegor, with an 18-hole course (58.43.56.59) and the first-rate Ardilouse golf course between Lacanau-Océan and Le Moutchic (coaching, accommodation; 56.03.23.15).

NATURAL PARK: Parc Naturel Régional des Landes de Gascogne — Main information office at the village of Sabres (58.07.52.70; fax 58.07.56.85): exploration of the pine forest, walks, cycling, riding, canoeing, wildlife reserves etc.

RIDING: There are riding clubs with stables, hire, lessons, and forest riding trails, at Arcachon, Dax, Hossegor, Hourtin-Port, Lacanau-Océan and other towns. Contact the Comité Régional Sportif d'Aquitaine at 5 cours de Verdun, Bordeaux (56.52.80.90) for full details.

SAILING/WINDSURFING: Arcachon — Yacht Club (56.83.22.11), several firms hire boats and surfboards (contact OTSI); Hourtin-Port — Sailing Centre (enquire at the Maison de la Station, 56.09.19.00) has instructor and hire of windsurfers, catamarans; Lacanau-Océan — good hire and instruction facilities for lake and ocean watersports; Le Moutchic — noted centre for windsurfing (on Lac Lacanau).

SURFING: Most of the Landes' Atlantic coast provides exhilarating surfing, but can be dangerous even at supervised beaches. Hossegor — supervised surfing (58.43.55.88); Lacanau-Océan — hire, instruction, club facilities, supervised beach (56.03.27.06); Pyla-sur-Mer — surf club (56.22.78.72); Vieux-Boucau — surf club, board hire, on Plage Nord.

SWIMMING POOLS: Many towns have free (or inexpensive) municipal swimming pools.

TENNIS: Arcachon — 22 courts at the Tennis Club, 7 av du Parc (56.83.07.77); Hossegor — Le Garden Tennis Club (58.43.55.39) private club with 6 courts open to public, with instruction, and inclusive accommodation possible; also at Parc Municipal des Sports (58.43.53.54), 11 courts; Hourtin-Port — 8 courts (coaching); Lacanau-Océan — 11 courts (coaching, accommodation), Centre UCPA Lacanau, Pôle de l'Ardilouse (56.26.37.37); Pyla-sur-Mer — tennis club with court hire, coaching (56.22.70.48); Vieux-Boucau — 17 courts (58.48.32.47).

WALKING: GR8 runs the length of the Landes just inland from the sea. It occasionally gets lost amid urban development, as at Arcachon, but most of the way follows a course of dunes and forest which captures the essence of this region. If you are planning to use any GRs in the Landes, useful advance information and topo-guides may be obtained from Comité National des Sentiers de Grande Randonnée (CNSGR), at the SI in Pyla-sur-Mer. In addition some municipalities have prepared shorter marked forest walks and have details at their tourist offices.

Theme Parks and Activities for Children

ARCACHON: Aquacity, route des Lacs, 33470 Gujan-Mestres (56.66.39.39), extensive water playground with other amusements.

HOURTIN-PORT: extensive facilities for children, with play-leaders, a vast playground for 6–13 year olds, and purpose-built area for under-sixes.

Ferries

ACROSS THE GIRONDE — ROYAN-POINTE DE GRAVE: several daily each way. Single fares — car approx 120F, passenger/pedestrian 15F. Enquiries 56.09.60.84.
ACROSS THE MOUTH OF THE BASSIN D'ARCACHON — ARCACHON–CAP FERRET: frequent service throughout the day from June to September. No cars. Enquiries 56.83.06.62.
TO BIRD SANCTUARY ÎLE AUX OISEAUX: Summer excursions from Arcachon. Enquiries 56.83.06.62.

5
The Pays Basque (Euskadi)

The Basque people, probably descendants of a native Iberian tribe which was never fully Romanised, have long occupied a small region at the western end of the Pyrenees. It has perhaps not been to their advantage that the Pays Basque, or Basque Land, straddles the border of France and Spain, so that their little nation is effectively divided into two. But to the Basques this frontier is as nothing; their culture, customs and language are the same on both sides of it. Of the seven Basque provinces — three in France, four in Spain — they like to say 'Zaspiak-bat'. which means roughly that seven are one. Of the total Basque population, estimated at about 1½ million, some 250,000 live north of the border. The Basques call themselves Euskaldunak, their country Euskadi (or Euskardi), and their language Euskara, Sound the 's' in these words almost like 'z'.

Much uncertainty remains about the origin of the curious speech of the Basque people. Although sprinkled with Latin, Spanish, French and Occitan words, Euskara survives essentially unaffected by these more recent languages. Euskara, being basically unconnected with Latin (and indeed having seemingly little relationship with any other language group either) has for outsiders a surprisingly impen-

etrable quality. It is just as well for visitors that the Basques have been bilingual for centuries, speaking their own tongue first and foremost but learning either French or Spanish as a second language. Indeed for many Basques — perhaps most — nowadays it is Euskara which is the second language.

Not only their language, but the people themselves are remarkable. With certain important exceptions — for instance, they embraced the Christian religion with fervour — Basques over the millennia proved highly resistant to outside influences, 'uncolonisable', and still guard elements of a culture and society some of the characteristics of which long pre-date the Roman, or even the Celtic conquest. Even racially they stand apart from all other nations; one interesting indication of this is that they have the world's highest incidence of Rhesus negative blood groups — over 50 per cent of the population in some districts.

Their Pays Basque is lushly green, productive, and hilly, and its towns and villages are distinctive with their strikingly picturesque whitewashed houses of large dressed stones and heavy timbers. Scenically, this is certainly one of the most satisfying regions in France. Its Atlantic climate is mild and often wet, although British visitors should be reassured that the Basque country's scattered white clouds billowing across brilliant blue skies, and its frequent soft warm showers, having nothing in common with Britain's cold grey rainy days. Temperatures are pleasantly warm all year round, without extremes of heat in summer or of cold in winter. On the green slopes of the interior, the Basques have traditionally lived well as pastoral farmers, while on the coast they have distinguished themselves as sailors and fishermen, and in the past as whalers. Fishing and farming remain important to this day, although tourism is now, inevitably, another of the region's principal sources of income.

Many Basques live up to the popular image of being taller and leaner than the typical southerner, and, it is said, more energetic and enterprising too. The cliché of the homely, taciturn Basque man wearing his traditional *boina* (beret) and *espadrilles* or *alpargatas* (rope-soled shoes) — or, nowadays more likely, light canvas shoes from Spain — is still true to life.

Although preserving their culture within a small Franco-Spanish Atlantic region, the influence and impact of the Basques has been greater than one might suppose. Probably originating in the Ebro valley (although this remains uncertain), the Basque tribe came to occupy a broad area of northern Spain between the Ebro, the Pyrenees, and the Atlantic coast. It seems likely that Basques were driven north from the Ebro valley and became concentrated in their coastal and mountain areas first by their attempts to avoid contact with the Romans and then in the turmoil of the Visigoth invasion which followed the Romans' withdrawal. Known then as Bascons or Vascons, they founded the Pyrenean Kingdom of Vascony. As parts of the Basque nation came down from the mountains in the 7th century to merge with a local Romanised population in the Armagnac lowlands 'Vas-

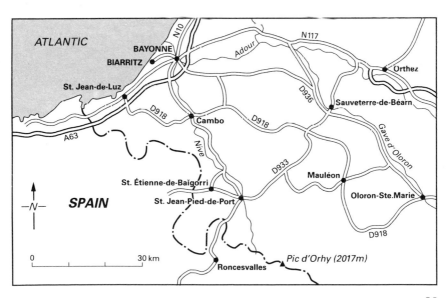

The Basque Language

Euskara, spoken by about one million Basques, is not a member of any known language group. (The only remotely similar language is spoken by a small group of mountain dwellers in the Russian Caucasus.) Euskara is not like the ancient pre-Roman Iberian tongue, and appears to be a remarkable survival of an even older palaeo-European language. At the time of the Roman conquest, it was spoken over a wider area of northern Spain, but many Basque speakers were converted to the Latin-based Romance languages of the occupation. Over the passing millennia, Euskara has absorbed words from Iberian, Latin, Occitan, Spanish, and French (many of these 'borrowed' words having kept their archaic form), but remains essentially unaltered.

Its syntax is complex, making abundant use of suffixes — of one or more letters — to denote which word in the sentence is the subject, object, etc. Transitive verb endings vary not only with tense but with the part of speech of the noun(s) to which they apply. Among other unusual elements is the insertion or substitution of letters in words to make slight changes in meaning, particularly the use of X to make a diminutive (eg: *hezur* means bone; *hexur*, little bone).

A stylised but recognisable form of Latin lettering is used, but pronunciation is difficult, with eight local accents. There are two types of glottal stops (B, D, and G, which are silent, and P, T, and K, which are sounded), and many slightly different sibilants (especially Z, TZ, S, TS, X, and TX). Pronounce X and CH as 'sh', TX as 'ch' or 'ks'. M, N, and Ñ are nasal. Sound LL as 'y'. S is often similar to 'z'.

A few common Basque words:
Boina — beret
Espadrilles — traditional light rope-soled slip-on shoes
Etche or **Etxe** — house
Euskadi or **Euskardi** — Basque name for the Pays Basque
Euskaldunak — the Basque people
Fronton — wall against which pelota is played
Gave — mountain river
Makila — decorative combination club/walking stick
Nive — river
Ongi Etorri — "Welcome"
Pelota — the Basque national game
Pottok — half-wild Pyrenean pony
Tchirula — three-holed flute
Trinquet — indoor court and wall for pelota
Ttun-Ttun — little drum
Txistus — three-holed flute
Xistera — leather and wicker glove for pelota (*chistera* in French)
Zortzicos — singing

Basque village houses

cony' expanded to become Gascony, while a purer Basque society remained in the coastal and western Pyrenees — today's Pays Basque. On the Spanish side of the frontier, the Basque country is still known as the Provincias Vascongadas or País Vasco.

The Basque provinces on the southern Pyrenees were, almost in their entirety, annexed by Spain's Castile over a period extending from 1200 until the 14th century (but they retained regional rights and privileges — called *fueros* or *fors* — right up to the beginning of the 20th century). On the northern slopes, the Basque country was at first held as part of English Aquitaine. During the 15th and 17th centuries most of the area that is now the French Pays Basque came under the control of Paris, but here too the *fueros* were respected until the Revolution. Since the Napoleonic period, when the Paris government was eager to eliminate regional differences, France's Basque territory has merely formed part of the département of Pyrénées-Atlantiques.

While Spanish Basques have become known for a resolute nationalism, seen at its most extreme in the violence of their separatist organisation ETA (which stands for *Euskadi Ta Azkatasuna*, Basque Freedom), Basques on the

French side of the border, though not themselves hankering for autonomy, have acquired a reputation for harbouring ETA activists who are being sought by the Spanish police. Yet, however much outsiders may or may not sympathise with the aims of ETA, it is important to realise that in truth the vast majority of Basques, whether Spanish or French, are not involved in any way with these activities and have little commitment to them. Especially since the Spanish Basque territory became an autonomous region in 1980, there has been a rapid decline in support on both sides of the border for the separatist idea and even more so for the violence — which ETA, undaunted, pledges will continue in Spain until the Madrid government allows the Basque country to detach itself as a completely independent nation.

One of this beautiful land's most picturesque features is the neat, distinctive domestic architecture. The typical village house, whether old or new, is prettily whitewashed, and has a lovely flowery garden: Basques are especially fond of hydrangea and wisteria. The building itself is constructed of large stone blocks and substantial vertical timbers; it has brown-painted shutters and wide eaves (sometimes supported by elaborate beams), and a shallowly pitched roof, often longer on one side than the other. Many of the houses have a first-floor balcony held up by Roman arches on the ground floor, and — a tradition most striking in the older houses — a carved lintel over the front door.

In many villages the dwellings do not cluster around a single centre as is common elsewhere, but are scattered over a wide area like two or three different hamlets. They do, nonetheless, have their focal points — particularly

85

the church. Indeed, the church is generally a notable feature of Basque villages, and the villagers are unanimous in the intensity of their religious devotion. Some of the distinct characteristics of Basque-style churches reflect their dominant role in communal life, and their need to accommodate the whole of the local population: a massive porch, a large aisleless interior crowded with pews, and wooden balconies. During services in a Basque church, the sexes are usually strictly segregated. The church and its parish graveyard are normally enclosed within an encircling wall, in what might be called the Celtic style (rarely seen elsewhere in France apart from Brittany).

In the graveyard, some of the graves are marked with traditional Basque headstones of a disc shape. Generally these are engraved with the heavy arms of the Basque cross (not crucifix-shaped); a few bear the ancient Basque swastika. Do not be disturbed if you see Basques wearing this esoteric symbol on jewellery; it has no sinister implications here, and is nothing to do with the German atrocities. Efforts to explain 'who the Basques are' and whence they originate sometimes point to the swastika — as well as certain features of the language — as evidence of a cultural link in antiquity with India.

Another focal point of the Basque town or village is its *fronton*. Just a tall wide wall beside a flat concrete or gravelled pitch, this is the place where Basque sports are played, especially pelota (or sometimes, in Basque, *pilota*). Many places also have, as is reasonable in this Atlantic climate, an indoor pitch and *fronton*, called a *trinquet*. It is almost certain that any summer traveller in the Basque country will come across pelota

being played. This is a fast and vigorous ball game between small teams of players, whose skill is in hurling and batting a small ball: it must hit the *fronton* and the ground within marked lines. It looks like a cousin of tennis and of squash, or a cross between the two, and indeed all three are derived from the same origin, the ancient *jeu de paume* (hand game). There are several forms of pelota, involving different rules and objectives and different hand-coverings; in most types a long wicker scoop-glove (a *xistera*, in French a *chistera*) is used, but surely the most impressive — and painful — version is the *mano* or *main nue* (bare hand), in which the hard ball is struck only with the player's palm or knuckles. Hand ball games using the pitch instead of the *fronton* wall — all variations on the pelota theme — are also likely to be seen.

Pelota, national game of the Basques, here being played à main nue, using only the bare right hand to strike the ball

Although it is the Basque national sport, pelota is not exclusive to this region. *Frontons* can be seen at a number of towns and villages in South West France, although outside the Pays Basque they tend not to have such an important place in local life. There are

Pelota

Still bearing a great resemblance to the ancient *jeu de paume* (*jeu* means game, *paume* is the palm of the hand), pelota has developed into a number of forms. All have their enthusiasts in the Basque country. The principle of all the pelota variations is that two teams oppose each other (a team being usually very small— perhaps two or three people), scoring points by the play of a small ball— generally hard— directed against a wall (the *fronton*) by being struck with the right hand. In most versions, a *gomme*— whether a racquet (*pala*), a scoop attached to the hand with a glove (*chistera*), or some other hand-covering— is used. In most forms of pelota, all players face the *fronton*, although the wall may be '*libre*' or '*à gauche*'. Between throws, a score-keeper (*chacharia*), on the pitch with the players, calculates and calls out the number of points scored. Not all types of pelota are played at the outdoor *fronton*; some are indoor games, played *en trinquet*. Players usually wear gleaming white outfits, with or without a coloured sash. In Basque, both the ball and the game itself are called either *pelota* or *pilota* (from the Latin *pilotta*, popular diminutive for *pila*, a ball), and players are called *pelotari*.

Versions of the game include:
Cesta punta— using large wicker scoop-glove, played in an arena or covered pitch walls with *fronton* on three sides (called a *jaï alaï*), hard ball with some 'bounce', 2 in team; this type of pelota has returned to the Pays Basque from South America
Chistera— using large wicker scoop-glove, *fronton*, hard ball, 3 in team
Frontennis— new variant using small stringed racket, *fronton* or *trinquet*, rubber ball, 2 in team
Jaï Alaï— see Cesta Punta
Joko Garbi— wicker scoop-glove, *fronton*, hard ball, 3 in team; an old form
Main Nue— bare hand (hit ball with palm or knuckles), *fronton*, hard ball, 2 in team, one of the oldest forms
Paleta— wooden racket, *fronton* or *trinquet*, rubber ball, 2 in team
Pasaka— large scoop-glove worn on hand, *en trinquet*, over a net, leather ball with some 'give', 2 in team
Rebot or **Lachoa**— long wicker scoop-glove, *fronton*, players face each other, hard heavy ball, 5 in team; probably the origin of the English game 'fives'
Xaré— stringed racket, *en trinquet*, hard ball, 2 in team

surprises though; on the Languedoc plain just inland from Montpellier, for example, a group of ten small towns and villages play an old pitch-and-*fronton* game called *tambourin*, which is clearly a close relative of pelota except that the ball is struck with a hand-held handleless circular bat like a tambourine; other versions of pelota are popular abroad, particularly in South America, and especially Argentina.

Quite apart from pelota, Basques enjoy many other sports and entertainments of their own invention. They can be seen at the frequent village festivals — including wood-cutting contests, trials of strength, poetry-reading competitions, jaunty musical performances on traditional instruments (pipe, drum, and more recently the accordion), and many colourful folk dances. Ritual Basque dances, always seen on these festive occasions, are often performed by men only, or with men and women strictly segregated. Striking embroidered costumes are worn for dances: the men's often mainly white, perhaps with bright streamers and sashes and head adorned with red beret; the women's maybe more richly coloured, but still with plenty of contrasting white and black and red.

Today nearly all French Basques live on the Atlantic coast between St. Jean-de-Luz and Bayonne, and it is here and in the beautiful ocean-facing hinterland province of Labourd that their traditions and way of life can best be appreciated. The two major cities of the Pays Basque are in this province: Biarritz and Bayonne, close neighbours which on the map seem to have almost, but not quite, merged into one. On closer inspection though, they are indeed quite separate, and each retains its own highly distinct character: the fundamental difference is that Bayonne has been for two thousand years a prosperous port and a capital of the Basque country, while Biarritz little more than a century and a half ago was a small, unimportant fishing village.

The obvious starting point for a visit to the Pays Basque is therefore **Bayonne** (pop: 40,000). The older part of the city stands on the south bank of the river Adour, regarded as the very border of the Basque country, while newer districts have spread onto the river's north

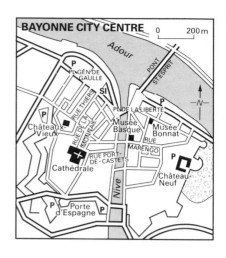

bank (St. Esprit), which now deserves to be brought into a visit to Bayonne if only for the fine view back across the water.

There is hardly a more congenial town in which to enjoy the best that South West France can offer in food, drink and art. One of its luxurious little pleasures is to sit at an outdoor table eating the famous handmade chocolates: any stroll in old Bayonne will soon lead past the door of a fine *chocolatier* or *confiseur*. Perhaps the most famous is *chocolatier* Cazenave, at 19 arceaux de Port-Neuf. Chocolate unexpectedly became one of the city's best-known specialities in the 16th century, after the Christian conquest of Spain, when the newly installed Catholic monarchy in Madrid ordered all Jews to be driven out of the country: they were, and most savagely. Portugal followed suit. While many of the refugees followed the conquered Moors back to North Africa, many others crossed the French border and were permitted to settle at Bayonne. Among the things they brought with them was a skill in making confectionery, especially chocolate and *touron* (like a soft almond nougat with pine nuts), both of which had previously been unknown in France. Other local specialities are the Basques' liqueur Izarra (advertised everywhere), and of course Bayonne cured ham.

The part of Bayonne which lies north of the Adour is called St. Esprit, mainly a 19th- and 20th-century residential development which now includes the railway station and several hotels and restaurants, as well as the St. Esprit church and, set well back behind protective gates, the pleasing early 19th-century classical-style synagogue (dated 5597) which serves Bayonne's remaining Jewish population. An older landmark is the rather uninteresting military citadel built by Vauban in 1679 to protect the harbour. On the waterfront, some big vessels and dock activity can sometimes be seen, although the busier quays lie downriver from this point. It was from Bayonne's port (as well as from St. Jean-de-Luz to its south), in the early Middle Ages, that so many Basques set out on their intrepid transatlantic whaling and deep-sea fishing expeditions. In the 10th century, sudden changes in the course of the Adour had a dramatically detrimental effect on the harbour; it recovered under French rule when, in 1578, the Adour was canalised to force it to flow to the sea at Bayonne again, instead of at Capbreton or Port Albret — for which places it also showed a strong predilection! Bayonne regained its position as a leading port, even as a notorious one, since it became well known as a base for much of France's lucrative piracy and privateering. That type of 'trade' has since been replaced by less dubious maritime enterprises, and Bayonne remains a major French port.

Look across the river towards Bayonne's old city; the view — the ensemble of place de la Liberté and place Général de Gaulle with their arches, the cathedral's spires, the dignified mansions — makes a noble introduction to the Pays Basque. Pont St. Esprit crosses the water, touches upon a slender peninsula which separates the Adour from its tributary the Nive, and continues (renamed as Pont Mayou) over the second river into place de la Liberté. This square is busy with traffic but nonetheless grand with the superbly arcaded façade of its theatre and Hôtel de Ville (housing the Syndicat d' Initiative-Office de Tourisme), adorned with café tables and chairs arranged in front. Behind the theatre, place Général de Gaulle is marginally quieter. Leading away from the place, rue Thiers is one of several bustling lively main streets of smart shops and bars. Off to its left are the narrower, mainly traffic-free shopping streets of the oldest quarter.

Rue Thiers soon reaches the sturdy walls and towers of the Château Vieux fortress and, beside it, remnants of the city's medieval fortifications. The ramparts still extend round the town centre in a broad defensive semicircle from the Château Vieux (built by the English in the 12th century, and reconstructed by the French in 1489) to the Château Neuf (newly built in 1489) on the other side of the Nive river. Both fortresses were further reinforced by Vauban in 1679. The Château Vieux stands on Roman ruins at the heart of former Lapurdum; the city's name was changed back, during the English period, to pre-Roman Baiona. As part of the French success at the end of the Hundred Years War, Bayonne was taken by the French in 1451 along with the rest of the Labourd province. The Château Vieux now houses the Foreign Legion.

The magnificent cloisters at Bayonne

Beyond the château, a few paces up rue des Gouverneurs you reach the Cathédrale Ste. Marie, which, together with its resounding bell, are among the most noticeable features of the town. This too stands on a Roman foundation — a temple which is itself believed to have taken the place of an even earlier shrine. The first sight of the cathedral, coming from this direction, is of the beautifully carved, gorgeously golden stone of the large porch. Coming closer, the whole is revealed as a superb building in the elegantly ornate Northern Gothic style. Dating mainly from the 13th century, the work continued until the 16th century and the north tower (still in the same style) and spires were added only in the last century. Inside, it

Bayonne: spires of the cathedral seen from rue du Port-Neuf

is dark, especially after Bayonne's blazing sunlight. The interior, tall and spacious, has three wide aisles as well as side chapels. Note that in one of the side chapels there is a representation of the Miracle of Bayonne which, if you want to believe it, occurred on 20 August 1451. This was the day that French troops besieged English Bayonne. A radiant white cross rising from a crown was seen in the sky, and was taken (retrospectively, one supposes, since it was seen by both sides) as a sign that God supported the French. The central aisle, with the heraldic arms of England on the keystone, reaches towards a high row of exquisite stained-glass windows. The choir and ambulatory, its side chapels, their superb stained glass, are inspiring and lovely. The choir is a magnificent achievement of Gothic art. Go out of the building into the cloisters, another marvellous example of Gothic work, with broad rib-vaulted arches and slender pillars, unbroken and enclosing a peaceful lawn. Walk round the cloisters, on the walkway paved in parts with 17th and 18th century grave-stones, to the south-east corner. This point gives the finest view of the cathedral's intricate stone-work: spire, buttresses, galleries and windows.

Emerge from the north entrance of the cathedral into pl Pasteur, and stroll down rue de la Monnaie. This street meets rue du Port-Neuf and rue Orbe in the heart of the oldest quarter. On this corner stands one of Bayonne's most striking old Basque-style mansions: five stories, including the arcaded street level, of handsome criss-crossed timbers and timbered windows. But all these streets have many other superb old houses worthy of a pause. Along rue Orbe, carrefour des Cinq-Cantons is where five of the old streets meet. Turn down rue Pont de Castets to the pleasant quayside of the river Nive. No. 1 rue Pont de Castets is a large rickety old timbered dwelling balanced on an arcaded stone base. Facing it is the Pont de Castets itself. In contrast with the Adour, very inadequately served with crossing points (Pont St. Esprit takes nearly all the Adour traffic; however a new bridge is soon to be constructed upriver), the river Nive has several picturesque little bridges like this. The old part of town on the Nive's left bank is called Grand Bayonne. On the right bank, the peninsula between the Nive and Adour, is Petit Bayonne. The *quais* along the right bank of the Nive make lovely walks.

Cross the pretty Nive on Pont de Castets. On the far side of the bridge is the Musée Basque, housed in a splendid Basque-style 17th-century mansion on the corner of rue Marengo and quai

Corsaire. Many French towns have a museum of local culture, but as often as not there is nothing of note to be seen in it. Don't fall into the trap of thinking that the same probably applies here. The Musée Basque is a really fascinating and enjoyable look at the remarkable culture and history of Bayonne, the Pays Basque, and its people. Exhibits, arranged in 40 rooms, give a valuable insight into such diverse subjects as pelota and Basque games, local Christian worship, Basque music and art, seafaring, the Jews in Bayonne, ceremonial costume, espadrilles and chocolate.

Nearby, in rue Jacques Laffitte, the extraordinary art collection donated to his native town by the portrait painter Léon Bonnat (1833–1922) now forms the basis of the Musée Bonnat. This is a first-class fine arts museum, with excellent examples of all major European schools of painting from the 14th to the 20th century, as well as some interesting sculpture including a Greek, Roman and Egyptian collection.

It is just a few paces from the museum back to the Mayou and St. Esprit bridges and place de la Liberté.

Anglet (pronounce the 't') is really neither Bayonne nor Biarritz, but between the two (pop: 33,000). It consists mainly of unpretentious detached houses, some old, some new, but almost all in traditional Basque style. It has an almost villagey flavour. Place Général de Gaulle, Anglet's small central square, has its parish church and the attractive administrative buildings of the little canton. They are not old, but are an excellent example of the Basque style.

Rue des Cinq-Cantons goes from Anglet to another little centre, less charming, called **Cinq Cantons**. This runs into **Chambre d'Amour** — wonderful name for a respectable residential district — which fronts onto a long, wide undeveloped beach, rather exposed to the Atlantic wind and waves. This is not the chic part of Biarritz. The beach is called Plage de la Chambre d'Amour. It is hard to know which was named first, the beach or the district, but the legendary explanation of the name, which would have to be translated as something like Love Chamber or Love Room, seems highly implausible. Apparently a loving couple, eager for a bit of privacy, retired to a waterfront cave; we do not know what occurred there, but it took so long that the tide rose without them noticing, filled the cave, and they were drowned. The cave itself can be seen at the southern end of the *plage*, in the massive rocky projection of the Pointe St. Martin.

On the other side of the Pointe begins **Biarritz** proper (pop: 28,000). Everything about Biarritz has to do with its magnificent waterfront; indeed there is little else of interest. The town follows the sweep of two broad bays (one of them a superb sandy beach), culminating in the turbulent shore of the Plateau de l'Atalaye, at the tip of which is a majestic rocky promontory, the Rocher de la Vierge. The town's streets and squares rise onto higher land behind the seafront, while the town centre is a small commercial area, close to the sea, built on the ridge which separates the two bays — the Grande Plage and the Plage de la Côte des Basques.

Along the full length of this spectacular stretch of coast, fluffy tamarisk and gaudy hydrangea follow a delightful promenade. The Biarritz seashore benefits from having this pleasant pedestrian walkway rather than a busy road beside the coast, even though in places there are short lengths of roadway beside the sea. Many sumptuous, fortunate mansions or 'villas' stand just behind the seafront in places, and in the shopping streets too it becomes obvious that there's plenty of money in Biarritz. It is, and has been for one hundred years, one of the most fashionable resorts in France. In the latter decades of the 19th century it was especially known as a winter resort of the British upper class. The 'Englishness' is scarcely apparent now, although perhaps Biarritz still does have a lingering affection for its British visitors.

Yet at the beginning of the 19th century, there was only a small Basque fishing and whaling community here (where the Port des Pêcheurs still is). In the early years of that century the village underwent an amazing transformation. At first, it attracted a few visitors of the less wealthy classes. In 1838, many supporters of Don Carlos de Bourbon's claim to the disputed Spanish throne (known as Carlists) were obliged to leave Spain in a hurry; these aristocratic rebels chose to spend their exile at Biarritz, which effectively 'put it on the map', at least as far as the Spanish were concerned. Victor Hugo wrote from Biarritz in 1843 that it was 'an adorable place', but added, 'My only fear is that it might become fashionable. People are already coming from Madrid and soon they will be coming from Paris.' He little knew just how fashionable it was shortly to become.

Overleaf: The beautiful ocean-front at Biarritz: picturesque Port des Pêcheurs in the foreground, with the stately Hôtel du Palais further back

During the next few years more and more, and wealthier, Spanish visitors came to Biarritz during the summer. One of them was a young lady from Granada called Eugenia Maria de Montijo de Guzman (1826–1920). In 1853 she married Napoleon III and became Empress of the French, and in 1855 began the construction at Biarritz of a palatial holiday home which came to be known as the Villa Eugénie. It was poised above the shore, at one end of the Grande Plage, with wonderful sea views, although evidently it was an unprepossessing sight itself ('like a barracks' according to one contemporary). In 1903, Villa Eugénie was badly damaged in a fire; it was acquired to become a hotel, and the subsequent reconstruction turned it into one of the Biarritz coast's most beautiful and impressive landmarks — the Hôtel du Palais. It is still truly palatial inside, offering real grandeur at a price only a privileged handful of people can afford. If room prices are more than the holiday budget allows, you can visit the hotel for a meal or for tea; but, be prepared, even that is far from cheap. Opposite the hotel is the lovely blue-domed church of the Eastern Orthodox community.

The arrival of Napoleon III and Empress Eugénie conferred the ultimate seal of approval on Biarritz. Almost at once British medical men started to proclaim the wonders of the town, its balmy invigorating ocean air and above all its salubrious winter climate. Elegant casinos and spa baths were constructed. During the latter decades of the 19th century the town became known increasingly as a British winter resort of standing. In 1861 it was felt necessary to build an Anglican church here, and visitors during the 1880s and 1890s and at the turn of the century included Queen Victoria, Edward VII and Gladstone.

Today, the broad sandy swathe of the Grande Plage — backed by the splendidly restored Art Déco Municipal Casino where King Farouk lost a great part of his fortune — spreads away south from the Hôtel du Palais. In summer it is covered with sunbathers. An interesting sight in autumn, when most of the tourists have gone home, is the massed audience of local people sitting along the promenade to watch the awesome waves of the equinoctial flood tides. At the southern end of the Grand Plage, the promenade joins boulevard Maréchal Leclerc briefly, climbs up the rising edge of the steep shore, then heads down away from the street again, skirting a rocky cove and an outcrop called the Rocher du Bastia before descending to the picturesque little Port des Pêcheurs, 'fishermen's port'. This popular little waterfront, with its café tables, its harbour, and the steep hydrangea-covered slopes behind, is a pleasant spot and very pretty seen from above.

Boulevard Leclerc, on the clifftop above, passes the sunny terrace of place Ste. Eugénie beside its church, and, in a short tunnel through the Plateau, goes directly to the Rocher de la Vierge.

The seashore walkway, leaving the Port des Pêcheurs, climbs again, partly in steps, clinging to the edge of the Plateau de l'Atalaye and giving another lovely view down onto the lazy activity of the harbour. Rising and falling with the contours of the cliffside, the path and steps make their way round towards the esplanade du Rocher de la Vierge. A walkway leads out, over a turbulent channel of water, to the Rocher itself:

down below is a dramatically ocean-beaten rocky shore, and in both directions superb views of all the Biarritz seafront. On the shore near the walkway, facing the Rocher, the large Musée de la Mer houses an exceptional aquarium of all local sea fauna, as well as having interesting sections on the history of fishing and local geology.

A few yards farther, on the other side of the Plateau, the Plage du Port-Vieux is a wide sandy cove sheltered by a semicircle of high cliffs. On windy days it is well protected and is something of a suntrap; the water though can be rough and unpredictable. More rocky outcrops separate this little bay from the long sweep of the Plage de la Côte des Basques. This is wilder, and backed by an immense cliff face, from the top of which the road called La Perspective has magnificent views. By tradition, on 15 August every year the Basques of the province's rural interior used to make a pilgrimage to this beach for a mass bathe. The Côte des Basques is now more associated with surfers, some of whom are amazingly skilled.

Behind the Plage du Port-Vieux, little place du Port-Vieux (which is little more than a car-park) marks one end of the original centre of Biarritz, now a popular district of pleasant, quiet shopping streets and agreeable squares with café-bars, and restaurants. From Port Vieux, these narrow streets lead to the bigger place Ste. Eugénie, and on to the much busier place Georges Clémenceau, through which pass the town's major roads. There are some enticing shops, with high-quality fashions and other goods, including lots of exceptional *chocolatiers* and *pâtissiers*. The main tourist office is at the bus station beside the glorious pink 'château' which houses the Mairie.

The coast from Biarritz to the Spanish border is known as the Côte Basque. Its high cliffs twist and turn high above the rolling waves, giving dramatic views in places — although on the whole there are few sea views from the road itself (despite which, the coast road can be very crowded).

St. Jean-de-Luz (pronounced like the English word 'loose'), on the north bank of the river Nivelle where it emerges into a calm and sheltered bay, is today a bright, popular modern resort. It has a considerable history too. Called Donibane-Lohizun by the Basques, its exact origins are not known, but it was a thriving seaport when the English took over in 1152. It has often been fought for since then, on account of its obviously strategic position, essential in the control of the Franco-Spanish border and the Bay of Biscay (the name Biscay, incidentally, comes from the Basque name Vizcaya for their coastal waters). Throughout the 16th and 17th centuries it was hotly disputed between France and Spain. Wellington, aiding the Spanish in the war with France, had the good sense to move his headquarters here to pass the winter of 1813–14 untroubled by any military activity. As soon as Biarritz began to become popular in the mid-19th century, St. Jean-de-Luz, with a reputation as a quieter and less ostentatious resort, was also favoured by the English. The town centre follows the bay's pleasant sandy beach. While much of the centre and waterfront consists mainly of large balconied apartment blocks, there are also many older buildings in traditional Basque style closer to the port.

The Nivelle estuary forms a busy fishing harbour at the southern end of the town. The port prospered from its whaling throughout the English period,

97

turning as well to piracy and privateering after the French conquest (1451). The important catches now are anchovy and tuna. Adjacent to the quaysides, place Louis XIV is the focus of the town. The Hôtel de Ville (1657) and the splendid Maison Louis XIV or Château Lohobiague (1635), where Louis XIV spent the month before his marriage with the Infanta Maria Teresa in 1660, are two landmarks close by. The future queen and her mother stayed in the imposing quayside mansion now called Maison de l'Enfante. Place Louis XIV marks one end of the old Quartier de la Barre district (now largely a pedestrianised shopping and leisure area) on the small spit of land which almost closes the harbour mouth — *la barre*. The main street through the Barre quarter is rue Mazarin (Wellington's headquarters was at No. 2), which passes place Louis XIV to become rue Gambetta, St. Jean's busy main street, in which stands the church where Louis and Maria Teresa's bizarre wedding took place, the

Église St. Jean-Baptiste. This superb example of the Basque style of church has the typical broad nave and fine oak galleries, as well as a striking gilt retable of about 1670. Although originally 13th-century, the church was largely remodelled during enlargements in the 15th century, and most of the interior is 17th-century. In a remarkable display of that absurd self-importance with which French monarchs (and later heads of state too) have been cursed, the main entrance was bricked up after the royal wedding so that no lesser mortal could pass through it!

Just across the Nivelle, **Ciboure** (or Zibiburu) fronts the south quays of the river with old, attractive timbered houses with balconies looking over the fishing trawlers in the port. The composer Maurice Ravel (1875–1937), perhaps best known for his Bolero symphony, was born at No.12 in the row of dwellings along the waterside. The bay curves round to the unusual lighthouse and small 17th-century for-

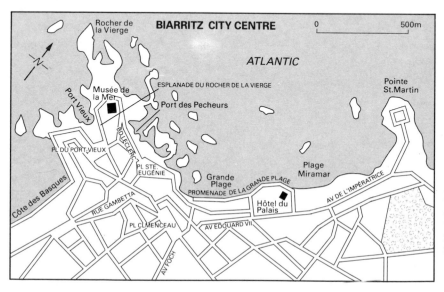

Inside a typical Basque church, with a single broad nave, ornate retable behind the altar and wooden galleries around the walls

tress at **Socoa**, from which there are fine coastal views. There's a good beach here. The coast road south (the D912), known as the Corniche Basque, closely follows the edge of high grass-topped cliffs which slope steeply down to the sea. The drive has several marvellous viewpoints before arriving at the border town of **Hendaye** and its resort area Hendaye-Plage. This was the unexpected location chosen by Winston Churchill for a holiday in 1945 after Hitler's suicide and when the Allied victory was secure. Colourful with flowering trees and shrubs which flourish in its mild climate, Hendaye rises sharply from the river Bidassoa, marking the Spanish frontier. In the midst of the river, the Île des Faisans has been for centuries the traditional 'neutral ground' for Franco-Spanish state

encounters: since the 1659 Treaty of the Pyrenees (which gave France the Roussillon and Cerdagne districts of Catalonia at the other end of the Pyrenees), the island has alternated every six months between Spain and France.

Inland from almost any point along the coast from Bayonne to the border, the country rises quickly into green and beautiful hills, hidden in the folds of which lie surprisingly rustic and unspoiled Basque villages.

From St. Jean-de-Luz, the D918 follows the Nivelle valley into the uplands. Its first stop is at **Ascain**, a rustic small town very conscious of its Basque identity, thoroughly 'discovered' but altogether rewarding a visit. Green fields penetrate almost to the main square. Picturesque traditional houses enclose the main square with its massive four-square tower-like church. The interior of the building is fascinating and atmospheric, dark and heavy. As usual, there are no aisles other than the central space between the pews, while three tiers of wooden balconies rise up around the sides. Behind the altar is a huge gilded retable. In the graveyard outside there are several traditional discoidal gravestones. One of them — dated 1657 — shows, curiously, a cock and hen on each side of a Basque cross. Note that a few of the tombs bear the ancient Basque swastika. Pierre Loti lodged in Ascain's Hôtel de la Rhune and while here wrote *Ramuntcho*, probably his best-known work.

Espelette is a centre of two very Basque things: red cayenne peppers and *pottoks*, the tiny, endearing semi-wild horse of the western Pyrenees. Hot peppers, used delicately, are an essential part of Basque cuisine, and the *piments de l'Espelette* are the most highly prized of them. The local variety is not terribly fiery, and balances its 'hot' spiciness with a subtle, almost sweet piquancy. Every year at the end of October Espelette celebrates with a Fête du Piment, during which garlands of red peppers can be seen all over the village. There's also, each January, an interesting Foire aux Pottoks, and it won't come as a surprise to any but the most sentimental (and optimistic) to discover that the main purpose of the commerce in *pottoks* is also gastronomic. The animals, which once were used in coal mines, now have little use except as meat.

After just 5 km more the road arrives at **Cambo-les-Bains**, rising from the river Nive. Not a typical Basque village in that it is a spa, for a brief spell Cambo was once quite cosmopolitan, although it is now much less so. It has a pleasant

leafy atmosphere and makes a good touring base, with easy and attractive access to much of the best of the Pays Basque. Edmond Rostand (1868–1918), author of *Cyrano de Bergerac* and many other dramatic works, lived just outside town on the D932 (the Bayonne road) in an ostentatious Basque-style mansion, the Villa Arnaga, built to his specifications in elaborate gardens.

The D932, a fast major road, goes to Bayonne by following the river Nive. A more scenic route to Bayonne would be to take the so-called Route Impériale des Cimes — the Imperial Summits Road. Leave Cambo to the east on the D10 (the Hasparren road), turning north as signposted after about 6km onto the Route Impériale. This high, winding military road was laid out by Napoleon (who, in his campaigns, was fond of using unexpected access routes through mountains). Though it is high up, the name means not so much that the road travels over the summits, as that it has a good view of them. **Hasparren**, east of Cambo, is a little workaday town dating back at least to Roman times: over the church door there is a 4th-century inscription. It has been known for many centuries as a centre of shoemaking and leather work. The D22 turns in the town, leading to the impressive caverns of the Grottes Isturits and Oxocelhaya (access is via the village of St. Esteben). Isturits has traces of prehistoric habitation, Oxocelhaya remarkable stalactites and stalagmites. Beyond, the road continues to St. Palais (see below)

Rising south from Cambo, the D918 travels towards St. Jean-Pied-de-Port (see below) through an increasingly calm, bucolic landscape. Almost at once it by-passes **Itxassou**, an enticing and charming village with several old dwellings and an attractive Basque-style church with its massive porch and interior galleries. There are discoidal gravestones in the churchyard, some with swastikas. Itxassou is another thoroughly 'discovered' village (it has nine hotels), yet remains quiet, unaffected and rustic. It is famous for cherries, and in spring the district is bathed in blossom. A steep minor road (the D349) works up the left bank of the Nive, while the main road travels more rapidly along on the other side of the river, passing from Labourd province into Lower Navarre and eventually reaching a junction at which one arm of the road leads on to St. Jean and the other turns towards St. Étienne-de-Baïgorri.

The road to St. Étienne passes through the vineyards of the Irouléguy *Appellation*, which produces the plain table wines, red, white and rosé, of the Pays Basque. **St. Étienne-de-Baïgorri** (or Baïgorry) lies in superbly attractive country in the valley of the Nive des Aldudes (*nive* meaning river). Crossing the river downstream from the much older crossing point called the pont Romain (although it is probably medieval rather than Roman), the road enters the town. St. Étienne has many fine Basque-style houses, several with excellent lintel carvings and impressive front doors. Spread out, like some other Basque villages, it is almost two separate places; one has the spacious main square with its *fronton*, the other has what must be the prettiest police station in France, and the intriguing and unusual church (with Syndicat d'Intiative opposite). On the day we arrived (3 July), St. Étienne was celebrating its Kermeza (village fête, called in French a *kermesse*). A procession of dancers in handsome embroidered costume (men and women keeping to opposite sides of the street) and musicians playing a

jaunty tune on traditional instruments, led by two tall models or 'giants' in female dress, danced its way from the square to the church. Returning from the church to the square, the whole village sat down to a banquet of Basque dishes. In the Pays Basque such things are not done for the benefit of tourists, and despite the friendliness of the people and the welcome they extend, one has a feeling, maybe only an intuition, that they wish they could keep all these customs a secret from outsiders.

St. Étienne has become popular among hunters, anglers and walkers as a base for penetrating the picturesque upper valley of the Aldudes. The valley, noted for fine quality charcuterie, rises through the small villages of Banca, Aldudes with its attractive little centre, and Urepel. Curiously, above Urepel, in the high pastureland of the Pays Quint, the local farmers have a long-held right to graze their animals over the frontier in Spain.

The D15 leaves St. Étienne for St. Jean-Pied-de-Port, again climbing and falling through the Irouléguy vineyards, and passing the village of Irouléguy itself, with its quaint church. **St. Jean-Pied-de-Port** (in Basque, Donibane Garazi), a superbly well-preserved little medieval town within impressive fortifications, and in a delightful setting, is the principal inland centre of the Pays Basque. A locally produced pear liqueur is Brana; its distilleries at rue 11-Novembre are open to visitors. The pretty Nive runs through the middle of St. Jean. The older heart of the medieval town — the *ville haute* — lies on the north bank, and is still surrounded by its 15th-century ramparts. South of the river the town and encircling fortifications date from the 1659 Treaty of the Pyrenees. Both districts are fascinating

and picturesque, with narrow cobbled streets lined with handsome old dwellings (mostly 16th–18th centuries). The two sides of the river are linked within the ramparts by the Vieux-Pont, while the town's one busy shopping street crosses on the Pont Neuf from place Floquet within the walled area south of the river to place du Marché and place Charles de Gaulle outside the walls on the north bank.

In place Charles de Gaulle, Monsieur Arrambide's well-known Hôtel des Pyrénées is a charming four-storey Basque mansion. The Syndicat d'Initiative is nearly opposite, close to the Porte de France. Go through this Gothic gateway into the medieval quarter. Inside, walk up rue de la Citadelle, lined with fine old houses, past the odd little Prison des Évêques, to the 15th-century Porte de St. Jacques, pretty with flowers. Remaining within the ramparts, a path leads from this gate steeply up to Vauban's 17th-century citadel, with good views. Either by the even more precipitous and difficult postern steps, or by returning along rue de la Citadelle, descend to the bank of the Nive, attractive with traditional timbered Basque houses, their balconies overhanging the water. Porte Notre Dame — built almost as a part of the Gothic church, the Église Notre-Dame — opens onto the Vieux-Pont, which crosses to rue d'Éspagne on the other side of the river. This street, with shops selling Basque linen or charcuterie from the Aldudes valley, rises again from the river towards the southern ramparts, and leaves town on the south side through the broken Porte d'Éspagne.

Houses by the Nive at St. Jean-Pied-de-Port

103

The Compostela Pilgrimage

Compostela, Jerusalem and Rome, were the three great pilgrimages of the Middle Ages, with up to 2 million believers visiting the shrine of Santiago (St. James) at Compostela each year. The basis of their journey was a story which had been created in the 9th century as a rallying point for the Christian struggle against the Islamic presence in Spain. It told that the apostle James the Greater had travelled to Spain after the crucifixion, worked for seven years to convert the country to Christianity, and returned to his homeland Judaea where he was killed by King Herod. His body, the tale continued, was taken back to Spain by his disciples (or, in some versions, by angels) and its unknown final resting place revealed for the first time some 800 years later to Bishop Theodomir, who in AD813 claimed to have been directed to the spot by a star (hence *compostela*, from *campus stella*, the field of the star). In one version, he personally saw the star; in another, he was told about it by some shepherds. The claim inspired Christians in their war against the Moors who at this time held half the Iberian peninsula. In AD844, Don Ramiro I and his men, in battle with Moors at Clavijo, claimed that St. James, in shining armour and bearing a white banner emblazoned with a cross, had ridden onto the battlefield and with celestial sword put the Moslems to flight. As Christians made steady advances against Moslem forces, they too would say, in the manner of the time, that St. James had aided them, slaughtering hundreds of men. James became known as the Slayer of Moors, symbol of the Christian conquest of Spain and the banishment of Islam from western Europe. As such he was greatly revered: the Bishop of Le Puy journeyed to give thanks at the shrine in AD951, which started the pilgrimage to Compostela in earnest.

Despite being completely at variance with all scholarly knowledge and with the biblical account of James's life and death, the story gained official credence from the pragmatic authorities in Rome. The church approved routes for pilgrims to follow, and these were waymarked by the Knights Templar. Board and lodging was provided along the way by the monastic houses, and medical treatment given free by the monks of Cluny. To receive this hospitality pilgrims had to be furnished with documentary evidence, usually a letter from their bishop, that they were genuine pilgrims — and had to be wearing the proper attire of a pilgrim: heavy cape with shoulder covering, sandals, leather belt, gourd, food pouch, felt hat turned up in front and adorned with scallop shells, and in the hand, a long stave.

During English attacks on Spain in 1589, the bones at Compostela were removed for safekeeping and subsequently lost. In 1879 it was claimed that they had been found again, were given the pope's blessing, and the shrine again attracts vast numbers, especially for 25 July, St James's day in the Catholic calendar.

Main Festivals in the Pays Basque

A brief selection from a full calendar of events throughout the Pays Basque.

Note that Biarritz stages many shows and performances during the year, especially in ballet and opera. Contact the tourist office for an up-to-date programme.

January
ESPELETTE — Foire aux Pottoks: fair for the buying and selling of pottoks, miniature Basque horses.

March
BIARRITZ — Carnival: traditional festivities and celebrations.

April–May
BIARRITZ — Fêtes Musicales: several days of classical music events, often with distinguished performers.

May
In many Basque villages — Procession de la Fête-Dieu (2nd Sunday after Whitsun).

June
ST. JEAN-DE-LUZ — Fête de la St. Jean: old Midsummer festival, with religious celebrations, music, pelota, bullfights, etc. (24th–25th).

July
HASPARREN — cow-running in the streets.

August
ASCAIN — Course à la Rhune: a mass run up the Rhune mountain and back.
BAYONNE — Fête de Bayonne: music, bullfights, processions, etc. (usually whole of first week).
BIARRITZ — Nuit Féerique: night firework displays (on the 15th); Fête de la Mer (on the 16th).
ST. JEAN-PIED-DE-PORT — Cheese Fair.
ST. PALAIS — Fête Basque.
All main towns of the Côte Basque — Festival de Musique: a succession of concerts (last week in August/first week in September).

September
BIARRITZ — Le Temps d'Aimer: about two weeks of arts and entertainment, mainly dance.

October
ESPELETTE — Fête du Piment: colourful festival of Espelette's red and green hot peppers (end of the month).

St. Jean is astonishingly festive during the summer months, with something 'from the seven Basque provinces' going on almost every day — singers, dancers, pelota players. Throughout the season the town is kept busy selling its history and charm to a constant stream of visitors. But there's nothing new in that; St. Jean has been 'harvesting' visitors for many centuries, especially the pilgrims who, during the Middle Ages, thronged through here on their way to the church of Santiago (i.e. St. James) at Compostela in north-western Spain. They came from all over western Christendom, pausing on the way at various churches and religious hospices which today can still be identified by their scallop shell (usually carved over the main entrance), which was the symbol of the Santiago pilgrimage. These travellers were truly the tourists of their day, for while many were motivated by intense religious passion — and it was common for large groups seized by mass religious hysteria to take the Compostela road *en masse* — a great many others were motivated not so much by spiritual feeling as by the desire to see the world. A guidebook was written for them in 1130, describing all the sights of interest on or near the principal routes, including details of language, local customs, and the food and lodging to be obtained. Others on the road were what was known as *faux pèlerins*, false pilgrims, who made money by begging, deception and theft while living on Church charity. One of the major routes to Compostela, and the most popular, crossed the crest of the Pyrenees at the Roncesvalles (or Roncevaux) Pass, known as the Port de Roncesvalle. At the foot of the last climb up to the Port — hence the town's name — was St. Jean-Pied-de-Port. Minor and

major pilgrim routes converged on Ostabat (about 18km from St. Jean), and the united bands of pilgrims continued from Ostabat to St. Jean. They would mostly arrive by the Porte de St. Jacques, cross the Vieux-Pont, and leave through the Porte d'Éspagne. From there the travellers climbed to Roncesvalles either by the steep, difficult, direct way on the old Roman road (Route des Ports de Cize, now the GR65) or the easier slope up the Petit Nive and, on the Spanish side, the río Luzanne. At the heights of the pass, they reached the welcome shelter and repose of the Ibañeta Monastery near Roncesvalles.

Perhaps there was something satisfying for Christians on their way to Compostela to descend into Spain through the Roncesvalles Pass, where in the year AD778 Charlemagne's soldiers, led by the great Roland, had been massacred — so the popular Song of Roland had it — by Saracens (that is, Moslems). The Song of Roland was, rather like the legend of St. James, a good example of how in the Middle Ages fact and fiction could be interwoven freely in any proportion; the mentality of the age permitted people to believe sincerely in tales founded more on imagination than truth. A whole type of story-telling, weaving fictional and dramatic episodes around the lives of real historical characters, thrived from the 11th to the 13th centuries — *chansons de geste*. Charlemagne (742–814), king of the Franks, crowned by the pope as Emperor of the West, was real enough. But the *chansons de geste* composed about him, based on a fictional idea that he was always

St. Jean-Pied-de-Port: the rue d'Espagne

accompanied by twelve 'paladins', turned his life into a series of spell-binding legends which were then referred to as historical fact. According to one of these, the Song of Roland, the bravest and most stalwart of Charlemagne's paladins was Roland, based on a real person, Hrodland of Brittany. In the year 778 — and this part is true — Charlemagne's army was returning through the Pyrenees from a battle at Pamplona. As they went through the Roncesvalles Pass, local Basques (or Vascons) ambushed the rearguard, among whom was Hrodland, and killed most of them by raining down large boulders from high above. The Song of Roland tells of this event by changing the Basques to Saracens, adding a thrilling tale of treachery and intrigue, and concluding with Charlemagne arriving to conquer the infidels — a version which the French considered infinitely preferable to the truth.

St. Jean-Pied-de-Port was the capital of Lower Navarre, which was cut off from the rest of Navarre in 1512 when Ferdinand of Spain took all that part of the kingdom which lay south of the Pyrenees. Nevertheless, the title of King of Navarre was always claimed by French monarchs after that time. None was more entitled to the honour than Henri IV (1562–1610) — the Protestant who decided that 'Paris is worth a Mass.' Born at Pau (see page 124), he acceded to the Navarre throne as Henri III of Navarre, married Margaret of Valois, daughter of the French monarch Henri II, and inherited the crown of France.

The pleasant main road (the D933), goes from St. Jean-Pied-de-Port straight through its older neighbour St. Jean-le-Vieux, where the church was for centuries an essential pause for the Compos-tela pilgrims, and on towards St. Palais at the northern margins of the Pays Basque. East of the road, Lower Navarre gives way to the Basque country's small Soule province, once English, taken by the Comte de Foix in 1449. At Larceveau, the D918 turns towards the Soule capital **Mauléon** (properly Mauléon-Licharre), on the way climbing over the scenic Col d'Osquich pass. An important agricultural and industrial centre, especially noted for espadrilles and shoes, Mauléon rises from the right bank of the river Saison, or Gave de Mauléon, with Licharre on the left bank. The ruins of the Château d'Andurain, originally a 15th-century fortress, transformed into a Renaissance mansion in the early 17th century, gaze down from the hilltop. From Mauléon, several routes cross the wooded hills to the east and north, leaving the Pays Basque and reaching the Gave d'Oloron in Béarn. The D918 remains in the Basque country, following the Saison valley south through pleasing rustic villages, to **Tardets-Sorholus**, which makes a good local base. Farther south, the Saison valley can be followed towards the spectacular scenery of the summits.

Staying instead on the main D933 as it leaves St. Jean-Pied-de-Port behind and follows the Bidouze river, the countryside changes, becoming less hilly, broader and more gently undulating. **St. Palais** likes to describe itself as *en Pays Basque*, which is quite true as it is within the province of Lower Navarre, but shows little of that genuine charm and character with which the rest of the Basque country is blessed. The D933 leaves Lower Navarre and enters Béarn, soon reaching the Gave d'Oloron and the waterside town of Sauveterre de Béarn (see page 115).

Hotels and Restaurants

AINHOA: Hôtel Ithurria (59.29.92.11), excellent restaurant, reasonable hotel, in superb old Basque dwelling, moderately priced.

BAYONNE and ANGLET (se also BIARRITZ): Mercure Hôtel, av Jean Rostand (59.63.30.90), large, modern, comfortable hotel with reasonable restaurant, fair prices.

Restaurant du Cheval Blanc, 68 rue Bourgneuf (59.59.01.33), Bayonne's long-established top restaurant, usually excellent, not cheap.

Restaurant François Miura, 24 rue Marengo (59.59.49.89), excellent modern cooking, good-sized portions, friendly and efficient service, and very reasonably priced menus for such high quality. In the old quarter.

Le Grand Hôtel and **Restaurant Les Carmes**, 21 rue Thiers (59.59.14.61), nice quiet reliable central hotel, moderate prices. Good restaurant.

Hôtel Loustau, beside Adour bridge on N bank (59.55.16.74), noisy at front, quiet at back, reasonably priced, well placed for Bayonne, good restaurant.

Château de Brindos, rte de l'Aviation, Anglet (59.23 17,68), luxurious Relais et Château with superb restaurant, in its own park, expensive.

Hôtel de Chiberta et du Golf, 104 bd des Plages, Anglet (59.63.95.56), smart well-placed hotel-restaurant adjacent to superb Chiberta golf course, prices above average.

BIARRITZ: There are many small hotels of modest standard and reasonable prices in the area close to the sea and to the centre of Biarritz between pl du Port-Vieux and pl Ste. Eugénie — e.g. Hôtels Beau Lieu, Montguillot, Port Vieux, Washington, Atalaya, Florida.

Hôtel du Palais, 1 av Impératrice (59.41.64.00), luxurious hotel and restaurant in the former Villa Eugénie, superb amenities and sea views, expensive.

Hôtel Miramar, av Impératrice (59.41.30.00), as luxurious as the Palais, with an even better restaurant, and just as expensive. Has own prestigious thalassotherapy spa complex.

Café de Paris, pl Bellevue (59.24.19.53), an outstanding restaurant with high prices. Centrally located.

Auberge du Relais, 44 av de la Marne (59.24.85.90), modest, agreeable little hotel restaurant with moderate prices.

Hôtel Carlina, bd Prince-des-Galles (59.24.42.14), excellent hotel-restaurant with sea view — rooms expensive, but reasonable *menu*.

CAMBO-LES-BAINS: Hôtel Errobia, av Chanteclerc (59.29.71.26), fine Basque house in park, quiet, inexpensive.

Relais de la Poste, pl Mairie (59.29.73.03), good inexpensive 3-star Logis with rather pricey restaurant.

ESPELETTE: Hôtel Euzkadi (59.29.91.88), appealing, comfortable 2-star Logis with excellent restaurant.

GUÉTHARY: Hôtel le Briketenia, rue de l'Empereur (59.26.51.34), reasonable hotel and superb restaurant both with very acceptable prices.
Hôtel Pereria, rue Église (59.26.51.68), agreeable rustic-style family home with pleasant shady garden, decent accommodation, good food, low prices.

ITXASSOU: Hôtel du Fronton, next to *fronton* (59.29.75.10), agreeable, friendly 2-star Logis with good *menus*, inexpensive.
Hôtel du Chêne, next to church (59.29.75.01), attractive old 2-star Logis with enjoyable *menus* of local dishes, inexpensive.

ST. ÉTIENNE-DE-BAÏGORRI: Hôtel-Restaurant Arcé (59.37.40.14), one of the most pleasing hotels in the Basque region, comfortable, well-equipped, with good views, and for very reasonable prices; the restaurant is superb.

ST. JEAN-DE-LUZ: There are several reasonably inexpensive hotels and restaurants of fair standard in rue Thiers and rue Gambetta.
Le Grand Hôtel, 43 bd Thiers (59.26.35.36), splendid old building in the main street, best hotel and best restaurant in town, expensive.
Hôtel Chantaco, at the Chantaco golf course (59.26.14.76), excellent tranquil stylish hotel and restaurant, expensive.
Hôtel Madison, 25 bd Thiers (59.26.35.02), traditional little town hotel, not dear.

ST. JEAN-PIED-DE-PORT: Hôtel des Pyrénées, pl Gén. de Gaulle (59.37.01.01), famous Basque restaurant with exceptional cuisine, together with comfortable rooms, Relais et Château, attractive building, nice atmosphere, above average prices but not expensive for this standard.
Hôtel Etche Ona, pl Floquet (59.37.01.14), very cheap small hotel with excellent higher-priced restaurant.
Hôtel Ramuntcho, rue de France (59.37.03.91), modest, very inexpensive 1-star Logis with restaurant.

ST. PÉE-SUR-NIVELLE: Hôtel-Restaurant du Fronton (59.54.10.12), small moderately priced 2-star with excellent restaurant.

SARE: Hôtel-Restaurant Arraya (59.54.20.46), magnificent Basque mansion, excellent restaurant, very fair prices.
Hôtel-Restaurant Pikassaria, in the Lehembiscay quarter (59.54.21.51), charming and very inexpensive 2-star Logis.

Museums and Caves

BAYONNE: Musée Basque, corner rue Marengo/quai Corsaire. Large, comprehensive and fascinating overview of Basque culture with emphasis on Bayonne *9.30–12.30, 2.30–6.30. Closed Sun and j.f.*
Musée Bonnat, rue Jacques Lafitte (59.59.08.52). Impressive collection of fine arts, all European schools 14th-20th centuries *15 June–15 Sept: 10–12, 3–7 (exc. Fri, open till 9). Rest of year: weekday mornings reserved for school parties; Mon, Wed, Thu 1–7; Fri 3–9, Sat, Sun 10–12, 3–7. Closed Tue and j.f.*

BIARRITZ: Musée de la Mer, Plateau d'Altalaye. Extensive displays of the flora and fauna of the Bay of Biscay, local fishing industry, local geology *7–7 daily*.

CAMBO-LES-BAINS: Villa Arnaga (59.29.70.57), Museum of Edmond Rostand in his former home *Guided tours only. Mar, Apr and Oct: 2.30–6; May–Aug, 10–12, 2.30–6.*

ISTURITS & OXOCELHAYA: Grottes, near St. Martin-d'Arberoue, 12km from Hasparren (59.29.64.72). Impressive caverns with rock formations, signs of pre-historic human habitation *Guided tours only. Mar–Nov, am & pm. Closed Mon & Tue mornings exc. Jun–Sep.*

ST. JEAN-DE-LUZ: Maison Louis XIV (59.26.01.56). Where Louis XIV lodged *Guided tours (½hr) throughout day from Jun–Sep. Closed Sun am and some j.f.*

ST. JEAN-PIED-DE-PORT: Musée de la Pelote Basque, at the Mairie (59.37.00.92). All about pelota *July and August only.*

ST. PALAIS; Musée de la Basse-Navarre et des Chemins de St. Jacques, at the Mairie (59.65.71.78). Local history. Compostela pilgrimage *All year.*

SARE: Grotto de Sare (59.54.24.16), *Jun–Sep: 9–6 daily; May, Oct: Sat & Sun only.*

Tourist Offices

CRT office (regional information for whole of Aquitaine): 10 rue René Cassin, Bordeaux 33049 (56.39.88.88; fax 56.43.07.63).

Agence de Tourisme du Pays Basque (information on the Pays Basque): 1 rue de Donzac, 64108 Bayonne (59.59.28.77; fax 59.25.48.90).

OTSI offices (local information): ANGLET — av de la Chambre d'Amour (59.03.77.01); BAYONNE — pl des Basques (59.46.01.46; fax 59.59.37.56); CAMBO-LES-BAINS — in Parc St. Joseph (59.29.70.25); ESPELETTE — rue Principale (59.29.91.66, July–August only); GUÉTHARY — pl du Fronton (59.26.56.60); HASPARREN — pl St. Jean (59.29.62.02); HENDAYE — 12 rue des Aubépines (59.20.00.34); MAULÉON — 10 rue J. B. Heugas (59.28.02.37); ST. ÉTIENNE-DE-BAÏGORRI — pl de l'Église (59.37.47.28); ST. JEAN-DE-LUZ — pl Maréchal Foch (59.26.03.16); ST. JEAN-PIED-DE-PORT — 14 pl Charles de Gaulle (59.37.03.57); ST PALAIS — pl de l'Hôtel de Ville (59.65.71.78).

Where there is no tourist office, apply to the Town Hall (Mairie or Hôtel de Ville).

Sports and Leisure

GOLF: excellent Chantaco course at St. Jean-de-Luz (59.26.14.22) and Chiberta course at Anglet/Bayonne (59.63.83.20); other first rate 18-hole courses at Biarritz (59.03.71.80) and Ciboure (59.26.18.99). All available with accommodation and tuition. Contact the Aquitaine CRT for brochure on the region's courses.

RIDING: Centre de Randonnée Equestre en Pays Basque. Centre Hippique de la Côte Basque, and other riding organisations, enquire at Comité Regional Sportif d'Aquitaine; also enquire locally at SIs in Anglet, Biarritz, Hendaye, Iraty, St. Palais, St. Pée-sur-Nivelle.

SAILING: contact SI for details of local clubs etc. in Biarritz, Bayonne, Hendaye.

SCUBA DIVING: Ciboure — Centre de Plongée, rue des Usines; Biarritz — ask at SI.

SQUASH: very popular in the Pays Basque; many towns have municipal squash courts.

SURFING/WINDSURFING: there are many first-class surfing locations along the Basque coast, especially Biarritz, where equipment-hire is readily available. Contact Federation Française de Surf, Plage Nord Bd. Front de Mer, 40150 Hossegor (58.43.55.88) for more information.

SWIMMING: Biarritz Olympic Pool at the Parc des Sports d'Aguilera (59.24.25.96).

TENNIS: Biarritz Olympic at the Parc des Sports d'Aguilera (59.24.25.96). Clubs with tuition at Anglet (59.63.83.58), Bayonne (59.52.22.55), Ciboure (59.47.10.36) and Hendaye (59.20.02.73). Many other towns have municipal tennis courts.

THALASSOTHERAPY/SPAS: Anglet — Centre Atlanthal (like a resort hotel, (59.52.75.75); Biarritz — Thermes Marins (59.23.01.22) and Thalassothérapie Louisson Bobert (59.41.30.00 — at 4-star Hôtel Miramar); Cambo-les-Bains — Établissement Thermal (59.29.79.54); Hendaye – Centre Serge Blanco (59.51.35.35); St. Jean-de-Luz — Hélianthal (59.51.51.60).

WALKING: several good sections of GR10 can be covered in the Pays Basque. GR65, called the Compostela route, crosses GR10 at St. Jean-Pied-de-Port. For general advice and information on walking in the Pyrénées-Atlantiques contact the Délégation départementale du CNSGR, 83 av des Lauriers, Pau.

6
The Pyrenees

Drawing a straight line from Atlantic to Mediterranean, the Pyrenees mark the clear southern edge of France. Yet this border has not always been so unambiguous; for a thousand years Spain and France vied for control of these high peaks, and indeed for much of the time neither was able to master them. For the Pyrenees are not mere barren, snowy rock. They are lived in, they have a history and a culture, and a people who fought to be free of either side.

The mountains can be experienced in different ways. For one, the grand central summits — and these, certainly, are barren and snow-covered — can be explored and touched, and all their majesty inhaled, by walkers, climbers or skiers. Secondly, magnificent views of these peaks can be enjoyed from far away, even from the gentle unmountainous country well to the north. Or instead, one can get right into the life of the French Pyrenees, its simple farms and pretty villages, in a refreshing landscape of hills draped with green pasture and watered by running streams. This verdant countryside covers the slopes of the whole range in the middle and lower altitudes.

Much of the area in this chapter is not in the high mountains but is dominated by them, and satisfies the second option — appreciating the peaks from below. In any case, travel from one part of the Pyrenees to another often requires a descent to the main roads: the autoroute A64 and the route nationale N117 skim along just north of the slopes. But for those who are not pressed for time, and can cope with some steep and winding mountain routes, there are magnificent journeys to be made in the heart of the mountains. The main body of the range is dealt with here; for its extremes, where the hills fall away into the Atlantic in the west (the Basque country) and the Mediterranean in the east (Roussillon), see Chapter 5 — the Pays Basque or the Roussillon chapter of the separate guide *Languedoc & Roussillon*. It is this peaceful greenery and distant rugged scenery which gives the Pyrenees much of their appeal. In addition, the mountains possess sedate spas of the Second Empire, modern ski resorts, fantastic caves and grottoes with awesome traces of humanity's origins, imposing austere medieval monasteries, and many reminders of the clamorous past.

Inhabited since prehistoric time, the Pyrenees were gradually taken over by the Basque people, who moved off the lowlands to the south to escape from Celtic and then Roman colonisation. The Romans did nevertheless penetrate the mountains; the northern slopes

were early brought under control as part of Aquitania. They were unable though to impose much of their rule on the higher ground. Visigoths took over the area after the Roman withdrawal in the 5th century, and two centuries later they too lost power to the conquering Franks under Charlemagne, but neither group made much progress towards a real conquest of the scattered and independent-minded mountain people. The Pyrenees were divided between local rulers whose areas of influence led to the creation of virtually autonomous mountain provinces. The largest of them were Soule, Labourd and Navarre in the Basque west; Béarn and Bigorre in the central zone; Comminges and Foix towards the east; and the Catalan-speaking provinces on the eastern slopes.

All of them as far east as the border of the county of Foix were included in Eleanor of Aquitaine's dowry when she married the Plantagenet count who became Henri II of England (1152). The Hundred Years War wrested Aquitaine and the Pyrenean provinces away from the English, but still did not place them firmly in the hands of the French crown. As the Middle Ages progressed, it was the ruling *seigneurs* of Albret in Armagnac who made themselves masters of more and more of South West France including Navarre and several Pyrenean provinces. Eventually — in 1589 — most of them did become united to the French crown: when Henri III of Navarre, Count of Albret, of Foix, of Béarn, of Bigorre, of Soule, and of Labourd, succeeded to the throne of France as Henri IV.

The union was made official in 1607. Under the Treaty of the Pyrenees

Winter snow at the Col du Tourmalet

in 1659, the Spanish ceded to the French crown the remainder of the mountain territories which today form part of the French Pyrenees. Even at that stage the unyielding mountaineers retained their staunch independence. This was recognised by the creation in 1620 of the Parlement de Navarre, which governed its Pyrenean domain as an autonomous region. It remained to a large degree administratively independent of France right up to the Revolution. With the setting up of départements and Napoleon's efforts to unify the country and eradicate regional differences, Béarn and the Pays Basque were placed together in the département now called Pyrénées-Atlantiques; Bigorre largely became the Hautes Pyrénées; the county of Foix formed the basis of the Ariège département. Despite this reorganisation, each old Pyrenean province or county keeps many signs of its unique character, its history, and local dialect.

The major highway N117, coming from Bayonne, leaves the Pays Basque and enters Béarn shortly before Orthez. A more scenic approach out of the Basque country is on the D933, coming from St. Jean-Pied-de-Port (page 101). This reaches Béarn at the Gave d'Oloron (*gave* means river), and crosses the water into **Sauveterre-de-Béarn**. Everything in this picturesque town fronts precipitously onto a big curve in the *gave*. The best views and the most congenial spot from which to admire them can be found at the tables on the terrace of the Bar-Hôtel du Château. Parts of the old ramparts and remnants of a 13th-century keep survive. Within them the 12th–13th-century church of St. André mixes Romanesque and Gothic styles. Below the town, an arch of a fortified medieval bridge sets out to cross the Gave d'Oloron and stops short.

Just north along the *gave* the village of Athos was the home of the real-life musketeer on whom Athos in Dumas's *Three Musketeers* was based. In the other direction along the river, the D27 makes an enjoyable journey to Navarrenx and on to Oloron-Ste. Marie (see below). The D933 continues from Sauveterre to **Salies-de-Béarn**, an exceptionally likeable and good-looking old town straddling the Saleys river. It has lovely squares, arcades, terraces, and magnificent old houses. There are new squares and modernised streets in the centre as well, but these have all been well designed, and are very pleasing. The town's and the river's names are apt, since the river water is curiously salted, and the town has long been known for its saltwater springs. Salt extraction became an important source of revenue for Salies, as well as making it a little spa. The highlight of the town is the little Pont de la Lune which crosses the rather insalubrious-looking river; or rather, not so much the bridge as its delightful view of timbered, balconied waterside dwellings, decorated with flowers, overhanging the river.

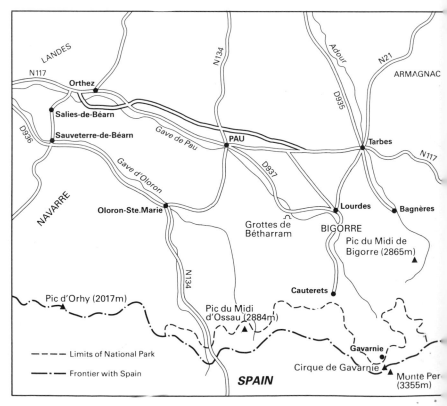

The road meets the N117, the main road along the broad valley of the Gave de Pau. Turn right here and 8km beyond is **Orthez**, a large market and industrial town. Once the capital of Béarn, it is still an important regional centre and a good place to find all the specialities of the Pyrenees, the Pays Basque and Armagnac. Much of Bayonne's famous ham, *jambon de Bayonne*, comes not from the Basque hills behind that city but from around Orthez. Some of the counts of the unified Foix and Béarn in the Middle Ages based themselves here, including the notorious Gaston Phoebus (Gaston III).

The main square is place d'Armes, on the edge of the older part of town, which has some attractive corners. Pont-Vieux, the fortified 13th-century bridge over the river, is the most striking relic of the town's medieval heyday. Rue Bourg-Vieux, near the bridge, has some fine old stone houses; the best of them is the one known as the Maison de Jeanne d'Albret (now occupied by the Office de Tourisme). On higher ground, the Tour Moncade fortress was built in 1242 for Gaston IV. Just north of the town, in 1814, the battle was fought in which Wellington defeated Soult in the course of the Peninsular War.

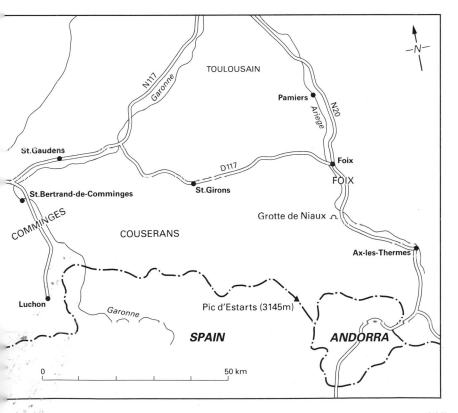

The N117, heading south-east directly towards Pau, comes to a highly industrialised region. Particularly around Lacq and Artix on the north side of the river, and Mourenx on the south, the country is marred by the sight and smell of extensive areas of natural gas extraction. Much more enjoyable is the D947, which climbs back into the hills to rejoin the Gave d'Oloron at **Navarrenx** (in this region, X is pronounced as in English), an old town protected by fine 16th-century ramparts. From here minor roads on the river's right bank or the D936 on the left travel upstream to **Oloron-Ste. Marie**, a likeable if surprisingly large town (pop:12,000) within the green hills. In the middle of Oloron, the Gave d'Aspe and the Gave d'Ossau meet to form the Gave d'Oloron. The town has a calmly busy, agricultural atmosphere. Being on two rivers gives it considerable character. The outskirts are fairly extensive and have some industry. The focal point, on the Gave d'Ossau's right bank, is place Gambetta, dominated by the town's main church, the Église Notre-Dame. Rue Justice descends across the gave onto the steep ridge of land which separates the two rivers; this is the Ste. Croix quarter, the old heart of Oloron where the town first came into being as a Roman camp. Now it has many appealing old dwellings, some with arcades. It's a steep walk to the top of the hill; or one can have fun driving up on the Lacets du Biscondau which switchback their way up the steep escarpment from the river. Promenade Bellevue, on the hillside below the church is a leafy walk with wide views — not as pretty as they

must once have been: now one can see the modern development stretching well away from the confluence of the gaves. At the summit, the Romanesque church of Ste. Croix, built in 1080, has a marvellously disorganised exterior with Gothic additions, yet inside retains the simple beauty of the earlier era. The choir and side chapels are especially attractive; there are good capitals; and note two unusual confessionals forming part of an ornate retable.

Return down the hill to the Gave d'Aspe, cross the river at place de Jaca; take rue de Révol opposite. This climbs to the Ste. Marie quarter, previously a separate village and still standing slightly apart from the rest of the town. It is quite a hike from the main centre of town to the Ste. Marie quarter, but it leads to Oloron's superb Église Ste. Marie, once a cathedral. Almost the whole structure dates from the 13th century, except for the choir, which had to be rebuilt in the 14th century after fire damage. The towers of grey slate roofs and grey stone give a stern but admirable equilibrium. An exceptionally fine Romanesque west portal in marble is magnificently carved on the arch and capitals with a multitude of strange stonework and craftsmanship. The most arresting features are the choir with immense painted pillars; the apsidal side chapels; the painted walls and ceilings; and the later organ loft.

There are some fine houses near the church and in this quarter. There is a useful unpretentious café-bar on the corner of place de la Cathédrale. Returning to the main town centre, rickety picturesque grey slate roofs along rue Révol catch the eye more than they did on the way up. For a quiet sit down or a picnic, turn left on reaching the river, and walk along rue Carrérot to the

Previous page: *Beside the river in Salies-de-Béarn*

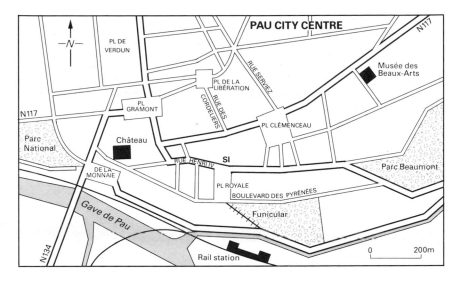

green, shaded public garden in place Général de Gaulle.

From Oloron, the D919 goes south-west into the Pays Basque (on the way passing through Aramitz whence came the real musketeer who became Aramis in *The Three Musketeers*). The N134, an ancient Roman highway, heads due south from Oloron up the Gave d'Aspe through several interesting and peaceful little towns and villages enclosed by the slopes of the beautiful Vallée d'Aspe — Sarrance (with unusual 17th-century church spire and cloisters), Accous and Lescun — and into the Parc National des Pyrénées. It eventually climbs over the Col du Somport (1632m) on the Spanish border — the only Pyrenean pass which remains clear of snow throughout the winter, a vital passage-way for Roman legionaries and later for Compostela pilgrims. In the other direc-tion, the N134 curves round from Olo-ron to Pau through green hills gentle and inviting.

Pau (pop: 82,000), historic capital of the Béarn, seat of the Parlement de Navarre and now préfecture of the Pyrénées-Atlantiques, has long been the principal town of the western Pyrenees. It keeps that role today, as an important industrial, agricultural, and military centre, and a university town. Pau occupies a curious site: the centre stands along the edge of a high cliff facing south across the Gave de Pau towards the mountains; newer districts sprawl away far to the north; while cutting through the middle of the high ridge is a deep channel carved by the Hédas.

Pau frequently finds itself named on French weather forecasts during the winter months as 'the warmest town in France today'. Spring and early summer, too, are very balmy, though sometimes wet. Its mild climate was discovered in the early 19th century by British troops who were sent here during the Peninsular War. At the close of the war the town quickly became a popular place for wealthy British families to pass the autumn and winter season, and continued to be so until well into the 20th century. Indeed large numbers of

121

British settled here permanently (about 3,000, it was estimated), and set up their own church, societies, race course and even fox hunts (an un-French pastime still practised at Pau). Contemporary literature suggests that many were people who had fallen foul of convention at home, made unsuitable marriages, lost fortunes, or in one way or another had reasons to feel that they might be better off living at some distance from Britain. For all that they could have done a good deal worse than to set up house at Pau — and no doubt among the British exiles there were a few who had come here for sheer love of the place. In the depths of winter, the pleasant, balmy weather is made all the more enjoyable by the sharp proximity of high mountains thickly covered with snow.

Pau's most distinctive feature is the Boulevard des Pyrénées, a promenade on top of the long southward-facing cliff face which drops to the valley of the shallow Gave de Pau. On a fair day the Boulevard has a stirring view of range upon range of hills, growing higher as they recede into the misty distance. The view was probably better before the placing of a railway goods yard in the foreground. On a really clear day (these though are said to number only six per year) fully 150km of jagged mountain horizon can be traced, with all the highest Pyrenean summits visible. The sight is at its most spectacular on a winter's day, the palm trees along the Boulevard, and the blue sky, making a dramatic contrast with the white summits. The Pic du Midi d'Ossau (2885m), almost due south, can usually be identified. To the south-east can be seen the Pic du Midi de Bigorre (2877m). On the

Exquisite carving in the portal of Église Ste. Marie at Oloron-Ste. Marie

slope of the escarpment below the Boulevard grows a profusion of vegetation which seems almost tropical, with gaudy blooms, thick-leafed laurel, luxuriant palm.

The Boulevard des Pyrénées runs from the large wooded Parc Beaumont and its casino, at the eastern end. Along the length of the Boulevard are grandiose buildings with superb views. Place Royale, an agreeable esplanade (with SI) adorned with a few shaded benches, comes right down to the Boulevard. At this point a funicular railway and a footpath descend the cliff from the Boulevard to the Gave de Pau (and the railway station). At its western end the Boulevard des Pyrénées reaches Pau's château and the extensive wooded public gardens of the Parc National.

The château combines sturdy medieval fortress with decorative Renaissance palace. In its original form it was built for the Counts of Béarn in the 12th century on the heights commanding the confluence of the Soust and other tributaries with the Gave de Pau. The periods of later additions were principally in 1370 under Gaston Phoebus, a colourful and tempestuous character who has passed into local legend, then during the 16th century under the *seigneurs* of Albret, and finally during the 19th century when some parts, being reconstructed by King Louis Philippe and Napoleon III after damage inflicted during the Revolution, were considerably altered. Nonetheless, the end result is a very pleasing structure, its disparate elements combining without discord. From Gaston Phoebus's brick keep a stone bridge crosses the former moat to the stone château. An impressive Porte d'Honneur leads into a charming triangular courtyard with a deep well. A lovely ensemble of buildings

123

encloses the courtyard. Each one is quite different, one of stone and brick, another of dressed stone, one with grey facing, another of older stone, and a pale dressed-stone tower; only a delicate frieze at roof level unites them into a single building.

A second gateway into the courtyard was the original entrance. It now opens onto a terrace with Pyrenean views in the distance. Along this (south) side of the château is a most unusual and interesting garden.

The interior of the château, on three floors, contains several interesting apartments and rooms, notably the vaulted kitchen and a dining room for 100 guests. Crests with the motifs M or H recall the Château's 16th-century occupants, Marguerite d'Angoulême and Henri d'Albret. Their daughter was Jeanne d'Albret, who gave birth in the château to the next Henri d'Albret — who was destined to become King Henri IV of France. The 16th-century Gobelin and Flemish tapestries, portraits of Henri IV and Jeanne d'Albret, and memorabilia of Henri IV are noteworthy. There's also a Musée Béarnais, containing collections illustrating local life, history, and archaeology.

At the west side of the château, another bridge connects the castle grounds to a broad esplanade of chestnut, lime and plane trees. This is a little offshoot of the adjacent riverside Parc National, in which a calm pathway wanders under the deep shade of mature trees.

East of the château lies the Vieux Bourg — the original Pau — contained in the area with the Hédas ravine on one side and the Gave de Pau escarpment on the other. Just outside the château

Henri IV

Henri d'Albret, son of Jeanne d'Albret and Antoine de Bourbon, was born in the château at Pau on 13 December 1553. The legend is that his grandfather, Henri d'Albret the elder, gave him a single drop of Jurançon wine at birth before he had even tasted milk. Although brought up as a Protestant, he was married in 1572 to Marguerite de Valois, sister of the French king and daughter of the fanatical anti-Protestant Catherine de Medicis. The last of Marguerite's brothers, Henri III, died in 1589, leaving Henri d'Albret, already king of Navarre since Jeanne's death, next in line for the throne of France — from which Protestants were forbidden. Henri was violently opposed by the Catholic establishment. With the irreverent words 'Paris is worth a Mass', Henri d'Albret renounced his Protestantism and so became Henri IV of France. But one of his first acts was the Edict of Nantes which legalised Protestant worship at certain towns and cities throughout France. Despite continuing vehement opposition from the Catholic hierarchy, Henri became one of the most popular monarchs ever to reign in France. He was admired for his conviviality, his liking for good food, good wine and good company, and his freedom from pomp or affectation. Henri declared that his ambition for France was simply 'a chicken in every pot'. He was assassinated in 1610.

rises the Tour du Parlement, part of what is now the office of the Conseil Général, once the Parlement de Navarre (the independent government of the French Pyrenean provinces after 1620). Walk along the Boulevard des Pyrénées or rue Gontaut-Biron to place St. Martin with its 19th-century church; beyond is the district known as the Borguet, originally a 16th-century extension of the town. Continue along rue Henri IV, one of the main roads of the old town, to place Royale, a pleasing square with the Hôtel de Ville and Maison du Tourisme.

On the left, beside the Hôtel de Ville, rue St. Louis is one of the shopping streets; cross over rue Maréchal Foch and carry on up rue des Cordeliers, the main shopping throughfare (in which is a good travel bookshop, Librairie du Palais). This arrives at place de la Libération, a nice little meeting point of some of the streets of the old quarter, dominated by the imposing 19th-century Gothic-style spires of St. Jacques church and the white columns of the Palais de Justice (behind which is the district mainly occupied by the British community). A few paces down rue Tran, the Musée Bernadotte gives some insights into 19th-century Béarnais domestic life but is primarily concerned with Jean-Baptiste Bernadotte (1763–1844), a native of Pau who became a general under Napoleon and subsequently went on to be crowned King of Sweden (under the name Charles XIV): his descendants remain the reigning royal house of Sweden. In the other direction from place de la Libération, rue St. Jacques is another popular shopping street, as is the turning off it, rue Serviez, the main street in this quarter. Rue Serviez leads to place G. Clémenceau, one of the town's main squares. From here rue Maréchal Joffre goes directly back to the château, while in the opposite direction rue Maréchal Foch (which becomes cours Bosquet) leads to Pau's important Musée des Beaux-Arts (fine arts museum). Its small, manageable collection of 17th–20th-century paintings contains many high-quality works.

Place Clémenceau is linked by a short modern street, the grandly colonnaded avenue de Maréchal de Lattre-de-Tassigny, to the Boulevard des Pyrénées; the approach to the Boulevard is dramatic if the mountain view is clear.

Old Pau deserves a longer, more aimless wander than this. And all around the city too, many places of interest reward a visit. Some of them now fall within the city's expanding suburbs.

The N134 heads north into Armagnac and the Landes. The D943 takes a course more directly into the most attractive parts of Armagnac; just 12km from Pau it reaches **Morlaàs**, an ancient town which was capital of Béarn from AD850 until the 12th century. It has an interesting Romanesque church, parts of which date to 1089: the beautifully carved portal is remarkable. West of Pau, **Lescar** was another early Béarnais capital (up to about AD850) and preserves considerable traces of the medieval period. Its 12th-century Romanesque cathedral (with parts rebuilt in the 17th century) has good capitals; two curious mosaics on the floor of the choir depicting hunting scenes (one of the hunters having a wooden leg); and the tombs of twelve members of the Navarre monarchy.

The Boulevard des Pyrénées in Pau, a magnificent 700-metre promenade with superb mountain views

Going south from Pau across the Gave de Pau, the N134 by-passes residential **Jurançon**, which gave its name to the best wine of the Pyrenees. Indeed the unusual but agreeable flavour, and a curious restrained sweetness, make it among the most interesting wines in South West France. It is usually drunk either as an aperitif or with *foie gras*. There are dry white Jurançons as well, which though less striking do deserve attention. The Jurançon vineyards extend over some 25 villages from Jurançon itself along the left bank of the *gave*. Most of the other vineyards in the region farther west of Pau are producing the light Rosé de Béarn. The N134 (and the more enjoyable little D234 on the other side of the Nez valley) travel south towards the high peaks, after Gan (with Gothic gateway, and a few Renaissance houses) forking left onto the D934. This rises to the attractively-located **Larun** and the small spa **Eaux-Bonnes**, both good starting points for further exploration, by car or on foot, into the mountains.

The fast main road (the N117) and the autoroute (the A64) from Pau pass out of Béarn and enter Bigorre, reaching **Tarbes** (pop: 48,000), préfecture of the Hautes-Pyrénées département. Although an old town in its origins, it was virtually destroyed by the inhuman savagery of Protestants and Catholics during the 16th-century Religious Wars. In modern times Tarbes has become a large workaday industrial and commercial centre. It is exactly what my taxi driver called it as he was showing me round: 'Une ville normale' (a normal town). Place de Verdun is its focal point; within a short walk are the *Haras* (national stud), the cathedral (12th-century, much altered later), and the Jardin Massey, a beautiful public

garden with remnants of a 15th-century cloister (transported here from out of town!) and a municipal museum of which possibly the most interesting section is devoted to Tarbes' tradition of breeding cavalry horses.

The other main route out of Pau is the D937, which — with a village every couple of kilometres — follows the Gave de Pau away from Béarn and into Bigorre. **Nay** and neighbouring **Coarraze** invite a little pause; the château of Coarraze was where Henri IV spent many years of his childhood, this being a safer place for him than Pau. While here, it is said, he went barefoot and played with local children. If that is true it may account for his later lack of ostentation and his anachronistic concern for the welfare of ordinary working people. The Grottes de Bétharram, off the road at the Bigorre border, are spectacular underground caverns and passageways with stalagmite pillars; the guided visit includes a cave railway and a boat ride on an underground lake. Soon after, the road and the Gave reach Lourdes, which is also quickly accessible from Tarbes, 20km away on the straight, flat N21.

Lourdes is extraordinary; a weird, maybe a wonderful place, or marvellous, or nauseating, depending on your temperament and outlook. Some four million people visit the town every year, and many have travelled to France from distant countries for no other reason than to come to Lourdes.

Sprawling and untidy, Lourdes lies on the west bank of the Gave de Pau in lovely green Pyrenean foothills, with peaks clear in the distance. It is surrounded by woods, fields of maize, and some light industry. In the middle of town is a fairly characterless old quarter, with a castle raised up on high ground at the centre. In the medieval period Lourdes was known only as the site of this fortress. Subsequently the castle lost all military use, and the town likewise declined to complete insignificance, pursuing the quiet agricultural life. It was, by all accounts, an unappealing ill-kept little place, by-passed by the growing number of wealthy visitors who made their way to Pyrenean mountain resorts and spas. On 11 February 1858, a 14-year-old local girl called Bernadette Soubirous, belonging to a wretchedly poor family — so poor, indeed, that they were almost starving and lived all in one room without facilities — reported that she had seen a vision of 'a lady' in the shallow cavern of the Grotte de Massabielle, which at that time was being used as a pigsty. The cave, in fact hardly more than a dent in the rock face, was in the steep bank of a little stream which ran, at that time, on the east side of the Gave de Pau and very close to the larger river. The 'lady', luminous, stood on a ledge of rock. Eventually she identified herself as 'the immaculate conception'.

At the time, despite, or because of, their extreme poverty, the Soubirous family attached great importance to Bernadette's forthcoming first communion. 11 February was a rare day free of catechism; tired, hungry Bernadette had been sent out to use her 'leisure' collecting firewood beside the stream with her sister and a friend. They had to cross the stream, which Bernadette did not want to do because, she told her friend, the water was cold. At that instant she heard a noise, looked up, and saw her vision, for the first time. What she saw was what she described as 'a lady dressed all in white: she had

on a white dress with a blue belt and a yellow rose on each foot, the colour of her rosary. The vision crossed herself. When I had finished saying the rosary, the vision suddenly vanished.'

Bernadette returned to the same spot a few days later and had the vision again. On 18 February, Bernadette asked the lady to sign her name, and received the reply, in the local language, 'What I have to say to you need not be taken down in writing. Would you please come here for a fortnight. I cannot promise to make you happy in this world but in the other.' From then until 4 March was 'the fortnight of apparitions'; after which Bernadette saw the vision only a few times more before the final appearance on 16 July. She was sometimes alone, but usually watched by an ever-increasing crowd of local people, although unlike many of the other cases of religious visions (which were very common during the 19th century in all Catholic countries) no one else ever saw Bernadette's apparition. As she had her vision for the ninth time, Bernadette was being observed by over 300 people, and was seen to kiss the ground, crawl on her knees, and eat the grass — all of which 'the lady' had told her to do, 'for sinners'. Then she scratched the ground around a little pool of water, enlarging the puddle until she could drink from it, as she had been instructed. The next day, water began to bubble from the muddy pool, and the more credulous proclaimed that she had discovered a previously unknown spring. On 2 March, 'the lady' said 'Tell the priest to build a chapel here and have people come in procession. 'On 25 March, Bernadette, still puzzled, again asked 'the lady' who she was. This time the reply came, in the local tongue, 'Que soy era immaculada

Lourdes' elaborate basilica, dedicated to the visions of local teenager Bernadette Soubirous

councepciou' — I am the immaculate conception.

Initial scepticism about Bernadette was usually banished by the sight of her in tranquil prayer and evident joy at the grotto, although this is slightly at odds with the idea that she herself was quite mystified as to who and what 'the lady' was. Some of the more sceptical observers came round to the idea of a divine presence when the 'miracle of the candle' occurred — Bernadette was holding a candle at the grotto, and was so lost in trance that she did not notice the candle burn down to her hand; flames burned on her hand for ten minutes, but left no trace on her skin. Nowadays 'divine intervention' would not be considered the most likely explanation for this (the villagers of 19th-century Lourdes did not know that such amazing events occur worldwide during

trances religious or secular, and in places are even performed for money). For whatever reason, the local ecclesiastical authorities accepted the veracity of her claims with relative alacrity. Just four years later, the diocese decided to erect a basilica above the cavern. Another two years after, the statue of the Virgin was erected on the ledge where the visions were seen. In two more years, in 1866, Bernadette left Lourdes to enter the convent of St. Gildard at Nevers as a Sister of Charity. She was 22 years of age, and was to remain there until her death only 13 years later, on 16 April 1879. Her coffin was placed in the vault in the garden of the Nevers convent.

The next thing to excite the credulity of the religious population was the phenomenon of Bernadette's body. In 1909, 1919, and 1925 the body was exhumed and formally identified as part of the canonisation process. The natural decay of the corpse was found to be proceeding at an exceptionally slow rate. Even by the third time, when doctors removed 'relics' from the body, Bernadette was still recognisable on sight and had retained her skin, eyes, hair, and internal organs in good condition. Since 1925, when slightly idealised wax masks, very lifelike, were placed over her face and hands — the rest of the body being concealed within her nun's habit — Bernadette's corpse has been displayed in a glass case in the chapel of the Nevers convent. She was declared a saint in 1933.

Pilgrimages to the Grotte de Massabielle began in the 1870s, comprising mainly sick people who came to beg the Virgin for a personal cure. Some claimed to have had their prayers answered, and Lourdes became known as a place where miraculous cures occurred. Soon, organised visits of the sick were a regular occurrence. In 1883, a Bureau of Medical Investigation was set up to document cures and assess which could be considered, if not miraculous then at least inexplicable. To be 'inexplicable' a cure had to be sudden, spontaneous, total, without the need for convalescence, and enduring for several years without a relapse; the disease cured had to be one normally regarded as incurable and life-threatening, and its presence proved conclusively by prior medical evidence. Even with such rigorous criteria the bureau found that a small number of cures could indeed be defined as 'inexplicable', and would be regarded by the ecclesiastical authorities as miraculous.

To date, 64 such cases have been documented. Of course, whether sudden remarkable cures are actually divine or whether they are rooted in the patient's state of mind depends entirely on one's religious outlook. Nowadays, each year Lourdes receives about 70,000 pilgrims suffering from severe illnesses, with special package tours for — to give an example — groups of people deformed by polio. One of the features of Lourdes is the large number of the sick being towed around on curious covered reclining chairs or beds with large wheels. Some dramatic cures do still occur, but since modern pilgrims have invariably had medical treatment, none these days fulfil the criteria of an 'inexplicable' recovery.

Inside the cavernous subterranean Basilique St.-Pie X at Lourdes, one of the world's largest churches

Commercialisation also proceeded at a rapid pace. In the early 1900s, writer Hilaire Belloc came here and described it as 'detestable', adding that 'to make it the more detestable, there is that admixture of the supernatural which is invariably accompanied by detestable earthly adjuncts'. He would not find it more acceptable today. The main streets in Lourdes are lined with tawdry souvenir shops selling Catholic paraphernalia in what most non-Catholics, and hopefully some Catholics, would consider to be appalling taste: plastic 'holy water' bottles in the shape of the Virgin Mary (her crown is the screw cap); crucifixes illuminated with flashing fairy lights; luminous flesh-coloured models of Bernadette Soubirous; thousands of 'likenesses' of Mary, each with the words 'Je Suis l'Immaculée Conception' (I am the immaculate conception) written around the head like a halo; 'portraits' of Mary, Bernadette, the Pope, and others, either individually or in any combination; and much more. Hotels, shops and restaurants also try desperately to profit from Bernadette's vision. In Lourdes nothing is sacred. There's even a cinema called Immaculée Conception (known as l'Immaculée for short).

You may find all this distasteful, yet it is, in a sense, worth seeing. The credulity of the pilgrims is amazing, their piety touching; and in western Europe there is little else quite like it.

However, unless you believe that Bernadette's 'lady' had some real existence outside her own mind, and therefore wish to be close to the scene of the apparition, it may be wiser to visit Lourdes in passing or while staying somewhere else. Accommodation in the town is of a generally low standard. Hotel star ratings in Lourdes deceive

visitors: the best hotels in Lourdes, with 4 stars, would warrant 2 stars elsewhere (although they charge 4 star prices).

The main streets of the town are rue de la Grotte, which descends to the right bank of the Gave de Pau and crosses the river on Pont Vieux to avenue Bernadette Soubirous; and boulevard de la Grotte, which crosses the river on Pont St. Michel directly into the Domaine de la Grotte. The Domaine comprises the grotto itself. and an interesting, highly elaborate structure in three levels. The first level is the Rosary Basilica; circular and domed in a mock-Byzantine style, it contains excellent murals in mosaic, but being built against the cliff rock is suffering from the damp. Above the Basilica is another church called the Crypt: it was built while Bernadette was still living at Lourdes, and she was present at its consecration. Above the Crypt, the upper Basilica was built during Bernadette's lifetime but after she had left Lourdes: it is in a complex rich style, and has stained glass showing the apparitions.

Leave the Basilica and walk round to the back, beside the gave. Here is the small Grotte de Massabielle. From Easter to October, thousands of people gather in perfect silence in front of the grotto. A statue of the Virgin Mary on a ledge shows the spot where Bernadette gazed, believing she could see her 'lady'. People queue to pass through the grotto and kiss one of the rocks. On the left, beside the cave, with sickly melodrama crutches hang high on wires. These are supposedly the crutches of people miraculously cured; I was unable to find out when they were placed here, but the same crutches were hanging there 30 years ago, and none have been added since. Irrespective of the divinity or otherwise of

Bernadette's visions, it is wonderfully affecting to have so many people standing in silence together. Beyond the grotto, pilgrims at a row of taps avidly fill containers with water from the 'miraculous spring'. In Bernadette's day, a tiny stream ran between the grotto and the gave; it has now been covered by the Basilica and the walkway. This, incidentally, was the stream which Bernadette crossed, not the gave.

On the far side of the gave a new 'overspill' church has been built, while within the Domaine de la Grotto there is the concrete underground Basilique St. Pie X, which is terribly functional and looks like nothing so much as an underground car park. Nevertheless, it is one of the largest churches in the world and can accommodate 25,000 people: to be here when it is full of singing is a magnificent experience.

Every evening at 8.45 thousands of people buy a candle (protected by a paper bearing a prayer) and throng along the streets to the grotto and the Basilica. Many are mumbling the rosary while others chat animatedly; there is a festive party atmosphere, at times almost unruly. In the voices one hears all the languages of the countries where there are Catholics. But not every pilgrim is a Catholic. In the crowd I have met devout Anglicans from England who believe, just as most Catholics do, that what Bernadette saw was actually the real Mary herself, no mere vision. More surprisingly perhaps, there are even Hindus and Moslems in the crowd who believe the same thing. They run the gauntlet of the souvenir shops where locals reap a rich harvest from the pilgrims, many of whom succumb and buy knick-knacks to take home. The candles are lit on reaching the huge open area in front of the Basilica, the esplanade du Rosaire. There they assemble, some with banners, to form an immense congregation while Mass, with a few words of the sermon in foreign languages, is celebrated in the balmy open air. The vast crowd all singing or praying or standing in silence, the flame of each person's candle flickering in the darkness, is a thrilling sight whatever one's beliefs.

It is refreshing though to get away from the crowd, to stroll along the right bank of the gave, or in the less commercial back streets. An enjoyable approach to the Grotte de Massabielle, for example, is to walk up the chemin de la Forêt and descend to the grotto by the footpath which winds down with views of the hills and the gave; the odour of burning candles below fills the air.

The old castle of Lourdes deserves a visit. It can be approached on foot or by a toll lift. During the Middle Ages this powerful fortress was considered strategic in the control of the Pyrenees, and was besieged without success by the Cathar hunting Simon de Montfort (1216); later, the English held it tenaciously (1360–1406). After the incorporation of all this territory into the kingdom of France, under treaties ratified by the Spanish as well as by the local provinces themselves, the fortress became of less importance. The existing building, largely a 17th- and 18th-century reconstruction with a 14th-century keep, now houses the Musée Pyrénéen, which has displays on traditional mountain life, mountaineering, and some paintings and etchings. Among the town's other 'sights' are the 'cachot' (the room where the Soubirous family lived during their years of misfortune) and the Boly mill (where Bernadette was born).

A traditional panelled door (this one is in Luz-St Sauveur)

Rising from Lourdes, the gave turns south towards the mountain heights, with the N21 running beside the river. On the left, close to Lourdes, a funicular to the top of the Pic du Jer (948m) is a popular outing. At the summit, a passageway penetrates surprising underground caverns and tunnels. The N21 enters the old region of the Sept-Vallées de Lavedan, seven valleys which formed a tiny federation of even tinier independent 'republics' right up until the 15th century. The scenery improves all the way into **Argelès-Gazost**, a small but popular historic spa beautifully located in a corner between the Gave de Pau and its tributary the Gave d'Azun. There's an old upper town and a lower thermal quarter. From Argelès-Gazost one road (the D918) follows the

Gave d'Azun into the mountains, eventually crossing high passes to reach Eaux-Bonnes, while another (the D921) remains in the lush valley of the Gave de Pau, over which the tiny well-placed **St. Savin** has a superb view. The village was once an important religious centre. It preserves a very interesting 11th-century Romanesque abbey-church which was fortified in the 14th century, and ruins of a well-defended 12th-century castle.

At the unappealing Pierrefitte-Nestalas the road again divides to follow two gaves. The D920 takes the route to **Cauterets**, an important mountain resort both as a spa in summer and as a skiing centre in winter. Its waters have been well known in France since the 10th century, and the town has prospered on their reputation, with such devotees as Gaston Phoebus, Jeanne d'Albret, Baudelaire, Victor Hugo, George Sand, and Chateaubriand. It continues to have a lot of appeal, and is an excellent base for touring the high mountains and reaching into the Parc National (an information office of which is in town). Magnificent scenery soars all around, with roads, footpaths, and telephériques giving access to several waterfalls, lakes, valleys, and rocky peaks close to the Spanish border.

The other road from Pierrefitte-Nestalas (the D921) goes through the Luz Gorge of the Gave de Gavarnie to emerge into a pleasant, more open stretch of the valley. A number of hamlets and villages cluster around the confluence of the Gave de Gavarnie and the Gave de Bastan, among them **Luz-St. Sauveur**, another attractively located little mountain spa. It is divided by the streams into Luz (the old town)

An izard, elusive native of the steep Pyrenean slopes

and St. Sauveur (the thermal quarter). Luz was a Templar village, and retains the order's unusual 12th-century sturdily fortified church.

The D921 picks its way from Luz through the St. Sauveur Gorge of the Gave de Gavarnie, eventually climbing to the unexpectedly crowded end-of-the-road village **Gavarnie** and giving spectacular views of the amazing mountain amphitheatre of the ice-covered Cirque de Gavarnie. If you like mountain walks this is the place for them. One of several superb paths from Gavarnie leads up to the great Grande Cascade, 442m of waterfall pouring from the glacier covering of the Cirque. Other paths penetrate the wilds of the Parc National. From the village of **Gèdre** an even narrower, steeper route climbs within reach of the even wilder Cirque de Troumouse.

The D918 rises sharply eastwards from Luz-St. Sauveur to the old mountain spa and new ski resort Barèges, with more superb mountain scenery. Beyond Barèges the road winds over higher altitudes, crossing Col du Tourmalet (2115m), giving access to the summit of the Pic du Midi de Bigorre (2865m), before twisting down through the large modern ski resort La Mongie to the Adour valley.

The river Adour follows an odd course through South West France, and has importance to four regions. It reaches the Atlantic at Bayonne, where the river forms the border between the Pays Basque and the Landes. Over the centuries the Adour has had a history of taking sudden changes in its course, causing havoc to the fortunes of three Atlantic ports. Farther inland, the Adour moves in a big curve from the Landes forest through the farms and vineyards of southern Armagnac. The river

135

Parc National des Pyrénées

The Pyrenees National Park covers a long narrow strip of about 100km along the crest of the Pyrenees, with a total area of about 46,000 hectares of high-altitude peaks, valleys and lakes. The object of the park is to protect the native wildlife and the environment of the high mountains, not to provide facilities for visitors (which are only available in towns and villages at its periphery). The principal access is on foot, with over 350km of clearly marked paths, including a stretch of the long-distance GR10. Simple accommodation, generally without staff, is available in mountain shelters and hostels. Among the most easily seen animals in the park are the thousands of izards (resembling chamois). Others, fewer in number and by nature even more elusive, include the lynx and the brown bear. Among the rare birds living here are vultures and eagles. To protect the natural balance of the environment, all hunting, gathering of plants or flowers, lighting of fires, and camping are forbidden within the park's borders. Information centres (Maisons du Parc) can be found at Tarbes, Arrens, Cauterets, Luz, Gavarnie, Gabas, Etsaut, and St. Lary. The main office is at 59 route de Pau, 65000 Tarbes (62.93.30.60).

emerges onto the rolling Armagnac countryside at the city of Tarbes, which lies at the foot of a long valley descending from the high Pyrenees.

The Adour comes into being at the village of Ste. Marie-de-Campan, at the confluence of the Adour de Tourmalet, which flows down from the Col du Tourmalet, with the Adour de Payolle, coming down from the Col d'Aspin. The two valleys are followed by two roads, both part of the D918. Beyond the Col du Tourmalet, it goes down to Barèges and Luz-St. Sauveur. Beyond Col d'Aspin, the road winds down to the Vallée d'Aure and the old Pyrenean small towns **Arreau** and **St. Lary-Soulan** (an important centre for high-altitude summer walking and for skiing in the winter).

Below Ste. Marie, the valley road (the D935) descends towards **Bagnères-de-Bigorre**, a well-established old spa and winter resort, although it is now also quite industrialised. The town

centre has a pleasing, leisured atmosphere, and preserves a few traces of its past. Its main square, place Lafayette and the shaded allées des Coustous, are midway between the Adour and the Thermal Park with the hot baths (the original Grands Thermes and more recent Néothermes).

The Adour road — passing a left turn (the D937) to Lourdes — moves farther down the valley to Tarbes (see page 128). North of the town, the Adour valley opens out, and two main roads, the D935 and the N21, run one each side of the river into the rich Armagnac farm country. The D632 heads off north-east to skirt Armagnac on its way to Toulouse. Meanwhile, the main Pyrenees highway, the N117, coming from Pau to Tarbes, continues its journey along the foot of the mountains from Tarbes to **Capvern-les-Bains** (a small spa) and industrial **Lannemezan**. This area has little to recommend it, although one point of interest is that many of the little rivers

136

of the South West radiate away from the heights of the Plateau de Lannemezan — very noticeable on the map of South West France. A more enjoyable hill road, the D938, goes directly to the Lannemezan area from Bagnères.

The busy N117 and the prettier, more relaxed D938, leaving Bigorre and entering ancient Comminges, converge on **Montréjeau** (pronounce with the 't' silent). The setting of this *bastide* (founded in 1272) is admirable, with excellent views of the country rising sharply to the south. It retains some picturesque corners. The river Garonne, pouring down from Pyrenean heights across the frontier in Spain, turns east at Montréjeau before beginning its wide sweep north and west. Passing many

other great rivers, the Garonne effectively marks the border of South West France. I shall cross it only to include the old Pyrenean counties of Comminges (or Cominges), Couserans and Foix.

Just 7km up the Garonne valley from Montréjeau a turning is signposted to **St. Bertrand-de-Comminges**, a wonderful little village perched atop a hill overlooking the river plain in a still, quiet, rural location. On the flatter ground below the village, take time to pause at two very worthwhile distractions before climbing the hill. First, to the left of the road, visit the ancient village of **Valcabrère**, especially its beautiful 11th-century church (St. Just and St. Pastor), with a fine Romanesque portal and incorporating fragments of Roman masonry from the nearby Roman settlement. Secondly, on the road itself at the foot of St. Bertrand, stop to see the remains of Ibero-Roman Lugdunum Convenarum, founded in 72BC. At its largest, the town's population probably numbered over 60,000. Excavations at the site have uncovered traces of its hot baths, forum, temple, marketplace, and — built just before the departure of the Roman administration — a Christian temple. With the subsequent onslaught by Germanic tribes, the local people moved onto the hilltop, which had been fortified by the Romans, but even there they could not defend themselves, and from the 6th century to the 11th the hilltop was hardly occupied. In the middle of the 11th century, Bertrand de l'Isle Jourdain chose the spot for a cathedral.

One of the lively carvings in the remarkable 16th-century choirstalls at St. Bertrand-de-Comminges

Even today the village is dominated, or possibly one should say overwhelmed, by the vast forbidding walls of the Cathédrale Ste. Marie and their immense, graceless buttresses. Visitors have to pay to enter the building, which seems a little unchristian; although entry is free if you are attending a service, which perhaps make it more excusable (but if you just want to go in to pray between services, too bad). There are unusual Romanesque carvings over the main entrance, dating from 1140. The interior of the cathedral has high bare grey stone walls pierced by impressive windows with some good stained glass. Most of the building is in Gothic style, dating from the early 14th century.

There's an astonishing 16th-century wooden organ loft with spiral stairs. A fascinating and intricately carved wooden screen separates the single aisleless nave from the choir. Within the choir, there are amazing woodcarvings, extraordinarily complex and skilful, which were installed in 1530. Most notable are the 66 superb choir-stalls, with exceptionally detailed carvings depicting all sorts of curious subjects sacred, symbolic, satirical — or rude! See too the south chapel with 16th-century tapestries, and 15th- and 16th-century tombs in the ambulatory. A side door leads out to exquisite little cloisters with double pillars and interesting stone carvings and a peaceful view of the

In the foreground, the interesting little church at Valcabrère; on the hill behind, the massive bulk of the cathedral at St. Bertrand-de-Comminges; between the two are the remnants of a Roman town

green fields and encroaching hills.

Concerts are held in the cathedral during an annual summer music festival. A tourist office can be found in the square in front of the cathedral. St. Bertrand is a walled village, roughly circular and the village street passes beneath one of the cathedral buttresses. In the main street and the back lanes, the village has many attractive and interesting buildings, some dating back to the 16th century. Note especially, just within the Porte Gabirole gateway, the remarkable post office in a lovely little mansion with a hexagonal tower.

Of course one would like to have such villages to oneself, but unfortunately that is far from being the case in St. Bertrand. It attracts quite large numbers of visitors and at times has difficulty absorbing them all. It also has the usual array of incongruous craft shops which threaten to spoil the village atmosphere. To see St. Bertrand in greater tranquillity, take some of the quiet back lanes where few people stray.

At the crossroads below St. Bertrand, the left turn (if descending from the village) goes to the Gargas Caves, one of the oldest — and perhaps most disturbing — of the prehistoric cave sites. On its walls there are marvellous line drawings of reindeer, bison, horses, and other animals, all drawn 30,000 years ago. In addition there are some two hundred 'hand outlines' of the sort seen in some other prehistoric sites — but here the hands are all mutilated, with one or more fingers missing. The effect is quite horrifying.

The N125, once a Roman highway, rises up the Garonne valley on the west bank. The D33 takes the east bank. The two roads meet at Chaum, where a bridge crosses the Garonne just below its confluence with the river Pique. This district is rather blighted by industry and quarries casting their soiled traces into the air.

Above this point, the N125 stays with the Garonne and heads away to the left, through **St. Béat** (with 14th-century castle, altered in the 19th century; 12th-century priory church; ancient high-quality marble quarries), to the Spanish frontier. The D125 chooses the Pique river instead, and goes through pleasant country to **Luchon** (or **Bagnères de Luchon**), a popular spa resort enclosed by high mountains with permanent snow.

There's nothing much to see here — unless it be the long tree-lined allées d'Étigny with its wide pavements running straight towards marvellously jagged white peaks. At No. 18, a grand 18th-century house accommodates the SI and a delightful museum of the town. Luchon did exist during the Roman period but disappeared almost completely for a thousand years to re-emerge in the middle of the 18th century. The museum covers all this in a lively, colourful way. Hardly anything in the town pre-dates the 19th century.

At one end of the allées, place Joffre is the sedate meeting point of roads at the town centre. Gathered around the square are some reasonable hotels and a conspicuous church. The church, which appears thoroughly medieval inside and out, with Romanesque arches, single nave, side chapels, traditional stained glass, dates largely (or so I was told both by the priest and by the town's archivist, although I find it hard to believe) from the 19th century.

The elegant 19th-century spa baths at Luchon

Leading off the *place*, rue Docteur Germes (!) — named after the man who was mayor of Luchon from 1919 to 1944 — is the main shopping street and goes into place Gabriel, where there is a market every day. At the other end of the allées, the classical-looking Thermes (1848) have handsome white marble columns. Inside, the Thermes have a convincingly 'Roman' atmosphere, with frescoes, steamy sulphurous air, and people wandering about in red or white robes. The speciality is treating disturbances of the respiratory tract.

Even today Luchon earns fame and fortune as a spa. Most visitors are genuine *curistes*, who come specifically to take the waters and to benefit from the town's bracing air. However it is an ideal base for non-*curistes* as well, with many excellent drives and walks, for

example up the Vallée de la Pique, the Vallée du Lys, or to the more resorty mountain base and ski centre Superbagnères, which directly overlooks Luchon (but is almost 20km away by road) and has magnificent views. A steep and winding mountain route climbs over the Col de Peyresourde (literally 'deaf stone'; 1569m), coming down on the other side to Arreau (see page 136) and the Vallée d'Aure.

Two principal routes continue eastwards. The most dramatic and scenic is the D618 which heads into the hills from Fronsac, twisting and turning to St. Girons (see below). The other possibility is to stay with the Garonne valley as it widens after Montréjeau: the D8 and the N117 travel either side of the river through an industrialised landscape to **St. Gaudens**. In theory, the town has a good view towards the mountains, and St. Gaudens was always known for its fine position, but this is now marred by natural gas processing and other industries. Between the town and the mountains billowing evil white clouds and nauseating chemical fumes hang in the air. For all that, if you do happen to find yourself here, pause to see the church, which has several good features (originally 12th-century, but with good later Gothic work); within a few paces of it, in place Mas St. Pierre, there's a tourist office and a local museum. From the architecture and the increasing use of brick it's easy to see that this is the edge of the Toulousain. While the N117 presses on towards Toulouse, a right turn (the D117) turns away from the Garonne and back into the mountains.

Almost at once it strikes **Montsaúnès**, where there are ruins of a 12th-century Templar church (also made of brick). A little farther, the larger **Salies-du-Salat**, is an ancient spa which takes its name (meaning roughly, the salt of health) from remarkable salt water springs. The town lies at the foot of a hill; from the summit a ruined château of the Counts of Comminges gazes down.

Running beside the river Salat, the road goes into the old region known as Couserans and arrives at **St. Lizier**. This was an important town when Couserans had a separate identity of its own, but today lives in obscurity in the hills. Its encircling ramparts though, a 17th-century Archbishops' Palace, and above all its cathedral (outside the walls) stand in testimony to the former stature of the town.

Originally built in the 10th century, partly using locally gathered Roman masonry, the cathedral was reconstructed in the 12th century. In the 14th century a pleasing octagonal brick tower in the Toulouse style was added. The building has a fine north portal; inside, it has a satisfying irregularity of shape; Romanesque frescoes depict biblical events. The delightful cathedral cloister of slender pairs of marble pillars dates from the 12th century, with a 16th-century wooden upper storey. In and around place de l'Église in the walled upper town (where the church of Notre-Dame de la Sède was also once a cathedral and has several points of interest) some very picturesque old medieval houses survive.

Little St. Lizier stands just a couple of kilometres away from the larger and

St. Lizier

more bustling crossroads town of **St. Girons**, at the meeting point of three rivers, the Baup, the Lez, and the Salat. It's in an attractive setting, and the town makes a good base for exploring this part of the Pyrenees. The D117 and D618 (the more scenic of the two) go over the hills into the Comté de Foix and the Ariège valley. A worthwhile detour off the D117 would be to the phenomenal caves of the Grotte du Mas d'Azil. The road actually runs through part of the caves — the superb arch of its entrance leads into what is effectively a long underground river bed, a tunnel with side caverns. Besides having spectacular rock formations, the Grotte is best known for the prehistoric finds which were made here (some of which are displayed at the cave and some others in the local village museum). The Grotte has often served as a refuge for local religious groups down the centuries, starting with the early Christians. Later persecutions followed — during the 13th century this area was strongly Cathar, and during the 16th and 17th centuries strongly Protestant. The neighbouring village of Le Mas d'Azil was a 13th-century *bastide*.

The D119 carries on beyond Le Mas d'Azil to Pamiers; the D117 keeps straight on to Foix; while the southern, mountain route, the D618, goes from St. Girons to Tarascon-sur-Ariège. All three are thriving little towns on the banks of the Ariège river in Foix county.

The Comté de Foix, with the Ariège passing through the middle of it, was one of the regions most strongly affected by Catharism, especially during its later period and during the 14th-century revival of the creed. (See page 189 for more on Cathars and what they believed.) The Ariège pours north from the high Pyrenees, its valley making a vital

highway not just for people and goods but for ideas. The Cathar 'heresy' was thus carried along this road through the succession of important market towns.

Rocky and wooded wild country, cleared in places for the vineyards of the Corbières, lies east of the valley. All of this secretive landscape nurtured Languedoc's Catharism and paid the price at the hands of the bloodthirsty Catholic nobles and mercenaries of the Albigensian Crusade (1209-29). Its unspoiled hills and craggy peaks topped by gaunt Cathar fortresses where the rebels made their last stand are still, for the people of Languedoc, a potent reminder of southern defiance against the march of northern power. Papal legates described the district as 'a nest of heretics'. Simon de Montfort passed this way, disturbed by such reports. He took many of Cathar fortresses in the countryside around the town, but felt unequal to the task of an attack on the castle of Foix itself.

Pamiers played a major role in the fight against heresy. Many of the influential discussions between ecclesiastical authorities and Cathars took place here; it was at Pamiers that the claims of Albigensian Crusade leader Simon de Montfort to all lands formerly belonging to the defeated counts of Toulouse were legally confirmed; and later the town was the base for a cruel inquisition into the Cathar heresy. Pamiers today is much larger than it was then, and most of it lacks either charm or interest. Although much damaged during the 16th-century Religious Wars, vestiges of the medieval centre do remain, and are dominated by the 14th-century octagonal brick tower of the cathedral.

All the way along the N20, the major road running beside the Ariège, there are enticing views of the Pyrenees. **Foix**

Foix: distinctive castle towers dominate the town

makes a powerful impact on first sight. Attractively located at the confluence of the Arget and the Ariège, it is overlooked by the three fine towers of a feudal castle poised on a lofty rock in the old town.

A steep walkway climbs up to the castle: vaulted rooms inside the towers date from the 14th and 15th centuries, like much of the rest of Foix, while most of the outer structure pre-dates it. A museum at the foot of the central and north towers has modest collections devoted to local culture, history and prehistory. Foix, still préfecture of the Ariège département, was the little 'capital' of the counts of Foix.

Thanks to its well-placed castle, Foix escaped the Albigensian Crusade, and the counts continued to deny the sover-

eignty of the French crown until 1272. In that year Philippe le Hardi (King Philippe III) came in person with his troops and successfully forced them to concede that their time was past. In the *vieille ville*, timbered houses line a labyrinth of lanes and narrow streets, and there are two fine 19th-century covered markets. The church of St. Volusian, often changed over the centuries, is what remains of the 10th-century Abbey of St. Volusian around which the town originated.

The N20, continuing south, passes another 'Cathar castle', the château of Montgailhard at the hill called Pain de Sucre, sugarloaf. East from here lies legendary **Montségur**, for many the most stirring symbol of Cathar resistance and the independent spirit of the

143

Main Festivals in the Pyrenees

January
TARBES — a week of café-theatre.

March
TARBES — a week of Occitan folk art and tradition.

Easter
LOURDES — major festival of religious music and art.

May
TARBES — Jazz Festival.

June
PAU — Theatre Festival.

July
OLORON-STE. MARIE — Pyrenees Folk Festival.
ST. BERTRAND-DE-COMMINGES — Classical Music Season.
FOIX — Journées Médiévales: colourful entertainment, son et lumières, period costume, etc.
LUCHON — Traditional local festival.

August
LUCHON — Flower Festival.
LOURES-BAROUSSE — Cheese Fair.
BAGNÈRES-DE-BIGORRE — important traditional local festival, with mountain singers.

September
ARGELÈS-GAZOST and LUZ-ST. SAUVEUR — Tonte de la Mude: gathering of the sheep returning from summer to winter pasture.

South: beside what is now a rather 'arty' little village looms a precipitous rocky pinnacle, on top of which the ruined fortress stands aloof. In this lonely refuge over one thousand Cathars, nobles and peasants together, held out against a nine-month siege by French royal troops. Eventually, in March 1244 the Cathars walked down from their retreat, on the promise that they would be spared if they would only renounce their faith. As many as 205 refused to do so even at this stage, and — according to a monument at the foot of the castle

144

hill — were burnt alive in the notorious *bucher* (pyre) *de Montségur*.

Farther up the Ariège valley, **Tarascon-sur-Ariège**, though industrialised, enjoys a beautiful setting of steep rocky hills all around. This is an area riddled with grottoes or caves, in many of which prehistoric man took shelter. The Grotte de Niaux, 5km away up a mountain road which leads right into the mouth of the cave, is the most outstanding of them. Far inside, magnificent line drawings in remarkably good condition date back 20,000 years. In **Niaux** village, there is a tiny Musée Paysan of the popular art and culture of the Sabarthès, as this little district is called. In the vast Grotte de Lombrive, one of the largest 'visitable' caves in Europe, beside the N20 about 4km from Tarascon, hundreds of Cathars hid to escape the royal troops. When found, they were walled in, so it is said, and starved to death. The morbid and the misguided sometimes come searching here for a mythical 'lost Cathar treasure'.

At the Roman spa of **Ax-les-Thermes** two rivers join the Ariège; in addition the town has 80 natural springs: the whole place seems to be bubbling and brimming with water. Ax is still immensely popular as a spa — it specialises in treating rheumatism. As well as having three *établissements thermals*, there are some intriguing outdoor hot baths and pools, notably in place du Breilh. Here there's a large foot-bath of soothing warm water; a water-pipe constantly pouring at 77°C (I feel sure that the local women collecting it in buckets use it for doing the dishes); and a smaller steaming pool of water near boiling point. There's more to Ax than the spa: it is a good base for touring the mountains by car or on foot, and in the winter season is active as a ski resort. Ax has some three dozen hotels.

South of Ax, the N20 carries on into Andorra and French Catalonia (or Roussillon). Going the other way, downriver beyond Pamiers, the river Ariège and the route nationale to Toulouse.

Tourist Offices

National office for Pyrenees information: Maison des Pyrénées, 15 rue des Augustins, 75002 Paris (1.42.86.51.86).

CRT office (regional information): MIDI-PYRÉNÉES — 54 bd de l'Embouchure, Toulouse 31022 (61.13.55.55). Note that part of the Béarn province falls outside the boundaries of the Midi-Pyrénées; see Béarn, below.

CDT offices (information on département): ARIÈGE — Hôtel du Département, Foix (61.02.09.70); BÉARN — contact the Agence Touristique du Béarn, 22 ter, rue J.J. de Monaix, 64000 Pau (59.30.01.30; fax 59.02.52.75). HAUTES-PYRÉNÉES — 6 rue Eugène-Ténot, Tarbes (62.93.03.30); HAUTE-GARONNE — 14 rue Bayard, Toulouse (61.99.44.00).

OTSI offices (local information): ARAGNOUET — phone 62.39.62.65; ARGELÈS-GAZOST — pl de la Mairie (62.97.00.25); ARREAU — pl du quai de la Neste (62.98.63.15); ARRENS-MARSOUS — phone 62.97.02.63; AX-LES-THERMES — pl du Breilh (61.64.20.64); BAGNÈRES-DE-BIGORRE — 3 allée Tournefort (62.95.50.71); BARÈGES — at the Mairie (62.92.68.19); BORDERES-LOURON — phone 62.98.64.12; CAMPAN — phone 62.91.70.36; CAPVERN-LES-BAINS — pl des Thermes (62.39.00.46); CASTELNAU-MAGNOAC — Maison du Magnoac (62.19.84.88); CAUTERETS — pl du Maréchal-Foch (62.92.50.27); FOIX — 45 cours G. Fauré (61.65.12.12); GAVARNIE — at the Mairie (62.92.49.10); GEDRE — phone 62.92.48.59; GOUAUX-DE-LARBOUST — SI des Agudes (61.79.17.88); LANNEMEZAN — Hall de la Mairie, pl de la République (62.98.08.31); LOURDES — pl Peymarale (62.42.77.40) and pl Champ Commun (62.94.15.64); LOURES-BAROUSSE — rte nationale (62.99.21.30); LUCHON — 18 allées d'Étigny (61.79.21.21); LUX-ST. SAUVEUR — pl 8 mai (62.92.81.60); LE MAS D'AZIL — phone 61.68.90.18; LA MONGIE — phone 62.91.94.15; MONTRÉJEAU — pl V. Abeille (61.95.80.22); NAVARRENX — pl des Casernes (59.66.14.33); OLORON-STE. MARIE — pl de la Résistance (59.39.98.00); ORTHEZ — Maison Jeanne d'Albret, rue des Jacobins (59.69.02.75); PAMIERS — bd Delcassé (61.67.20.30); PAU — pl Royale (59.27.27.08; fax 59.27.03.21); ST. GAUDENS — pl Mas St. Pierre (61.89.15.99); ST. GIRONS — pl Alphonse Sentein/quai du Gravier (61.66.14.11); ST. LARY — phone 62.39.50.81; SALIES-DE-BÉARN — 4 bd St. Guily (59.38.00.33); TARASCON-SUR-ARIÈGE — pl du 19 mars 1962 (61.05.63.46); TARBES — 3 cours Gambetta (62.51.30.31).
Where no tourist office is listed, apply to Town Hall (Mairie or Hôtel de Ville).

Loisirs-Acceuil (hotel booking service): apply to relevant CDT office as listed above.

Hotels and Restaurants

ARGELÈS-GAZOST; Hôtel-Restaurant Miramont, rue Pasteur (62.97.01.26), pleasant and moderately priced, well placed, attractive garden.

AX-LES-THERMES: Hôtel-Restaurant L'Oustal, at Unac, village 8km N (61.64.48.44), delightful old hostelry in the country, well equipped, good food, acceptable prices.

CAUTERETS: Hostellerie la Fruitière, in La Fruitière, 6km out of town (62.92.52.04), appealing little country hotel, beautiful tranquil location, good restaurant. Inexpensive.

FOIX: Hôtel Lons, 6 pl G. Duthil (61.65.52.44), inexpensive 3-star Logis. Good modern rooms in old inn beside the Ariège.

LOURDES: there are scores of hotels in and around Lourdes, but standards are mostly disappointing, prices excessive and star ratings deceptive. Hotel names are amusing (eg. Golgotha, Galilee-Windsor, etc.) but that seems an insufficient attraction on its own. Most satisfactory accommodation is out of town. Try **Le Relais Pyrénéen** at **SAUX** (62.94.29.61), good restaurant with modest, quiet rooms.

LUCHON: Hôtel Panoramic, 6 av Carnot (61.79.30.90), friendly but efficient 2-star Logis, central position, modest prices, good restaurant attached.

OLORON: Hôtel-Restaurant Alysson, bd Pyrénées (59.39.70.70), attractive modern accommodation, well-equipped rooms, and first class restaurant, at very reasonable prices.

PAMIERS: Hôtel de France, 13 rue Hospice (61.60.20.88), inexpensive 2-star Logis with good local cuisine.

PAU: Hôtel Montpensier, 36 rue Montpensier (59.27.42.72), modern, peaceful centrally located, moderate price.
Restaurant Pierre, 16 rue Louis Barthou (59.27.76.86), popular, animated, best restaurant in Pau, good wines, pricey.
Les Pyrénées, pl Royale (59.27.07.75), relaxed, informal eating place with good menu at reasonable price.

ST. BERTRAND-DE-COMMINGES: Hôtel l'Oppidum, rue de la Poste (61.88.33.50), sound 2-star Logis, modern, with restaurant. Modest prices.

ST. GIRONS: Hôtel Eychenne, 8 av P. Laffont (61.66.20.55), unusual and likeable hotel with excellent restaurant, bearable prices.
Hôtel Mirouze, 19 av Gallieni (61.66.12.77), inexpensive 2-star Logis with restaurant.

SALIES-DE-BÉARN: Hôtel-Restaurant du Golf, slightly out of town centre on D933, direction Pau (59.65.02.10), adequate little modern hotel with quite good restaurant, reasonably priced and usefully located.

Sports and Leisure

For fuller information on sports and leisure in the Pyrenees, also contact La Maison des Pyrénées, 6 rue Vital Carles, 33000 Bordeaux, and the Comité Régional Sportif d'Aquitaine, 5 cours de Verdun, 33000 Bordeaux (56.52.80.90).

CYCLING: there are many rewarding cycle routes through the Pyrenees, mostly on ordinary roads. The regional tourist offices have details. Mountain-bike hire and organised rides available at several towns and villages, for example Arette (59.88.90.61), Bedous (59.34.75.25) and Narcastel (59.82.09.36).

GOLF: the area was among the first in France to introduce golf. The golf links at Pau, still excellent, were established in 1856. A number of courses of international standing are open to the public (green fees around 100F–250F per day). Locations include — Artiguelouve (8km from Pau): Béarn Golf Club (59.83.09.29); Aubertin: Scottish Golf Club (59.82.70.69); Pau: rue du Golf, Billère (59.32.02.33); Saliès de Béarn: Domaine Hélios (59.65.02.10). Contact Aquitaine's CRT for their free brochure on the region's golf courses.

CLIMBING, CAVING, MOUNTAIN CANOEING: several local companies lead groups, give instruction, rent equipment for adventure and activity holidays in the Pyrenees. Contact CDTs and tourist offices for up-to-date lists.

PARC NATIONAL DES PYRÉNÉES: in addition to high mountain scenery, the National Park contains rare wildlife, including the last brown bears in the Pyrenees, small numbers of lynx and golden eagles, and large colonies of isard and marmot. Marked footpaths total almost 400km. Park Museums at Etsaut and Arudy. Main information office: Parc National, route de Pau, 65000 Tarbes (62.93.30.60). Other offices in Etsaut (59.34.88.30), Gabas (59.05.32.13), Arrens (62.97.02.66), Cauterets (62.92.52.56), Gavarnie (62.92.49.10), Luz-St. Sauveur (62.92.87.05), St. Lary (62.39.40.91).

Ski Resorts

In the central Pyrenees region (excluding the Pays Basque and Roussillon) there are some 17 major centres for skiing. The Pyrenees are generally characterised by a slightly shorter season than the Alps, more sunshine, a less fashion-parade atmosphere, and easier access to other sights and activities away from the slopes. Resorts can be divided into four types (each category is listed in order east-to-west, with a phone number for local information).

High altitude, well known, purpose built

Monts d'Olmes (61.01.14.14)
Les Agudes (61.79.17.88)
Peyresourde (62.98.64.12)
Val Louron (62.98.64.12)
Aragnouet-Piau (62.39.61.69)

La Mongie (62.91.94.15)
Artouste (59.05.31.41)
Gourette/Eaux-Bonnes (59.05.12.17)
Arette/Pierre-St. Martin (59.66.20.09)

Quieter, less well known, purpose built

Guzet Neige (61.96.02.90)
Le Mourtis (61.79.47.55)
Bourg d'Oueil (61.79.34.07)

Gavarnie (62.92.49.10)
Hautacam (62.34.22.03)

Lived-in villages, downhill or cross country

Ax-les Thermes (61.64.20.64)
Superbagnères/Luchon (61.79.21.21)
St. Lary-Soulan (62.39.50.81)

Barèges (62.92.68.19)
Luz-Ardiden (62.92.81.60)
Cauterets (62.92.50.27)

Easier, lower altitude, mostly cross country

Campan-Payolle (62.91.70.36)
Arrens-Marsous (62.97.02.63)

Iraty (59.28.51.29)

MULTI-ACTIVITY CENTRE: For white-water rafting, canoeing, climbing, caving, mountain cycling and more, in the Ossau valley area, contact the Centre Pyrenéen de Loisirs, BP3, 64800 Asson (59.71.03.28).

RIDING: Ligue Midi-Pyrénées de FEF, 17 av du 14ème RI, 31400 Toulouse, Association Régionale du Tourisme Équestre, 61 allée de Brienne, 31069 Toulouse (61.21.94.60). Riding in the Parc National — enquire at Maisons du Parc. Enquire also at CDTs.

SKIING: See box. Fédération Pyrénéenne des Stations et Centres de Ski, Mairie de Luz-St. Sauveur (62.92.88.92). Cross-country — ask CDTs for addresses of Associations Départementales de Ski de Fond.

SWIMMING: most large towns (and some small) have cheap or free municipal pools.

TENNIS: enquire at SIs or CDTs for details of local clubs open to the public.

WALKING: the GR7, the GR10 and the GR65 cross the region. There are hundreds of kilometres of other marked routes, notably in the Parc National. Useful IGN map — Parc National des Pyrénées. Information from CIMES — (Ariège) 3 sq Balagué, 09200 St. Girons (61.66.40.10); (Hte-Garonne) res. les Ormes, bat. G3, Castanet-Tolosan (61.81.77.69). Contact SIs or CDTs for addresses of walking associations and companies in each département.

Museums and Caves

BAGNÈRES-DE-BIGORRE: Musée Salies, (62.95.05.03). Fine arts, natural history *Mid-Jun—mid-Oct: 10–12, 2–6; closed Tue and some j.f. Rest of year: Thurs and Fri only, exc. j.f.*

BETHARRAN: Grottes, nr St. Pé-de-Bigorre (62.41.80.04). Spectacular caves with lake *Easter—mid-Oct: 8.30–12, 1.30–5.30.*

ETSAUT: Exposition du Parc National des Pyrénées in the Maison du Parc (59.34.88.30). All about the National Park *Mid-Jun—mid-Sept: 10–7.*

FOIX: Château/Musée. History and prehistory of the county of Foix *May—Sep: 10–12, 2–6.30. Rest of year: 11–12, 2.30–5.30. Guided visit (¾ hr).*

GARGAS: Grotte, nr St. Bertrand-de-Comminges (62.39.72.07). Prehistoric drawing and weird handprints of hands with fingers missing. *Guided tour (¾ hr); am and pm in summer; pm only rest of year. Closed during or after rainfall.*

LOURDES: Château Fort et Musée Pyrénéen, in the fortress (62.94.02.04). Traditional folk culture of the region *Apr—mid-Oct: 9–11, 2–6. Rest of year: 9–11, 2–5; closed Tue.*
Le Cachot. Where Bernadette Soubirous lived with her family *Apr—mid-Oct: 9–11, 2–6. Rest of year: 2–5.*

LUCHON: Musée de Luchon, 28 allées d'Étigny. History of Luchon, colourful and interesting *9–12, 2–6, Mon–Fri, exc. j.f.*

MAS D'AZIL: Grotte, on D119. Caves in which were found one of the most important prehistoric collections known *Apr–Jul: Sun and j.f. 10–12, 2–6; other days 2–6. Jul–Sep: 10–12, 2–6 daily. Oct–Nov: Sun and j.f. only 10–12, 2–6.*
Musée de la Préhistoire, in village. Overall view of prehistoric civilisation in France, with displays of objects found in and near the important Grotte nearby *10–12, 2–6. Apr–mid-Jun: Sun and j.f. only. Mid-Jun–Sep: daily.*

NIAUX: Grotte, outside village, signposted (61.05.88.37). Important prehistoric cave drawings of animals *Jul–Sep: guided tour every ¾ hr; 8.30–11.30, 1.30–5.15. Rest of year: tours at 11, 2, 4.30. Note: 20 max per tour — advance reservation possible.*
Musée Paysan, in village (61.05.88.36). Good, well-presented traditional art and craft of the region *Apr–Sep: 9–8; Oct–Mar: 10–6.*

PAU: le Château, at western end of Boulevard des Pyrénées (59.82.38.19/59.82.38.00). See page 123 for description. Includes **Musée Béarnais** (59.27.07.36), local folk art and tradition *Summer: 9–12, 2–6. Winter: 9.30–12, 2–5.*
Musée des Beaux-Arts, rue Mathieu-Lalanne (59.27.33.02). Good collection of painting, sculpture, coins; notable are works by Dégas, El Greco, Corot, Rubens *10–12, 2–6; closed Tue.*
Musée Bernadotte, rue Tran (59.27.48.42). Birthplace of Jean-Baptiste Bernadotte, museum devoted to his life and career as soldier, diplomat and eventually founder of the Swedish royal line *10–12, 2–6; closed Mon.*
Musée de Parachutisme, Camp Astra (59.32.05.97). History of parachuting *Mon–Fri: 2–6.*

ST. GAUDENS: Musée Municipal (61.89.15.99). Arts and crafts of traditional Comminges *Guided visit; closed Sun and j.f.*

SALIES-DE-BÉARN: Musée du Sel (59.38.00.33). All about salt *Open by request.*

Theme Parks and Activities for Children

ST. FAUST (just SW of Pau. W of Jurançon): Cité des Abeilles. Chemin des Crêtes (59.83.10.31). Open air bee park with everything there is to know about bees, their lives and work *May–Oct: 2–6. Closed Mon.*

7
Armagnac, the Heart of Gascony

Once anything south and west of the Garonne used to be called Gascony. Now, with greater awareness of the immense regional diversity within South West France — the Landes, the Pays Basque, the Pyrenees — the name Gascony has come to be most associated with the warm rustic central heartland of the region: the rolling farm country of Armagnac.

The region takes in most of Novempopulania — the 'nine peoples', the Romans' original colony in the South West which was to expand to become Aquitania. In the later years of Roman rule, when Aquitania had become far too large for a single administration, Novempopulania reappeared as Aquitania Tertia. The nine communities, as we would be more likely to call them today, were Auch, Lectoure and Eauze; Labourd, Tarbes, Béarn and Comminges; Bazas and Dax. The first three are in the midst of Armagnac, while the others — in the Pyrenean foothills, the edges of the Landes, and the easternmost vineyards of the Bordeaux region — mark its frontiers. That Armagnac was quite densely populated and thoroughly colonised is clear enough from the quantity of Gallo-Roman finds made since and the number of ruined 'Gallo-Roman towers' still standing. Those early peoples of Auch,

Lectoure and Eauze were the Ausci, Lactorate and Elusate tribes.

Their borders almost exactly coincided with those of the Vascon (Basque) domain established here in the 7th century in the wake of two centuries of violence and chaos following the Roman withdrawal. The Vascons in Armagnac, mixing with the Romanised population and the Germanic invaders, soon became quite separate from their Basque relations in the Pyrenees. Their kingdom became known as Gascony. Conquered by, and absorbed into, the larger Frankish duchy of Aquitaine, in 1152 Gascony passed with the rest of Eleanor of Aquitaine's dowry into the hands of the Plantagenet king of England, Henry II. The noble house of Armagnac, based at Lectoure and Auch, emerged after the eventual French victory at the end of the Hundred Years War. All of this rich central heartland of Gascony passed into their hands; but in 1472 the counts lost their independence, and the Armagnac territories were seized by the French king Louis XI.

Apart from elements in the local patois and accent, little now recalls the long years of English rule. Yet Gascony does retain a character and an atmosphere of its own. Noticeable is a certain Gascon flair and self-confidence (per-

151

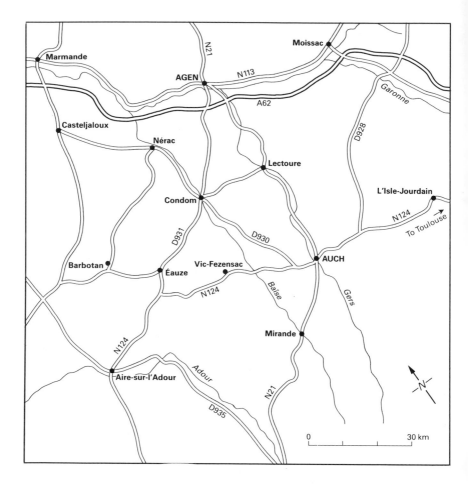

haps this is the root of the strange use, no doubt invented by envious outsiders, of the words *gascon* and *gasconnade* to mean showy exaggeration and boastfulness). In gastronomy, the region is distinguished by the fine quality of its farm-made meat preserves: *foie gras*, *confits*, and indeed almost anything else derived from goose, duck or pig. A favourite starter is the thick meat and vegetable stew called *garbure*. *Amateurs* of *garbure*, when reaching the substantial last few spoonfuls, will pour in some red wine from their glass

to restore a proper soup consistency to the mixture. Among Gascon desserts, the flaky pastry-cake *croustade* is filling and traditional.

When it comes to choosing something to drink, although Armagnac is best known for its elegant but fiery *digéstif*, the region is fortunate in wines too. The ancient Côtes de St. Mont vineyards in the region's south-west produce palatable *VDQS* reds, rosés and whites which are virtually unknown to outsiders. More widely seen, the reds, and especially those fragrant, slightly *pétillant* dry whites made with the Sauvignon grape, of the *vin de pays* Côtes de Gascogne, are remarkably good. Better still though, and the best bargain, is Madiran, a rich, full-bodied *Appellation Contrôlée* from the southern Armagnac, worth maturing and worth savouring. Armagnac's favourite aperitif is Floc de Gascogne, either red or white, a farm-made drink of complex flavour made by macerating grape must with Armagnac and fresh grape juice and maturing the blend in oak casks. Another is Pousse-Rapière, a simpler cocktail produced from maceration of the fruit with Armagnac. Floc, or *flouc de nouste* ('our flower' in Gascon), as it is sometimes called, has a long history and is only made within the Armagnac *Appellation* districts; served cool, it may be enjoyed not only as an aperitif but as an accompaniment to a good *foie gras*, or possibly with dessert. There are Gascon ladies who will even take a little Floc with their afternoon pâtisserie.

This is a profoundly rural region, quiet and undulating, full of golden sunlight illuminating fields of sunflowers, maize, and vines. Many of its villages are magnificently well-preserved old *bastides*, relics of the long war between England and France for control of the territory. Undefended by great natural

---

Bastides

In the troubled 13th and 14th centuries, hundreds of *bastides* were built in South West France. These were fortified towns, built in territory which was disputed, subject to violence, or over which sovereignty was uncertain, to protect the local population and consolidate control over an area. People were encouraged to live in them not only for the sense of security but because all sorts of inducements were offered, such as low taxes or freedom from military obligations. The first *bastides* appeared around the western borders of the lands held by the powerful counts of Toulouse, but the greatest number resulted from the fierce competition between the French and the English for control of Aquitaine (12th–15th centuries, especially the Hundred Years War, 1337–1453).

Whether constructed by the counts of Languedoc, the French, or the English, *bastides* were remarkably consistent in style. They nearly all followed a simple grid plan of streets (*carreyous*) and connecting alleys (*androne*), with a large central market square with covered pavements (*cornières*) and, usually close to the square, a fortified church. The whole town was enclosed within defensive walls entered through fortified gates, which could be locked shut and protected to keep out hostile forces. Nowadays *bastides* tend to attract rather than repel visitors, for those which retain their original features, especially the distinctive main square with its arcades, have great charm to the modern eye.

Other fortified 'new towns' of the Middle Ages were *sauvetés*, religious settlements which cleared and cultivated the surrounding land under the protection of a military or monastic order, and *castelnaux*, built, usually close to a château, as dependencies of a local lord.

The rolling farmland of Gascony

barriers, throughout the Middle Ages the people of Armagnac found it prudent to live behind sturdy ramparts; many fortified new towns — *bastides* and *castelnaux* — were built by local French lords, by the English, and by religious communities to protect themselves and their dependants. These today are among the most attractive features of the Gascon countryside.

The large département of Gers, justifiably, considers that it lies at the centre not only of Gascony, but of Gascon culture, tradition and gastronomy. The département effectively represents most of the territory held by the former counts of Armagnac.

Capital of the Gers, and an excellent base from which to explore the Armag-

nac region, is the rather sedate and civilised town of **Auch** (pronounced approximately as Osh). This was originally Elimberris, home of the Ausci tribe, conquered by Rome in 50BC. The pre-Roman settlement stood on a high ridge above the Gers river, but spread down during the Roman prosperity onto the river plain below. When Aquitaine was invaded by the conquering Visigoths and Franks, the town retreated within its hilltop ramparts, and there remained for most of the Middle Ages, Auch took over from Eauze, after that town had been sacked by Moslems in the 8th century, as an important ecclesiastical centre and seat of an archbishop. As the centuries passed, hilltop Auch suffered the sieges of the English, the

Auch: the imposing Escalier Monumental climbs to the Upper Town

counts of Armagnac, and finally the conquering French, and withdrew into a period of insignificance. It was re-awakened by the imaginative royal Intendant of the town, Antoine Mégret d'Étigny (in office 1720–67), who inspired much rebuilding and cultural life. He is buried in the cathedral and has been honoured in street names and statues. This old heart of the town, the *ville haute* — though still very much part of the day-to-day life of modern Auch — now stands in splendid dignity while the busier workaday newer part of town, the *ville basse*, has again spread down onto the plain. The higher district, seen from the lower, makes an evocative sight.

Certainly the most fitting approach on foot is up the majestic steps of the Escalier Monumental. This vast stone staircase ascends directly from the river to the centre of the old town. Half way up, a modern statue (1931) of d'Artagnan in a dashing outfit (he obviously rode a horse, because he couldn't possibly have walked in those boots) confronts visitors. It's a long slog to the top, with some 370 steps altogether (although curiously, opinions vary as to the precise number).

The Escalier emerges at last into the quiet tree-filled place Salinis, at the foot of the tall, pale stone tower called the Tour d'Armagnac (a former prison, not open for visits). The *place* looks out across an excellent view of the lower town and the Gascon countryside beyond.

Adjacent to the Tour d'Armagnac rises the massive cathedral, or Basilique Ste. Marie, all in pleasing pale stone blocks and with huge windows. Orig-

D'Artagnan — Fact and Fiction

In Alexandre Dumas the elder's thrilling novel *The Three Musketeers*, the hero of the tale is the 'fourth man', Monsieur d'Artagnan. In the story, d'Artagnan joins the King's Musketeers, fights duels with three of the most valiant of them, and subsequently becomes their firm friend. D'Artagnan's later exploits are followed in two sequels, *Twenty Years After* and *The Vicomte de Bragelonne*.

The character was closely based on a real man: Charles de Batz. Born in about the year 1615, probably at his family's manor house in the Gascon village of Castelmore, de Batz was an impoverished country gentleman who joined the regiment of the French Royal Guards. To further his acceptance in the highest circles, he took up the more distinguished-sounding name d'Artagnan from his mother's side of the family. Winning the personal respect of Louis XIV and of Mazarin, he was called upon to perform tasks calling for bravery and discretion. He was made Governor of the city of Lille, and raised to the rank of *Capitaine-Lieutenant* in the First Company of the King's Musketeers (the elite corps of the king's official bodyguard). Sent to the scene to inspire courage in the other troops, d'Artagnan died in combat on the field of battle at the Siege of Maastricht (1673). A romanticised account of his adventures, including the names of the three musketeers and the first part of the Milady episode, was written late in the 17th century by Gatien de Courtilz de Sandras under the title *Les Mémoirs de Monsieur d'Artagnan*; Dumas and his researcher Maquet discovered the book in the 1840s, and in 1844 Dumas published his own even more fanciful version of d'Artagnan's life, making him the very model of Gascon valour and *panache*.

The three musketeers of the story were also, in real life, Gascon *seigneurs*: Athos, squire of the Pyrenean village of Athos; Porthos (Portau) from the city of Pau; and Aramis (Aramitz), squire of Aramitz in Béarn.

inally 13th-century, rebuilt (after a fire) between 1489 and 1592, and with a good deal of later Renaissance work including the twin towers, the structure is attractive and interesting. Opening onto place Salinis, the cathedral's magnificent Porte du Midi entrance has impressive, ornate Gothic stone carvings. But round the corner in place de la République, the main entrance is quite different — an astonishingly large and imposing façade in Renaissance style, with three archways with gates opening onto an immense arcaded porch topped by the two strong square towers (added

1678). On the other side of the building, the Porte du Nord is another fine Gothic entrance; beyond it the grand former Archbishop's Palace, hidden behind a grand gateway, now houses the offices of the préfecture.

Unfortunately, the interior of Auch cathedral is an example of what one sees all too often in France: a splendid building cluttered with rubbish — hanging with dust-covered second-rate pictures which, if they had been found in an attic, would have been thrown out; awful paintings of the stations of the cross; and ghastly old statuary and

A flamboyant d'Artagnan stands on the Escalier Monumental at Auch

Place de la République lies in front of the cathedral, with a few tempting pavement café tables to one side. Across the square from the cathedral, on the corner of rue Dessoles, the Office de Tourisme-Syndicat d'Initiative occupies a really lovely 15th-century mansion, Maison Fedel, with intricate crossed timbers and brickwork. The tourist office can provide abundant information, not only about Auch but about the whole region. Place de la République opens into place de la Libération, the focus of the town. D'Étigny's solid Hôtel de Ville (with theatre inside), the ornate splendour of the luxurious Hôtel de France, and a popular, pleasant brasserie border place de la Libération, while at its centre waters spray high from a modern fountain, most attractive at night when it is illuminated. Raised up next to place de la Libération, the 250-metre tree-

furnishings. Some side chapels look as if they are being used as store-rooms. A *brocante* should be invited to bring a truck and get rid of it all. Then it would be possible to see how beautiful the cathedral is, and how much excellent medieval and Renaissance artwork it does contain: behind the altar, some excellent stone carvings, and 18 lovely windows by Arnaud de Moles (made 1507–13); a good 16th-century Misc à Tombeau and Face of Christ; an unusual retable of the Nativity (1662); a less interesting retable of the Assumption (1662, and looks as if it hasn't been dusted since that time); above the entrance, a fine organ by the 17th-century master Jean de Joyeuse. The highlight of the whole building is the group of 113 richly carved oak choir-stalls (1500–52), with outstanding craftsmanship (fee payable to see choir).

Auch: the cathedral's Porte du Midi

lined cours (or allées) d'Étigny is a fine looking esplanade, as well as a useful place to park the car and also a fairly agreeable spot to sit on a bench under the plane trees with a picnic.

The three squares, places de la Libération, de la République and Salinis, cut a broad open area through the middle of the upper town. A small network (for the centre of Auch is not large) of narrow old streets and back alleys, well worth exploring, extends away on both sides of this spacious corridor. Some of the streets have fine medieval and Renaissance dwellings. An interesting museum with an eclectic collection of local and foreign art, together with important archaeological finds, and a room devoted to Charles de Batz (alias d'Artagnan), occupies a former Jacobin convent behind the Préfecture/Archbishop's Palace. South of place Salinis, the *pousterles* (sometimes *poustrelles*) are an unusual feature: precipitous narrow alleyways that run down in steep steps from the upper town to the lower town. They were originally the postern steps of fortified Auch. Some have kept old, odd-sounding names — pousterle de las Houmettos, pousterle des Couloumats; on this side, the *ville haute* still preserves its medieval pedestrian gates into the town, although these are no longer the only entrances.

Along the busier main road, rue Gambetta (off place de la Libération), a 19th-century corn exchange has been transformed into the Maison Gascogne (open throughout July and August), an emporium of the region's products, and especially its gastronomy. Many local foods and wines can be sampled here free of charge and without any obligation to buy. On sale there are all the specialities of Armagnac, including the traditional fine preserved meats, *confits*

and *foie gras* of duck and goose, bottles of Floc de Gascogne, and of course, Armagnac itself. The building is an imposing stone structure with arcaded exterior, heavily beamed ceiling inside, and a gallery on which nowadays there are exhibitions of local arts and crafts.

In every direction from Auch, main roads and minor lanes lead through appealing villages which deserve a pause.

Heading east, the N124 quickly reaches the red-brick country of the Toulouse region, on the way passing through **Gimont**, formerly Francheville, a *bastide* (founded 1265) with a magnificent wooden covered market standing astride the steep main street; and through **L'Isle Jourdain** in the valley of the river Save, with remains (unusually) of two arcaded central market-places, at the meeting point of the ancient Aquitaine and Languedoc provinces. In all these little places the use of bricks in building is noticeable, presaging the character of the Toulousain towns. North of this major road, **Mauvezin**, with an even more splendid large central square and market-place, and **Cologne**, with its 15th-century dwellings and market, are other *bastides* on this border of Gascony and the Toulousain.

This country east of Auch, heartland of goose and duck farms, produces a huge proportion of France's epicurean *foie gras*. Going to the south of L'Isle-Jourdain, **Samatan** in the Save valley, a red-brick town much damaged during the Religious Wars is a major market centre for Gascon *foie gras*. Its neigh-

Pousterle de l'Est, Auch

bour **Lombez**, just 2km along the river, is dominated by the unusual and attractive octagonal tower, pierced by five storeys of windows, on the large, interesting brick-built 14th-century church. The D632 continues towards Tarbes (see page 128) and Lannemezan (see page 136), with increasingly good views of the Pyrenees, especially at Thermes-Magnoac on the stretch from Boulogne-sur-Gesse to Trie-sur-Baïse (see below). West of the road, small, attractive **Simorre**, once the site of a Benedictine monastery, still has an interesting fortified brick church (1304) with good woodcarving and windows. A little farther west, reaching the Gers valley, **Masseube**, originally a Gallo-Roman town, was recreated as a *bastide* in 1274. The main road through the town is the D929, which runs straight north and south beside the Gers river: turn onto this road to return to Auch, skirting **Pavie**, another former Gallo-Roman settlement (called Spartacus), which in 1281 was rebuilt as a *bastide*.

Leaving Auch on the south side, the busy N21 (the main road to Pau) passes through more delightful *bastides* with well-preserved central squares and churches. To see some good examples of these picturesque medieval towns start by travelling on the N21 to **Mirande**, a pleasant agricultural centre, founded in 1281. It retains the traditional grid plan and has an impressive main square with stone arcades, flowers and plane trees. Fifty metres from the square stand the Roman watchtower and the 15th-century former cathedral in Languedoc Gothic style, with its storeyed tower supported by an unusual belltower (locally known as the Arc de Triomphe). Next door, there's a rather good Musée des Beaux-Arts with

collections of 18th- and 19th-century costume, ceramics, painting, local history and archaeological finds. The Hôtel des Pyrénées is well placed at the centre of the town.

Miélan, farther down the N21, is another former *bastide*, which has become something of a holiday centre because of the nearby artificial lake, popular for watersports, created in the valley of the now-skimpy river Osse. The area west and south from Miélan is the Bigorre, a gorgeous rustic district, richly productive, with hills and valleys, woods, farms and traditional farmyards, and good views of the Pyrenees. The N21 crosses the high crest known as Puntous de Laguian (320m), with a marvellous mountain panorama, descending through Rabestens-en-Bigorre and Vic-en-Bigorre on its way towards Pau. The D3 branches away south from Miélan to **Trie-sur-Baïse**, an ordinary workaday industrial village around a huge central square with a fine covered market-place, a pleasing church in the local style with alternating stone and brick, and, down a side street, an old tower gateway, the only notable relic of its fortifications.

Turning north from Miélan on the D3, or perhaps cutting across country more directly from Mirande on the D16, one comes to **Tillac**. This small fortified village, entered through a tower gateway, was created as a miniature *bastide* in 1312. Within its walls handsome timber arcades support crumbling old brick and timber dwellings. The one short street leads to a simple Gothic church with a tiled spire; the gateway out of the village on this side has disappeared. The D3 curves round following the river Boués to Marciac, or one could take a longer, prettier route, the D156, over on the other side of the river. This would go first through the simple hamlet of St. Christaud, with surprisingly large brick church and fine views. **Marciac**, a *bastide* of 1298, is dominated by the twin octagonal belltowers of its 15th-century Gothic church and Augustinian convent, and has an astonishingly large market square lined by arcaded pavements. Marciac has become quite a popular centre for activity holidays. More remarkably, in August the village hosts an annual jazz festival of considerable standing, attracting well-known American, French and British names, mostly 'big band' style.

The D3 carries on to two *bastides*, **Beaumarché** and **Plaisance**, meeting the D946, which makes a good return route. The hills west of here, along the left bank of the Adour almost into Aire-sur-l'Adour, are the home of the Madiran *Appellation*, its vineyards producing the Armagnac region's best table wines. The village of Madiran itself is a 16-kilometre drive on country lanes from Plaisance.

Turning back to Auch, the D946 reaches the small one-street *bastide* of **Bassoues** (1360). The road passes right through a magnificent wooden covered market, and a large well stands in the roadway. Beside this splendid marketplace (*halle*), flower-hung carved wooden arcades run beneath old timbered houses.

To one side of the road, the large church of Notre-Dame is entered, unusually, by going down a flight of steps: the spacious interior has no aisles, the walls and ceiling are decorated with frescoes, and the choir has interesting vaults. There's a 16th-century *pietà* on display, and a curious pulpit is reached by stone steps constructed inside the church

A wooden covered market straddles one end of the main street of Bassoues; at the other rises the 14th-century donjon

wall. In short turnings off the road stand some marvellous old houses, heavily timbered.

At the other end of the street, the village's massively high 14th-century keep (*donjon*; SI inside) looms across the cornfields. Beside the keep, a little 'château' formed part of the former defences of the village. Outside the walls, the long narrow Basilica of St. Fris, towerless but with huge buttresses, stands ignored in the churchyard; not ignored by locals though, for many of them revere this obscure 'saint' who died in battle with the Moors.

The Auch road — now the D943 — goes through **Montesquiou**, with a ruined château and relics of once-powerful fortifications; **L'Isle-de-Noé**, an agreeable village with an 18th-century château, at the confluence of two little rivers; and the sturdily fortified, moated village of **Barran**, which deserves a stroll, and a perhaps a meal (if it's lunchtime) with the locals at the unpretentious, lively, and astonishingly inexpensive Chez Georgette in the main street. Note the 'heliocoidal' (as

161

they say here) spire on Barran's church: it is effectively octagonal, but with a twist in it, and rises from a square tower on a church of lovely golden stone. Inside, the building is Gothic, but simple; the choir-stalls are notable. There's a simple, arcaded main square, goldfish in the moat, and smallholdings in the very centre of the village. Nice little exhibitions are held in the tower above the old town gate. The D943 joins the N124 and enters Auch on the west side.

The N124 is a main axis of the South West. Coming from Toulouse, it cuts across Gascony, skirts the Landes, and turns south towards the coast and the Basque country. Leaving Auch through the western suburbs, it crosses a countryside dotted with Gallo-Roman towers and other relics.

Vic-Fezensac, after some 30km, is an exceptionally likeable market town in prosperous farm country. It lacks much in the way of 'sights', but has an enjoyable bustling energy. Place de la Mairie, part of cours Delom, is the main square (with SI in Hôtel de Ville); the Hôtel d'Artagnan overlooks the square, and has a popular café downstairs. The principal landmark is the tower of the Gothic church; inside, the church has unusual wooden vaulting. A number of old, arcaded dwellings survive in the town. Perhaps surprisingly, Vic has a reputation as a great centre of bullfighting, with *courses* and *corridas* — Spanish, Portuguese, Landaises and Languedocienne — especially at Pentecôte (Whitsun) in May but occasionally throughout the summer.

Wooden arcades in the little village of Bassoues

After Vic, the N124 turns directly west towards the Landes Forest, while the D626 stays within the ancient boundaries of Armagnac: from Vic to Eauze it is fringed by neat, well-tended vineyards planted in long rows with not a weed in sight. **Eauze** (pronounced 'Ayouze'), a refined small town with some picturesque brick-and-timber houses and several high-quality little food shops, was two thousand years ago the principal settlement — called Lesberous of the Elusate tribe of Iberian Celts. Conquered by the Romans and made capital of the Novempopulania colony (more or less corresponding to later Gascony), the *oppidum* was renamed Elusa. In fact the original pre-Roman settlement was slightly north of the existing town; almost nothing survives of it now, much of the stone having been used over the generations in the buildings of Eauze. During those early centuries Eauze held the rank of the most important town in Armagnac, and stood as the region's ecclesiastical centre until it was sacked by Saracens in the 8th century. The town still likes to call itself the Capital of Armagnac, a forgivable conceit considering its history. Certainly it is today one of the capitals of Armagnac the drink, being the main commercial centre for the Bas-Armagnac *Appellation* district, which generally produces the best Armagnac of all. In the town's main square, suitably named place d'Armagnac (SI on corner), there are several attractive brick-and-timber houses three and four hundred years old. Opening off the square, the 15th-century church (former cathedral) of St. Luperc, in stone and red brick, has an unusual asymmetric tower. Much of the stone used in the building comes from Roman Elusa. The impressive interior of the building has

163

Armagnac

Reputedly France's longest-established *eau de vie* (dating from the 15th or 16th centuries), Armagnac is a powerful fiery brandy softened by an intriguing combination of rusticity and refinement. Quality varies considerably, but a good Armagnac properly matured in oak should be extremely smooth and elegant, though retaining a certain 'farmhouse' earthiness. It is produced by a process of continuous distillation in a special pot still, which accounts for its having greater flavour and fragrance than other fine brandies. The grapes used — as in Cognac — produce only a thin, acidic, poor white wine which, however, proves ideal for distillation. The principal varieties are Folle Blanche, Ugni Blanc and Colombard, mixed with eight other permitted grape types. On leaving the still, the new Armagnac is sharp and colourless; its mellowness and the golden hue result from the ageing, which lasts about two years in one (new) barrel followed by as much as twenty years in another (older). The barrels are made of local oak. After bottling, no further maturation takes place — so there is no virtue in keeping Armagnac in the cellar.

The label reveals the length of time that the Armagnac has been aged in the barrel. Trois Étoiles is the lowest quality, aged for 1–4 years; VO, VSOP, and Reserve all indicate 4–5 years; Extra, Napoléon, XO and Vieille Réserve indicate increasingly long periods of over 5 years.

The Armagnac-producing region covers most of the Gers département and parts of Lot-et-Garonne and the Landes. It is subdivided into three areas of different character; Haut-Armagnac (the largest, based on Auch), Ténarèze (in the centre, with its capital at Condom), and Bas-Armagnac (in the region's west, with its commercial centre at Eauze). The finest Armagnacs come mainly from the Bas-Armagnac, those from the other two districts usually being blended to achieve a suitably fine quality.

A number of other local drinks are made with Armagnac, notably Gascony's aperitifs Floc and Pousse-Rapière. For details of Armagnac producers who welcome visitors to their *chais*, consult local Syndicats d'Initiative, particularly in Auch, Eauze, and Condom.

unfaced walls and a single nave with no separate choir.

Eauze stands at a crossroads: the D931 goes in one direction to Condom, and in the other to **Aire-sur-l'Adour**, a historic town on the western edge of Armagnac with some remnants of its Gallo-Roman and medieval past. Just west of it, the little spa of **Eugénie-les-Bains** has been put firmly on the map by the famous restaurant of the hotel Les Près d'Eugénie.

The other road intersecting at Eauze, the D626, crosses straight over in the direction of **Barbotan-les-Thermes**. Barbotan is a quiet little spa resort: at the entrance to the Thermal Park, there's a 12th-century church with an interesting porch-belltower which was once part of the town's fortifications. Beyond, the D626 passes a small endearing chapel dedicated to Our Lady of Cyclists, and goes on to the *bastide* village **Labastide-d'Armagnac** (founded 1291). Picturesque old stone and timber houses enclose its charming main square, place Royal. Here again we are on the abrupt margin of the Landes forest.

Condom is another important local centre of Armagnac brandy. While Eauze is the commercial capital of the Bas-Armagnac area, and Auch the centre of the Haut-Armagnac, Condom is the capital of the Ténarèze district. In addition, proximity to the road and rail links of the Garonne valley make it an important commercial focus for all other Armagnac produce.

In the standard northern French accent, the town's curious name is pronounced as if the last letter was nasal, the 'm' indistinguishable from 'n', however, in the local accent people say Condom unequivocally just as it is spelt. The name certainly startles some English-speaking visitors, and causes not a little merriment among others. It appears that the English word (which for that matter is the same in French, though less frequently used than *préservatif*) comes from the inventor of the modern male sheath, a Frenchman called Jean Condom. It is not known whether he personally lived in the town. Condom has a highly agreeable atmosphere, busy and unpretentious, with good little food shops, attractive old houses, and makes an excellent base for exploring one of the most interesting corners of Armagnac.

Everything of greatest note in the town clusters together around the large early 16th-century Cathédrale de St. Pierre. An excellent example — and one of the last to be built in the style — of Gascon Gothic, the building has an air of strength and dignity. The rib-vaulted stone ceiling, the flamboyant stonework in the windows and choir, fulfil all the aspirations of Gothic art.

The superb cloisters at Condom

There are some good later features too — notice the impressive organ of 1605 — and certain elements do survive from the earlier church on the site. Beside the building there is a tower dating from the 13th century. Adjoining the cathedral, superb 16th-century cloisters now form part of the Hôtel de Ville. Next to that, the Gothic Chapelle des Évêques (Bishops' Chapel) is now the Palais de Justice, and the 18th-century Évêché (Bishops' Palace) has become part of the offices of the local sous-préfecture administration (both are open to the public). Close by, a former gendarmerie houses the Musée d'Armagnac, where some intriguing historic Armagnac-distilling equipment is on display.

All around Condom there are interesting and attractive *bastides*, churches and country mansions, and farms producing local food and drink specialities. A few kilometres west on the D15, **Larresingle**, built (in the 13th century) as a stronghold of the Condom bishops, survives as a superb fortified village with ruins of its episcopal castle and Romanesque church. The road continues to the *bastide* of **Montréal** (built 1255, charter granted 1289). Everything in the town is very badly sign-

One of the Gallo-Roman mosaics at Séviac

posted, but go upwards — for the old town was constructed on a high ridge of land — to reach the arcaded main square. Although severely damaged during the Religious Wars, Montréal keeps its traditional layout, with narrow streets in a grid pattern, and the church standing at one corner of the market square. The edges of town give extensive views into countryside, including whole hills entirely yellow with sunflowers during the summer months. On the western edge of Montréal, the archaeological site at Roman Séviac reveals the beautiful mosaic floor of a luxurious Roman villa.

Also discovered on the site have been numerous coins dating from the first century, objects carved in ivory and bone, and hot baths. Just north of Montréal, on the D29, **Fourcès** is a delightful little English *bastide* of similar age (built 1279, charter 1289); most unusual because of its circular plan. Enter the village on a small bridge over the Auzoue. At the village centre, lovely old stone and timber houses surround the large shady circular *place*.

Going north from Condom, the D931 and the D930 make good time through Armagnac vineyards to the Garonne valley, the latter road passing close to hilltop **Moncrabeau**, where the village bar is also a good cheap hotel with an excellent restaurant. The village and neighbourhood make the strange claim — probably an outright lie — that its people are the most boastful in all Gascony; and they have a local Académie des Menteurs (Academy of Liars) to prove it. Membership of the Academy, founded in the 18th century, is open to 'All boasters, liars, storytellers and other idle persons expert in the fine art of untruthfulness'. Academicians, numbering forty at present, entertain each

The lovely cloisters at La Romieu

other at *soirées* with tall but credible stories.

Close to Condom, the minor D41 turns away from the D931 to enter **La Romieu**, an incredibly pretty village of old cottages dominated by a huge twin-towered church. Most of the houses are stone, some are timbered. Roadside verges have been tended and planted like gardens.

The central square, place E. Bouet, has arcades on two sides. A doorway leads into a beautiful Gothic cloister, badly weatherworn and partly damaged, but still complete on all four sides. This gives access into the 14th-century church. A separate square tower formed part of the former Cardinal's Palace. The village has few visitors — often none at all, even in high summer.

East from Condom, the D7 makes an enjoyable drive through cheerful farm country towards Lectoure. Country lanes to the right go between the fields, past casual, crumbling, comfortable Gascon farmhouses to **Terraube**, an enticing little fortified village. It has several attractive houses, a château (originally 13th-century, much restored in the 16th–18th centuries), and a couple of pleasant restaurants with regional dishes.

The D7 winds up into **Lectoure**, a likeable town, enclosed by ramparts and with many unusual fine houses, the result of its having been for centuries the seat of the counts of Armagnac and then the main commercial centre of the Armagnac region. It was the taking of this town by royal troops in 1473, and the killing of the count of Armagnac, the megalomaniac tyrant Jean V, which marked the end of Armagnac's regional independence. The road climbs into the *centre ville*, giving more and more extensive views across the countryside. At the hilltop, promenade du Bastion is a leafy esplanade with chestnut trees, a well-placed café, bandstand, and tremendous view (a jocular viewing table shows the positions of Peking, New York and Moscow as well as neighbouring villages like Terraube). Near the *promenade*, a most impressive belfry rises from an attractive pale stone Gothic church, originally 13th-century, largely reconstructed about 1488 and 1540. Previously a cathedral, it is in fact two buildings, St. Gervais and St. Protais, which were joined. It can be seen clearly that they are in different styles, one with the far more perpendicular, more pointed arches, of the north, the other in the rounder and broader southern Gothic. The more 'pointed' church is really just a large choir and ambulatory; the other is a single nave with stone balconies and side chapels. The church stands on the site of a Roman temple, which itself replaced an important Celtic religious site. Lectoure, as a centre of Celtic religion, did not adopt Christianity until well into the 6th century. In place Charles de Gaulle, beside the church, the old Bishops' Palace has become Lectoure's Hôtel de Ville; in its basement, the municipal museum has a remarkable collection of Mithraic bull-sacrifice altars found on the church site. The district surrounding Lectoure, called Lomagne (of which Lectoure is historically the capital), was the territory of the Lactorate tribe, one of the original 'nine peoples' of Aquitania. The whole area is covered with Gallo-Roman remains, many good examples of which have found their way into the

museum. (The same building houses the SI). At the bottom of rue Fontelie, off place Charles de Gaulle, steps descend to the level of the Fontaine Diane, a water source emerging in a handsome 13th-century enclosure — the fountain's name implies perhaps that it had some religious significance in pre-Christian time. Along the main street several superb arcaded houses of pale stone have big double doors opening into spacious and enticing private courtyards.

The Lac des Trois Vallées near Lectoure has been made into a leisure and watersports area with campsites. Among many things to see in the countryside farther east, **St. Clar**, a well-preserved little hilltop *bastide* (English, 1274), has some unusual features. In particular it has two arcaded central squares — place de la République and place de la Mairie, indicating its past importance as a local market: place de la Mairie has a splendid wooden covered market dating from the 13th century. Indeed St. Clar remains an important agricultural centre today, and is sometimes called Gascony's Capital of Garlic.

The N21, linking Tarbes and Agen via Auch, has caused some unsightly industry to cluster along the Gers valley, although the surrounding landscape is rolling with woods and wheatfields, meadows and maize. Unfortunately the main road conceals much of this countryside, and even the river cannot be seen. Lying beside this dull highway close to Lectoure and St. Clar, **Fleurance** appears (despite big bowls of flowers lining the route into town) fairly unpromising: a large, sprawling village with modern outskirts. Yet the old centre of this *bastide* (of 1274) has a great deal of charm. The main market square, place de la République, has a fine arcaded covered market; the town hall, over the market, is bedecked with flowers; and all around are beautiful stone and timber arcaded pavements.

The Gothic church adjacent to the square has a distinctive octagonal tower, the principal landmark of the town, while the interior has some outstanding 16th-century stained glass by Arnaud de Moles, some frescoes, and a good organ loft.

South of Condom, the country is full of places amply rewarding a visit. At **Cassaigne**, a pretty village between the D930 and the D931, the Château de Cassaigne, once a residence of the Condom bishops, has become an Armagnac *chai* open for tours and tastings. Originally 13th-century, the château derives much of its present interest from the 16th-century reconstruction: note especially the magnificent vaulted ceiling of the old kitchen. There are several

other *chais* in the district where Armagnac can be tasted and its distillation explained (ask at Condom SI for addresses). Just 4km from Cassaigne, back on the D930, the Abbaye de Flaran stands quietly beside the road. It looks like nothing so much as a large Gascon farmhouse, of pale golden stone with red-tile roof and a beautiful old doorway joined onto a later building. The simplicity of its surviving Romanesque lines reflect the abbey's Cistercian origins; it was built in 1151. But Gascony's turmoil during the Hundred Years War, then the violence of the Religious Wars, made many changes to that basic structure. The Revolution put the abbey into private hands, and the final disaster was a devastating fire in 1970. After the fire though, the département bought the buildings, restored them, and now the Abbaye de Flaran at least retains its 12th-century Cistercian church, remnants of a 14th-century chapter-house and cloisters, and an 18th-century refectory. All sorts of exhibitions and

Main Festivals in Armagnac

May

CONDOM — Festival de Bandas: a lively festival of traditional music played in the streets (2nd Sunday).
VIC-FEZENSAC — Pentecôte (Whitsun): the main bullfighting season.

August

MARCIAC — Festival de Jazz: annual event with some big names.
MIRANDE — Fête Locale: cycle races, horse races, street parades (on the 15th).
MONCRABEAU — Fêtes des Menteurs: Liar's Festival, with prize-winning tall stories and a tournament of pulling faces.
LABASTIDE-D'ARMAGNAC — historical costume parades and candlelit meals under the pavement arcades (last Saturday, or first Saturday in September).

events are held during the year at the abbey, which is now designated as the département's cultural centre.

The nearest village to the abbey is **Valence-sur-Baïse**, a sleepy little *bastide* on the D930, the main Auch road. The road runs diagonally through the main square, with its stone arcades and a small simple Gothic church adorned by two low octagonal towers and a strange parapet. Beyond, **Castéra-Verduzan** was a spa village (specialising in mouth and gums, and digestive and metabolic problems) in Roman times; the healing power of its waters was rediscovered in the 18th century. There's a charming little arcaded *établissement thermal* in the village centre. A pleasant spot for a little cure if you've got sore gums!

The landscape here is abundant with yellow fields of corn, attractive with steep little hills, and populated by beautiful farmhouses satisfyingly rambling and unpretentious. Left turns off the main road lead along country lanes to **Lavardens**, a small hilltop village dominated by its large semi-ruined early 17th-century château. The château, built around the natural shape of the rock on which it stands, has tremendous views over the rolling fields and farms. A windmill can be seen atop a distant crest. Part of the building has been restored: there are daily visits, and it hosts exhibitions, concerts, and the like. Adjacent to this huge edifice rises a massive buttressed square tower, surmounted by a tiled spire, which is now the elaborate porch of the simple village church but which once formed part of the earlier castle of the counts of

Fleurance: Place de la République — the covered market with town hall above

Armagnac. Passing beneath the tower, through narrow arches, notice over the church doors a curious mosaic tympanum. It depicts an angel in armour, bearing a sword, while beside him unfortunates tumble into hell. The narrow interior has a pious simplicity, but here too is some old mosaic decoration, together with good stained glass and woodcarving and, unusually, excellent photographs hanging on the walls (a great improvement on the more customary incomprehensible paintings). From Lavardens it is not far, either on the main road or on exquisite back lanes, through the hills to Auch (see page 154).

Just as the Pyrenees form the southern boundary of the Armagnac region, so the Garonne river marks its limit to the north, and the Gironde border its western edge. Most of the towns and most of the country along the Garonne are densely populated and intensively developed whether for industry or for agriculture, which does not detract from the places of interest often found along this historic river highway.

The most rewarding route approaching from the Gironde would be the D655, well south of the river, for the first town along the N113 on the north bank is **Marmande**, large, industrial, and not one of the Garonne's jewels: a 13th–15th-century church and Renaissance cloister are its main feature. Continuing along the valley, the N113 then passes through **Aiguillon**, a *bastide* of 1296, and the old river harbour **Port Ste. Marie**, each retaining a few attractive reminders of its past, before reaching Agen (see below). By contrast, the D655 — running right beside the edge of the Landes forest — first reaches **Casteljaloux**, a picturesque well-preserved old *bastide* at the meeting of Landes, Armagnac, and the Bordeaux vineyards. Among several impressive timber-framed houses, most striking is the one known either as La Maison de Xaintrailles, after Joan of Arc's companion Jean de Xaintrailles, or alternatively as La Maison de Jeanne Albret, after the mother of Henri IV (though neither seems to have had any connection with the house). A former convent now accommodates Casteljaloux's Hôtel de Ville.

The D655 crosses the wooded countryside. At the Carrefour du Placiot crossroads, a minor turning (the D141) goes off towards the Château de Xaintrailles, a 12th-century fortress rebuilt in the mid-15th century for Jean de Xaintrailles, (it has good views), while the D655 keeps straight on. Later, a right turn (the D665) leads to **Durance**, an attractive remnant of a *bastide* with ruins of a 13th-century castle calling itself the Château de Henri IV. The D655 continues its course through Barbaste (with Gothic bridge and fortified 14th-century mill), from which a turn (the D642) up the left bank of the Baïse leads to **Vianne**, another well-preserved *bastide* (of 1284), with impressive ramparts and Romanesque church.

From Barbaste take the D630 into **Nérac**, a historic town on the river Baïse, once very important, and still an appealing place today, but with little left to see. It was important because it was the capital of Albret. Initially, Albret was as insignificant as many another small French *pays*. In the course of time though, thanks largely to a policy of prudent marriages, the *seigneurs* of Albret found themselves wielding more and more influence in Gascony. By the 16th century they held, as well as little Albret itself, the tit-

les and the lands of Foix, Béarn, and Basse-Navarre. Furthermore, they were intellectuals — and toyed with religious reform and what was then called humanism. In 1527, Henri d'Albret married Marguerite d'Angoulême, sister of the French king François I (1515-47). Under their rule, the Béarn capital Pau and the Albret capital Nérac became centres of art, literature, and also of religious dissent. Marguerite is traditionally credited with the authorship of the astonishing *Heptameron*, seventy ribald but moralistic anti-clerical stories.

Marguerite and Henri's daughter, the outspoken and forthright Jeanne d'Albret (of whom it was said that 'the only thing feminine about her is her sex') married a member of the Bourbon family, Antoine de Bourbon, and they too held court at both Pau and Nérac. They had a son, whom Jeanne named after her father, as Henri d'Albret.

Succeeding to the throne of Navarre (which women could do in all the Pyrenean provinces), within a few years Jeanne d'Albret officially renounced Catholicism and embraced Protestantism. The French monarch Charles IX (1560–74) sent troops to seize Pau and reconquer all the Albret territories for Catholicism. This proved an impossible task: they managed to conquer Pau, but only for a few months. Jeanne returned with troops of her own, under Lieutenant General Montgomery, recaptured Pau, and, basing her army at Nérac, waged outright war against all Catholic influence in Gascony, promoting Huguenots (as Protestants were called) to all positions of importance, and urgently encouraging religious reform. She made Nérac a formidable Protestant military and intellectual stronghold.

Of course, Jeanne d'Albret brought up her son Henri as a Protestant. With exceptional foresight and sense of poetic justice she was able, as part of a 'peace deal' with Charles IX, to arrange for Henri a particularly astute marriage. Since he was (through his father) a Bourbon, it was agreed that Henri d'Albret would marry Marguerite de Valois, sister of the king and daughter of the fanatical anti-Protestant Catherine de Medicis. Jeanne died before the wedding (1572), but although she did not see it, her plans were to come to fruition.

Since Marguerite de Valois had three older brothers, it might have been assumed at the time of the marriage that the throne of France was safely in Catholic hands, but all three were physically weak, and incompetent rulers, who enjoyed but brief reigns. When the last of them, Henri III died in 1589, Henri d'Albret, already King of Navarre since Jeanne's death, rose to take the crown of France. It's as well that Jeanne did not live to see the very end of the tale, for Henri, pragmatic Gascon that he was, did not insist on the right to sit on the Paris throne as a Protestant. Instead he decided, with the famous words 'Paris is worth a Mass', to be rebaptised as a Catholic. In fact, he was quite a well-practised apostate, because he had already given up Protestantism once before — for just long enough to escape being killed in the St. Bartholomew's Eve Massacre of Protestants (1572), which his mother-in-law Catherine de Medicis had organised while he was in Paris for his wedding.

What survives of all this in Nérac? Most of the town dates from the 19th century. Of the fine Renaissance riverside château reconstructed for Jeanne d'Albret, only a single wing remains

(housing a municipal museum devoted mainly to the Roman period). The streets close to the château preserve a few old buildings. A Gothic bridge, the Pont-Vieux, crosses the Baïse to the right bank, where the quarter called Petit Nérac retains more buildings of Nérac's 16th-century heyday.

The D656 meanders from Nérac towards the Garonne, and crosses the river to enter **Agen** (pop: 33,500), préfecture of the Lot-et-Garonne département. Pronounce its name as 'Ajenn'; sometimes it can even sound almost like 'Ajunn'. This large commercial town has a centre of interesting old buildings and pleasant medieval streets. Admittedly they are sometimes rendered intolerable by loudspeakers blaring out a more-than-usually ghastly jumble of music and advertisements (this is a feature of some French provincial towns). The vieille ville lies in the angle between the north bank of the Garonne river and the south side of the Garonne canal. The town's busy main shopping street, boulevard de la République, cuts east–west through the network of narrow lanes. Another busy road, rue Palissey-cours Victor Hugo delineates the southern limit of the old centre. Both intersect another main boulevard, boulevard Carnot (with SI), which goes north–south through the centre of town.

The Gallic oppidum of Aginn stood on the high ground of the Côteau de l'Ermitage just north of the present-day canal. In time of peace it would spread down onto the fertile river plain. The community followed the usual history of a Gascon town until the year 1196: a period of Roman rule gave way to the Frankish dukes of Aquitaine, and Eleanor of Aquitaine gave Agen with the rest of her domain to Henry II of England on

her marriage to him in 1152. But when Eleanor and Henry's daughter Joan wanted to marry Raymond VI of Toulouse (the Count of Languedoc), they included Agen and its surroundings in her dowry. In theory, such friendly links between England and Languedoc were to the advantage of both, and to the disadvantage of France. Yet when, hardly more than twenty years later, Languedoc was invaded and ravaged by the French during the Albigensian Crusade (1209–29), England did not come to its defence. In consequence, the French subdued Languedoc and brought it under the control of the king of France; that included its territories at Agen. In 1360, during the Hundred Years War, the English retook Agen and held it until the end of the war in 1444.

As a market town in good fruit-growing country, having excellent water communication with other regions, Agen grew and prospered. It is still a major centre for the production of fruits, especially peaches, eating grapes and plums. The greatest speciality of Agen is prunes (dried plums). This might sound a bit odd to the British, coming as they do from a dreadful land in which the prune is served in syrup, sometimes with instant custard, and is seen as an object more risible than gastronomic. By contrast, the *pruneaux* of Agen are the object of the craftsmanship of the best *confiseurs* in France. Whether plain, sugared or stuffed, they are delicious. Packets of *pruneaux fourrés* (stuffed prunes) can be seen displayed in the windows of numerous shops in the town.

Place de la Halle, the quaint marketplace at Auvillar

Much of the area between boulevard Carnot and the river consists of medieval alleys and backstreets, with a number of interesting and attractive old houses. Certain of the more important old lanes, notably rue Montesquieu, have become agreeable shopping streets. There are countless individual buildings of note to be discovered on a stroll. Esplanade du Gravier, beside the swift, swirling Garonne, is a large waterside area with boules, plane trees, riverbank benches, and parking space convenient for the town centre. A suspension footbridge goes over the river from the esplanade to the residential area on the west bank.

The best way to see Agen is to park the car in esplanade Gravier and walk: the weather is usually ideal for it. From the esplanade, take rue Lomet (opposite the pedestrian bridge). On reaching rue Vivent, glance to the right down this back street at the houses inside a curious old square archway, but turn left to walk up rue Richard Coeur-de-Lion. On the left, opposite the 13th-century redbrick church of Notre-Dame des Jacobins in place des Jacobins, the Crêperie les Jacobins is a nice place for lunch. Farther along, rue Richard Coeur-de-Lion has several fine houses. Turn right down rue Beauville, a charming old back lane with good examples of these lovely brick and stone buildings, some of them being used as the cheapest form of housing. (Some of the most striking medieval and Renaissance buildings in Agen's vieille ville, with their overhanging upper floors supported on sturdy wooden beams, line what are really just malodorous alleys).

Rue Beauville reaches place Docteur Esquirol, a delightful square (in fact roughly triangular) with the 17th-century Hôtel de Ville on one side; a group of Renaissance hôtels in one corner, including a striking brick and white stone mansion, all now housing the Musée des Beaux-Arts (Fine Arts Museum); and next to that, the impressive round-fronted white stone Théâtre Ducourneau (or Théâtre Municipal), often with art exhibitions in the foyer. Beside the Hôtel de Ville, the tables of the Café des Arts complete the picture, making this an ideal spot to linger. The Musée des Beaux-Arts contains prehistoric collections (in a vaulted basement which used to be a prison), some high-quality Gallo-Roman artwork found locally (notably the 1st-century Venus du Mas d'Agenais), some good examples of 18th-century faïence (ceramic) work, and a rather variable collection of paintings, mainly 17th- and 18th-century French works, including a number by well-known portraitists, and 19th- and 20th-century early Impressionists. The interior of the buildings themselves is another considerable attraction of the museum.

Several of the many roads leading away from the place are tempting: rue Molière, rue Chaudordy, rue Moncorny, rue du Paradis, rue des Colonels Lacuée, rue de Cessac. Take rue Moncorny and turn right (round the back of the theatre) into rue Garonne. In nearby rue Voltaire there are several good little inexpensive restaurants. In rue Garonne note an absurdly florid Renaissance hôtel at No. 12, as well as some interesting modern buildings; many of the new constructions in the heart of old Agen do have good and unusual architecture, although whether it will last for three or four centuries as the older buildings have done seems doubtful. You arrive at place des Laitiers, a pleasing arcaded medieval square sheltering shops and cafés, though spoiled by the surrounding modern developments.

Cross the busy boulevard de la République and continue on the arcaded rue Cornières; here, and in rue du Puits-du-Saumon, rue Barnabéra, and rue Floirac, there are more old houses of character. The road changes at its end to rue François Arago, where you turn right along rue Neuve des Augustins to reach the Cathédrale St. Caprais. Previously a collegiate church of the 12th century, much of the cathedral dates from post-Revolutionary rebuilding. Quite apart from being made entirely of attractive pale stone, it has an interesting appearance. It has an octagonal clock-tower beside a taller square belfry. What purports to be the front entrance is really at the side; the main door in place Maréchal Foch comes in close to the altar. The interior has an unexpected simplicity, with a single nave and no side chapels; but the disproportion between the sizes of the 15th-century nave and 12th-century apse and transept is striking. 19th-century frescoes adorn the walls and ceilings.

At the other end (from the cathedral) of quiet place Foch, a useful shop sells all the gastronomic specialities of Armagnac, especially of course Agen's own dried plums, stuffed and sugared. Go round the corner, along rue des Héros de la Résistance, for more *pâtissiers* and *confiseurs*. Turn right into boulevard de la République and left into place des Laitiers again, but this time go down rue Montesquieu, the narrow main street through the *vieille ville*. This soon reaches (on the left) the delightful little 13th-century brick church of Notre-Dame du Bourg. Only one bell survives in its simple brick belfry-façade. You enter the church by going down some steps; the utterly simple white interior bathes one in peace.

Beside Notre-Dame du Bourg, in the magnificently named rue des Droits de l'Homme (The Rights of Man Street), the English-run Le Pancake (lunch and dinner) serves crêpes, soup, salads, scones and tea, and *'pâtisseries anglaises'*. Rue Montesquieu leads down to place A. Fallières, at the meeting of rue Palissey and cours Victor Hugo. This square with gardens and war memorial, is looked over by some grand 18th-century buildings, including the imposing Palais de Justice and the Préfecture, behind which is the site of a Roman amphitheatre. From here a few paces along rue Palissey return to esplanade du Gravier.

The N21 goes due south from Agen towards Auch; worth seeing on this road are the huge 11th- and 12th-century domed church (note the 11th-century mosaic on floor of apse) at high **Layrac**, and the fortified village and castle of **Ste. Mère**.

Continuing eastward along the Garonne, the main N113 follows the north bank, while a multitude of minor lanes, as well as the autoroute, run south of the river. Many small bridges link the two banks. To the left of the N113, **Puymirol** is a likeable small hilltop *bastide* (built 1246). **Valence-d'Agen**, farther along the road, is another *bastide* (1279) which still preserves a few of its features.

On the far side of the river at this point, **Auvillar**, an old hilltop village of great character, has an unusual market hall and triangular market square. Once, Auvillar thrived from *faïence* and the manufacture of quill pens made from goose-feathers, of which there were rather a lot in Armagnac — there still are, but the demand for quill pens is somewhat less than it was.

The N113 keeps to the Garonne's north bank as far as the confluence with the Tarn, where it turns up the Tarn river into Moissac. On the south side of the Garonne, by-passing Moissac, the D12 heads directly to Castelsarrasin. See chapter 8 for these two towns, for upriver of its meeting with the Tarn, the river Garonne is not only outside the Armagnac region, but has left Aquitaine altogether and crossed into the old Languedoc county of Toulouse.

Hotels and Restaurants

AGEN: Hôtel Provence, 22 cours du 14-juillet (53.47.39.11), pleasant little 3-star Logis at a moderate price.
Restaurant Michel Latrille, 66 rue C. Desmoulins (53.66.24.35), charming, attractive restaurant with excellent cooking.

AIRE-SUR-L'ADOUR: Chez l'Ahumat, 2 rue des Ecoles (58.71.82.61), incredibly low-priced simple popular restaurant (tending more to the Landes style than to Armagnac), with equally inexpensive accommodation.
Hôtel-Restaurant du Commerce, 3 bd des Pyrénées (58.71.60.06), 2-star Logis with modestly priced rooms and *menus*, food very good.

AUCH: Relais de Gascogne, 5 av de la Marne (62.05.26.81), satisfactory though unremarkable hotel-restaurant on a busy road in the *ville basse*.
Hôtel de France, pl de la Libération (62.05.00.44), luxury hotel in grand mansion, with famous restaurant; Gascon specialities — especially *foie gras*, duck, Madiran wines, and Armagnac — are near to perfection here; André Daguin's cooking well deserves its high reputation, but for best value stick to the reasonably-priced *menu* of traditional dishes; fascinating wine list with comments by Daguin; Relais et Château.

BARBOTAN-LES-THERMES: La Bastide Gasconne, (62.69.52.09), well-equipped Relais et Château with excellent restaurant, not cheap.

BARRAN: Chez Georgette, in main street (62.64.13.98), cheerful, popular, satisfying local eating place, offering astonishing value for money. No choices, no English spoken, just sit down and eat.

CASTELJALOUX: Hôtel des Cordeliers, 1 rue Cordeliers (53.93.02.19), decent, agreeable hotel in town centre.

CAZAUBON (near Barbotan-les-Thermes): **Château de Bégué,** (62.69.50.08), comfortable, quite stylish country château hotel in huge private park, prices remarkably bearable.

CONDOM: Hôtel des Trois Lys, 38 rue Gambetta (62.28.33.33), excellent little hotel in superb 18th-century house. Central location. Remarkable value.

EUGÉNIE-LES-BAINS: Les Près d'Eugénie, (58.51.19.01), Michel Guérard's great restaurant *avec chambres,* one of the most highly regarded in France, some say the best of all; a keen exponent of the *nouvelle* style, he perfects the art of light, delicate fragrant cooking inspired by local ingredients; prices are high, but not excessive. Accommodation (Relais et Château) in exquisitely elegant 19th-century mansion in its own grounds. Rooms are quiet, restful, beautiful, but expensive.
La Maison Rose (58.06.07.05), more accommodation for Les Près d'Eugénie, peaceful, charming accommodation among flowers and greenery.

LAYRAC: La Terrasse, pl de la Mairie (53.87.01.69), good cheap hotel with excellent restaurant.

LECTOURE: Hôtel de Bastard, rue Lagrange (62.68.82.44), unfortunate name for a reliable modern hotel and restaurant at moderate prices.

MONCRABEAU: Hôtel de la Phare, in main street (53.65.42.08), ordinary village bar, with simple hotel above, but with excellent smart restaurant.

MONTRÉAL: Hôtel-Restaurant de la Gare, 3km out of town on D29, direction Eauze (62.28.43.37), charming, most reasonably priced little restaurant with rooms, in converted former railway station.

PLAISANCE: Hôtel-Restaurant Ripa-Alta, 3 pl de l'Eglise (62.69.30.43), reasonably priced rooms and good value *menus* at this outstanding restaurant with Gascon specialities.

PUYMIROL: Hôtel-Restaurant l'Aubergade, 52 rue Royale (53.95.31.46), Michel Trama's famous and outstanding restaurant in 13th-century house; food superlative, yet prices not excessive. Hotel rooms are charming, elegant, stylish, spacious.

SÉGOS (S of Aire-sur-l'Adour): **Domaine de Bassibe** (62.09.46.71), lovely Relais et Château in depths of the country, with superb restaurant.

TRIE-SUR-BAÏSE: Hôtel de la Tour, 1 rue de la Tour (62.35.52.12), pleasant unassuming 2-star Logis, perfectly acceptable as a stopover.

VIC-FEZENSAC: Hôtel d'Artagnan, pl de la Mairie/cours Delom (62.06.31.37), traditional basic 1-star in main square with popular pavement bar below; very cheap.

Places of Interest

AGEN: Musée des Beaux-Arts, pl Esquirol (53.66.35.27). Good collections of 17th–19th-century paintings, *faïence*, antiquities including Venus du Mas d'Agenais *10–12, 2–6. Closed Tue and some j.f.*

AUCH: Maison de Gascogne, pl Jean David (opposite post office in rue Gambetta) (62.05.12.08). Exposition of all specialities of Armagnac, and exhibitions by local artists etc. *Approx mid-Jul–mid-Sep: 10–12.30, 2.30–7.30.*

Musée des Jacobins, pl Louis Blanc (62.05.74.79), Gascon art, archaeology, and folk tradition; also, good collection of pre-Columbian and colonial Latin-American art *9–12, 2–5. Closed Mon, Sun am Nov–Mar, and j.f.*

Musée de la Résistance, rue Pagodéoutés. *Tue–Fri: 2.30–4.30.*

CASSAIGNE: Château (62.29.12.02). Evocative old château of bishops of Condom, Armagnac distillery *9–12, 2–7.*

CONDOM: Musée de l'Armagnac, (62.28.31.41). All about Armagnac the drink, its vinification and distillation. *Approx 10–12, 2–5. Closed Mon, Sun from Oct to May, and 1 Jan.*

FLARAN (near Valence-sur-Baïse): **Abbey** (62.28.50.19). Cistercian abbey in open country, arts centre *July and Aug: 9.30–7. Rest of Year: 9.30–12, 2–6. Closed Tue.*

LECTOURE: Musée Municipal, pl Charles de Gaulle, remarkable collection of locally discovered Gallo-Roman artefacts, especially the bull-altars *Open daily.*

MIRANDE: Musée des Beaux-Arts (62.66.68.10). Collections of historical costume, 17th–19th-century painting, *faïence*, ceramics *Open daily exc. Sun and j.f.*

NÉREC: Château (53.65.21.11) *Guided tour am and pm. Closed Mon and all Jan.*

SÉVIAC (nr Montréal): **Villa Gallo-Romaine** (62.28.43.18) *Guided tours daily in summer.*

Tourist Offices

CRT offices (regional information): AQUITAINE (for Landes and Lot-et-Garonne) — 10 rue René Cassin, Bordeaux 33049 (56.39.88.88; fax 56.43.07.63). MIDI-PYRÉNÉES (for Gers, Tarn-et-Garonne, Haute-Garonne, Hautes-Pyrénées) — BP166 or 54 bd de l'Embouchure, Toulouse 31022 (61.13.55.55; fax 61.47.17.16)

CDT offices (information on the départements): GERS — 7 rue Diderot, Auch (62.05.37.02); LANDES — 22 rue Victor Hugo, Mont-de-Marsan (58.06.89.89; fax 58.06.90.90); LOT-ET-GARONNE — 4 rue André Chénier, Agen (53.66.14.14; fax 53.68.25.42); TARN-ET-GARONNE — Hôtel des Intendants, pl Foch, Montauban (63.63.31.40); HAUTES-PYRÉNÉES — 6 rue Eugène-Ténot, Tarbes (62.93.03.30); HAUTE-GARONNE — 14 rue Bayard, Toulouse (61.99.44.00).

OTSI offices (local information): AGEN — 107 bd Carnot (53.47.36.09); AIRE-SUR-L'ADOUR — pl de Gaulle (58.76.64.70); AUCH — rue Dessoles (62.05.22.89); BARBOTAN-LES-THERMES — pl d'Armagnac (62.69.52.13); CONDOM — pl Bossuet (62.28.00.08); EAUZE — pl d'Armagnac (62.09.85.62); LECTOURE — cours de l'Hôtel de Ville (62.68/76/98); MIRANDE — rue de l'Évêque (62.66.68.10); MONCRABEAU — rue Principale (53.65.42.79); MONTRÉAL — pl de l'Hôtel de Ville (62.28.43.10); NÉRAC — av Mondenard (53.65.27.75); SAMATAN — 3 rue du Chanoine Dieuzaide (62.62.55.40); TRIE-SUR-BAÏSE — 33 pl de la Mairie (62.35.52.39); VIC-FEZENSAC — 2 rue des Filatiers (62.06.34.90). Where there is no tourist office listed, apply to the Town Hall (Mairie or Hôtel de Ville).

Loisirs-Acceuil (hotel booking service): apply to relevant CDT office as listed above.

Sports and Leisure

ARMAGNAC CHAIS: several Armagnac producers are open to the public, notably the *domaines* and châteaux at Auch (Château de St. Criq), Avezan, Cassaigne, Cazaux-Saves (Caumont), Flamarens, Lavardens, Mansencôme (Busca-Maniban), Terraube, Vic-Fezensac; apply to local SI for visiting details. For more names, enquire of SI at Auch, Condom, and Eauze.

CYCLING AND RIDING: details of tracks, trails, paths and suggested itineraries are available from the Comité Régional Sportif d'Aquitaine, 5 cours de Verdun, 33000 Bordeaux (56.52.80.90); the Midi-Pyrenees CRT, 54 bd de l'Embouchure, 31022 Toulouse (61.13.55.55); and départemental tourist offices.

SWIMMING: many towns have free (or inexpensive) open air municipal swimming pools; there is an indoor pool at Auch.

TENNIS: some 50 tennis clubs scattered throughout the region are open to non-members; enquire at SIs.

WALKING: the region has some 1000km of marked footpaths, including a section of the GR65, the Compostela Route. Contact CDTs, CRTs and local SIs for details.

WATERSPORTS (on lakes): ideal locations include Barbotan, Lectoure, and Miélan.

8
The County of Toulouse

At the eastern margins of South West France, at the border of Languedoc, the landscape becomes less appealing, somewhat flatter and a good deal more industrialised. In the midst of this sun-pounded setting sprawls France's fourth city, **Toulouse** (pop: 359,000 within the *commune* of Toulouse; or 680,000 within the whole metropolitan area). For devotees of the French countryside this edge of our region seems to hold little promise; but lovers of a great city, a historic capital which today is fairly bursting with energy and *joie de vivre*, will not be disappointed. Toulouse has a tremendous atmosphere, exhilarating, animated and youthful, with an inexhaustible variety of cafés, restaurants, art and entertainment. There's plenty to see as well, reflecting the city's changing fortunes over the passing centuries. Its story takes a little time to tell, but is worth hearing and gives a better appreciation of modern Toulouse.

All Aquitaine shares a common history, of conquest by Rome and by Charlemagne, and three centuries as part of the English kingdom. Toulouse has grown from quite a different past. It shares common ground with the rest of South West France, and even had a spell as capital of Aquitaine, but while Aquitaine looks to the Atlantic, Toulouse belongs to the ancient civilisations of the Mediterranean. When the Romans first moved round the coast from Italy into Gaul in 118BC, they incorporated all of Mediterranean France into their world, not as a colony, but as a senatorial province. They called this province Narbonensis, with its capital at present-day Narbonne (in Languedoc). For 500 years the whole region lived and prospered under the Pax Romana, and in AD381 for administrative reasons was divided into two: Narbonensis Prima, from the Pyrenees to the Rhône; and Narbonensis Secunda, from the Rhône to Italy. The main towns of Narbonensis Prima were seven in number — their modern names are Toulouse, Uzès, Maguelone, Agde, Lodève, Béziers and Nîmes.

Even before the Roman annexation, there had been a large community of the Volques tribe of Celts at Toulouse, which even then was named Tolosa and was noted principally for a legendary sacred pool. The Volques, a relatively sophisticated group, conducted a considerable degree of trade, and had already in 154BC formed an alliance with Rome. Tolosa was amicably transferred to Roman rule, as part of Narbonensis, in 108BC. However, the draining of the sacred pool, in 106BC, sparked off intense uprisings against the

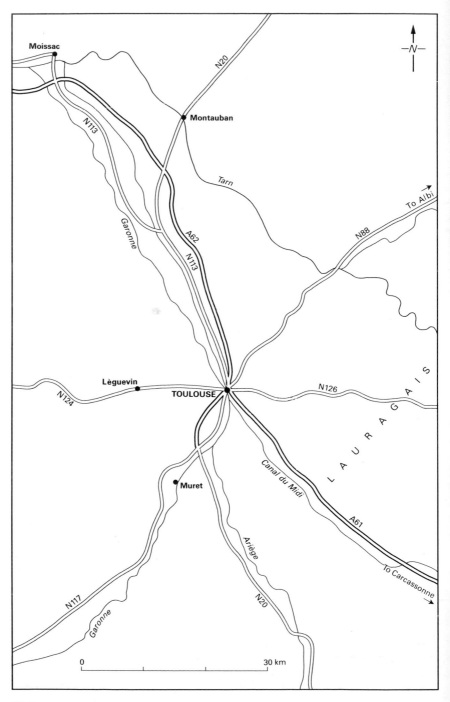

Roman presence and led to some surprising defeats for the Roman troops in other districts. But eventually Toulouse was subdued, and under Rome became one of the most important towns in Narbonensis. The nine Gallic tribes farther west were ignored for a few years more, but by 28BC they too had been conquered and colonised under the name Aquitania.

The Visigoths, coming into possession of Narbonensis Prima after the Roman withdrawal (AD419), renamed it (in honour of its seven cities) Septimania, with Toulouse as the capital. Less than a hundred years later the Visigoths were pushed south by the more warlike Franks, who by AD628 had taken control of all former Aquitania and Septimania. The Frankish leader Dagobert carved from this vast conquered territory a kingdom of Southern Aquitaine, with Toulouse as its capital. North African Moors coming up from Spain swept through the area during the 8th century but held it for barely twenty years; after they had been driven out by the Franks in AD778 Charlemagne redivided southern France, creating the Aquitaine duchy (or kingdom) and separating Septimania into a county of Toulouse and a marquisate of Gothia. Charlemagne it was who effectively brought into being the concept of France as we know it today — but over the centuries there were to be many obstacles in the way of a unified France, and the county of Toulouse was one of them.

The long-civilised southerners, speaking their langue d'oc, looked upon their northern barbarian conquerors with contempt, and this attitude soon rubbed off onto the Frankish counts of Toulouse who were never willing to honour their nominal allegiances to a northern crown. The dynasty of the counts grew rapidly in wealth and power. They learned the southern language and supported learning, the arts, and religion, encouraged trade, and were vastly more open to contact with the rest of the Mediterranean than their more narrow-minded and insular cousins in the north. By the time of Raymond III, in the year 936, Toulouse was in a position to annexe all of former Septimania. Raymond IV (1093–1105) went on to expand well beyond these borders.

Raymond IV (who liked to call himself Count of St. Gilles, after his favourite possession on the edge of the Camargue) was truly a great statesman of his day, at a time when statesmanship meant the diplomatic acquisition of territory and titles, honourable conduct towards allies, mercilessness towards the infidel, and devotion to the cause of Christian imperialism. He led a holy war against the Moslems who occupied much of Spain. He made close bonds with the pope. He married Princess Elvira of Aragon to create friendly links with another important southern domain. And in later years he took possession of the equally wealthy and cultured marquisate of Provence. Toulouse had become the capital of all of the lands that had once been Rome's Provincia.

Thus unified, with Toulouse at its head, southern France saw an unparalleled flowering of art and literature. The langue d'oc, or Provençal as it should perhaps more properly be called, became the leading European language of song and poetry. This was the beginning of the age of the troubadours, which was to end abruptly with the Albigensian Crusade at the beginning of the 13th century. Troubadours, travelling from one segneurial court to

another, composed long lyric poems — *cansos* — almost all on the theme of courtly love. The concept of courtly love, which sprang up in Languedoc, was that of an intense, unrequited spiritual love between a lord and a lady: the most popular version was *amor de lonh*, love from afar. Some *cansos* were symbolic, for instance, of man's devotion to God, or a vassal's admiration for his lord. Later, some troubadours were able to carry the message of Catharism beneath the mask of this romantic symbolism. Hand in hand with the growth of courtly love as a subject of poetry grew the cult of *courtoisie* — chivalry and courtliness.

By the end of his life Raymond IV was one of the richest and most powerful members of the Western nobility, although this gave him little comfort as he spent his last years fighting in the Holy Land. He died in 1105 from injuries in the fortress which he had built on the edge of Tripoli, a fortress which the Arabs called Qalat Sanjil — the Castle of St. Gilles.

The countess returned to Toulouse with Raymond IV's legitimate son Alfonso-Jordan (1105-48), while his illegitimate son Bertrand (not entirely illegitimate, since he was born in wedlock when Raymond was married to a Provençal cousin, but this marriage was later annulled) taking over his father's struggle, eventually made himself Count of Tripoli. Alfonso-Jordan reigned over an increasingly prosperous domaine which stretched from Gascony to the Alps. In 1147 he too took the cross, and returned to the land of his birth, only to die almost as soon as he arrived (1148).

Rue St. Rôme, one of the shopping streets in the heart of old Toulouse

The greatest achievement of the next count of Toulouse, Raymond V (1148-94) was to prevent any incursion into his vast territories by the expansionist Plantagenets of Aquitaine. This was the period during which the destiny of Toulouse was further separated from that of Aquitaine. For while Henry II of England brought all of South West France firmly under his control, the county of Toulouse keenly protected its western borders and lost no ground on that side. Henry II actually attacked Toulouse in 1159, and then Richard the Lionheart returned for a second attempt on the city in 1188, but both were seen off by Raymond's forces. However, in the east, across the Rhône his county was disintegrating, with local lords asserting themselves, too far away to be controlled. One of the features which made the area which was later to be called Languedoc so different from France was the large number of free men, who owed no allegiance to anyone, and also of vassals who refused to honour their allegiances and could not be forced to do so. In addition there were many traders, free men and vassals alike, who had built up far larger fortunes than the nobility.

There was an atmosphere, perhaps unique in medieval Europe, of personal liberty at all levels in society. In Toulouse this democratic air gave rise to an extraordinary political development: the capitouls. In 1152 Count Raymond V decided to relinquish much of his own power in favour of an elected body of councillors or capitouls, as they were known. The experiment worked, and in 1180 he extended it, widening the franchise and giving the capitouls full legislative and judicial powers. Another, odder indication of the atmosphere prevailing in Toulouse at the time (while the rest of Europe emerged from the Dark Ages) was that in 1190 the capitouls gave birth to Europe's first public limited company, with the ordinary citizens buying shares in the city's water-milling industry. All this libertarianism made an explosive mixture when combined with the still undiminished opinion of southerners that they were a greater people with an older and a nobler civilisation than the French. Throughout Raymond V's reign, the seeds of a heretical Christian belief, Catharism, were being blown in from the Balkans. The climate of freedom and dissent in the county of Toulouse at the time was perfect for them to take root and flourish.

One would only have to observe the murderous power-seeking, treachery and vice of orthodox Christians at the time (the crusaders, for example) to realise that to espouse a creed, and even to believe in it, did not require one to live according to its principles. So it was too, in large part, with Catharism. Although the majority of people did remain loyal to the established church, the Cathar doctrine was eagerly adopted by a large minority, members of all classes, as an expression of southern separateness, a rejection of outside authorities — Crown or Church. Perhaps the most important reason of all for its success in the extensive lands of the county of Toulouse was that Cathar preachers addressed their listeners in the local language, the *langue d'oc*.

Cathars, quite apart from opposing the whole idea of an organised church hierarchy, won a lot of support by vigorously condemning the corruption and greed of the Catholic Church and its officials. And by refusing to pay tithes, Cathars posed a direct threat to the Church establishment.

Despite, or because, of his humanitarianism and tolerance, the reign of Raymond VI (1194–1222) was to witness the most tragic episode in the history of the county of Toulouse, and indeed was to prove a calamitous turning point for the whole of Mediterranean France and its culture. During the upsurge of support for the Cathars, Raymond was moving ever closer to forming an alliance with the kings of Aragón, also powerful and hostile to France. The kings of Aragón already controlled a large area, including parts of France; a union with Toulouse would create a vast, unmanageable neighbour for the French, who had just lost half their territories to the Plantagenets. It was vital for King Philippe Auguste of France to take control of the county of Toulouse before King Pedro II of Aragón beat him to it. This would, furthermore, give France a longer border from which to attack English Aquitaine.

As part of his planned take-over, the king of Aragón, though a devout Catholic, had declared his willingness to tolerate the Cathars (the creed was in any case rapidly crossing the Pyrenees). Pope Innocent III was even more concerned than Philippe Auguste about the turn events were taking. In 1198 the pope sent envoys and preachers throughout the county to urge people against the Cathar 'heresy'. In 1208, the papal envoy Pierre de Castelnau was assassinated at St. Gilles; the pope excommunicated Count Raymond for complicity in the crime.

In 1204 the pope had proposed to King Philippe Auguste that they join forces to crush Catharism; he had added that the king would have his blessing if any land which had ever been owned by a heretic, or used to offer shelter to heretics, were confiscated and added to the royal possessions. At first Philippe Auguste had delayed, being caught up with other wars, but in 1209 he and the pope launched the 'Crusade against the Albigenses' with much fanfare and preaching. Here was a wonderful opportunity for people to take the cross and slaughter infidels without all the inconvenience and hardship of a long journey in foreign lands. Vast numbers of volunteers and mercenaries came forward, including many lesser nobility who hoped to be awarded various of the

What Cathars Believed

It is not true that there is one God. All creation is a struggle between two great forces, Good and Evil. The material world, and everything in it, including human life, is the domain of the Satanic evil god. The good power governs the spiritual world, the unseen, the divine. The good god has no physical form, no human emissaries, and no material trappings. As a man, Jesus was not divine. His holiness was something without substance, a breath of spirituality which moved the souls of men. Arguably, Jesus had never existed physically at all; he was only an idea, an inspiration which came from the spiritual world to show the way to a good life.

That was the Christianity preached by the Cathars. By their definition, the works of the evil one included the organised Church, the Old Testament, Mass, marriage, burial in consecrated ground, prayers for the dead, the priesthood and all hierarchy. Cathars considered the Church of Rome as a vile heresy working against Christ's message of poverty, charity, and love. They called themselves Christians or Good Christians, and their wandering preachers were called *Bons Hommes*, Good Men. Outside sympathisers, of whom there were many, referred to them as Cathars (from the Greek *katharos*, pure), and knew the Good Men as *parfaits*, 'perfect ones'. To their enemies the Cathars were *Albigenses*, from the diocese of Albi where there were early concentrations of Cathar supporters.

The Good Men or *parfaits* formally renounced the pleasures of the world. They remained celibate, wore only a simple black robe, lived sparsely on charity, fasted frequently, and ate no food which resulted from sexual union (meat, eggs, milk). Although opposed to an organised church, Cathars would elect local leaders whom they called bishops; women as well as men could be chosen. Cathars did not entirely reject the Bible, and carried with them a copy of the Gospels. There was only one important Cathar ritual, the *consolamentum*, through which *parfaits* could initiate others into the life of the spirit. The rite involved baptism, the laying on of hands, kissing the Gospels, and explanation of the Lord's Prayer, for which they offered an arcane and symbolic interpretation. While many people professed to be *croyants*, believers, very few undertook to become 'perfected' themselves until they felt that death was near. Then they would ask for the *consolamentum*, many afterwards renouncing the physical world so completely as to die from starvation.

confiscated southern territories when the war was over. Arnald-Amaury, the Abbot of Cîteaux took the ecclesiastical leadership of the crusade. Simon de Montfort the Elder was given the principal overall military command. The pope granted everyone complete forgiveness for all sins committed in the past and any which they might commit during the first 40 days of the crusade, and they set off to conquer Languedoc. It was to take forty years.

The first town the crusaders reached which had any Cathars at all was Béziers, a thriving, ancient city of the Languedoc plain. By the end of the onslaught most of the city's population of 20,000, whatever their religion, were dead. Most were Catholics, who had been burned alive inside their churches. Abbot Arnald-Amaury declared the result 'a miracle'. Carcassonne was the next to fall, followed by a number of smaller Cathar centres in the countryside to its south — all this area had to be conquered with urgency as it was in the hands of the viscounts Raymond-Trencavel, a family growing in influence, who unchecked would soon have had almost as much power as the counts of Toulouse themselves. In 1211 the crusaders turned on Toulouse.

However, the city was fully prepared for the attack and the crusaders were unable to penetrate its walls. The siege was never fully lifted, but most of the crusaders under de Montfort spent the next few years taking on smaller Cathar centres, notably Moissac and Muret, inflicting barbaric massacres on the defeated towns. Meanwhile, in 1215, the future Louis VIII succeeded in breaking through the walls of Toulouse, and fierce battles raged inside the town. Raymond managed to retake the city in 1217, just as Simon de Montfort

returned to lend his weight. This time de Montfort initiated a heavy and relentless siege which was to last well into 1218. It was only halted when Simon de Montfort himself was killed in the course of the battle. Raymond VI died in 1222. Taking over an almost entirely destroyed inheritance, neither his son Raymond VII nor the populace had the morale to put up much more of a fight when a new body of crusaders, again under the leadership of Louis VIII, arrived in 1226. Raymond VII decided to make terms which would at least allow him to keep his life.

The Treaty of Meaux, which he signed in 1229, officially brought the Albigensian Crusade to an end, and placed most of the county of Toulouse under the direct authority of the French crown (although the French and Catholic battle to root out and kill the southern heretics went on until the middle of the century). In fact Raymond was allowed to retain some of his lands during his lifetime. In exchange he had to arrange the marriage of his daughter (his only heir) to Alphonse de Poitiers, brother of the future king of France, Louis IX; he also had to fund, for its first ten years, a new University of Toulouse which was to act as a bastion of orthodox Catholicism. An inquisition was set up at Toulouse to extract confessions from supposed Cathars and mete out punishments. Raymond, the last count of Toulouse, died in 1249. His daughter died in 1271, and the county of Toulouse became a French royal province under the name Languedoc, so called after the language spoken here.

The 14th century saw battles with the English, a terrible outbreak of plague, and an immense fire which destroyed over half the city. Yet that was far from being the end of Toulouse. It was completely rebuilt in red brick, many fine new buildings were constructed, and although the Crown and the Church continued to keep a close watch on Toulouse — being particularly harsh on any tendencies to wander from absolute orthodoxy — the city was allowed a good deal of autonomy. In the early 16th century another transformation was brought about by an unlikely new crop in the fields east of Toulouse: the plant Isatis Tinctoria, from the leaves and yellow flowers of which 'pastel', a variety of indigo, is made. This valuable blue dye, previously found only in the tropics, sold at a new Merchants' Exchange, became the source of immense wealth in the city. It led to another era of grand building, in the lavish southern Gothic style, producing some of the best that Toulouse has to offer to this day. But at the same time, the city's rise seems to have brought its natural heterodoxy again to the fore: Reform churches were built, Protestantism was preached. The watchful Catholic authorities soon cracked down: hundreds of Protestants were massacred on St. Bartholomew's Eve in 1572. Any who survived were driven out of the city. Even as late as 1761 a Protestant, Jean Calas, was broken on the wheel in the main square in punishment for a trumped-up charge of murdering his son to prevent his conversion to Catholicism (he was later proved innocent). It is incredible to think, and it puts such pious barbarism in context, that this happened while the writer Lawrence Sterne — who seems an almost modern character — was staying in Toulouse. Only three years afterwards, Adam Smith spent some time in the city while working on *The Wealth of Nations*. In any case the great prosperity

had passed after only one hundred years, as cheap imported indigo from America began to flood the market.

Developments in the city during the 19th century are still deeply regrettable: disorderly expansion and unplanned urban development caused numerous fine buildings to be demolished without reason. At the time Toulouse was dubbed 'the Capital of Vandalism' as speculators tore down whole streets of magnificent Renaissance mansions. But of course much escaped, and the 20th century has seen another astonishing turn in fortunes for Toulouse. A massive influx of people has led to a phenomenal expansion in the size of the place, and in its economic activity. During the last twenty years this has carried on apace, with a tremendous growth of high-technology enterprises around the suburbs, most notably of France's aerospace industry which is based here.

The charms of the old centre of the city are undimmed by this. Indeed they are enhanced, as the sunlit streets and squares of its past have become alive with things to do and pavement cafés at which to do nothing, good restaurants in which to enjoy the best of both Aquitaine and Languedoc, and an endless succession of art, music and theatre events.

With the creation of new administrative provinces in 1972, the Midi–Pyrénées region came into being with Toulouse as its capital. Of course, the Midi–Pyrénées is a sort of imaginary region, with no historical existence at all, and is something of a cultural and geographical absurdity. For the Toulousains, to be capital of such a truncated hybrid, when once one was the capital of everything from Gascony to Provence, and north into Auvergne, must seem a dubious honour.

191

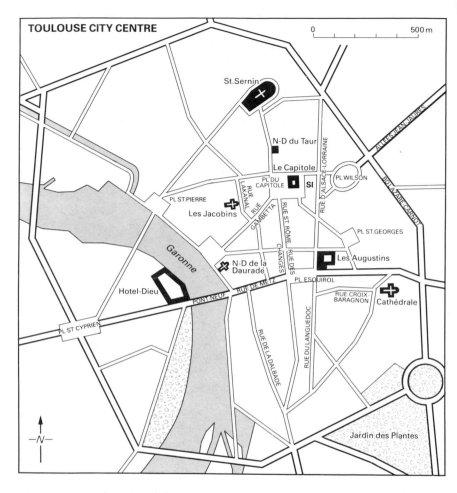

TOULOUSE CITY CENTRE

0   500 m

St.Sernin

N-D du Taur

Le Capitole

PL'DU CAPITOLE

SI

PL WILSON

RUE D'ALSACE-LORRAINE

BD LAZARE-CARNOT

ALLÉES JEAN-JAURÈS

PL ST.PIERRE

RUE LAKANAL

RUE GAMBETTA

RUE ST.ROME

RUE DES CHANGES

Les Jacobins

PL ST.GEORGES

Garonne

N-D de la Daurade

Les Augustins

PL ESQUIROL

Hotel-Dieu

PONT-NEUF

RUE DE METZ

RUE CROIX BARAGNON

Cathédrale

PL ST CYPRIEN

RUE DE LA DALBADE

RUE DU LANGUEDOC

Jardin des Plantes

—N—

But, ever in the same defiant spirit, the Midi-Pyrénées has chosen as its symbol the old Languedoc cross. Once more it adorns the flag which flies from the Capitole at the heart of Toulouse.

Old Toulouse, still with its medieval network of narrow streets and lanes, stands on the right bank of a sharp bend in the river Garonne. Busy boulevards, following the track of medieval ramparts (dismantled in the 19th century), encircle this central district. Less ancient areas on both sides of the Garonne, with an outer complex of major roads, and (on the east side) the Canal du Midi, form another circle around the centre. Beyond that is a broad outer ring of modern industrial and residential suburbs.

For a quick transit from the Jolimont quarter on one side of town to the Mirail district on the other, hop on the new automatic underground railway. Of its 15 stops, some of the most useful for the visitor are Marengo-SNCF (for Gare Matabiau, main SNCF station), Esquirol, Capitole and Allées Jean-Jaurès. The service is easy to use, a single ticket

La Langue d'Oc

The ancient language of southern France — known as Occitan, Provençal, or the *langue d'oc* — developed directly from spoken Latin (as did the other Romance languages: Italian, Spanish, French, Catalan, Portuguese, Romanian, and Swiss Romansch). Within the Romance group of languages there are broad similarities as well as many differences. One of the differences between the language of the south of France and the language of the north was in the word for 'yes'. The Romans — strange as it might seem to us — had no word for 'yes'; the expression they used was *hoc ille* (literally, 'this that'). In the colonies of northern Gaul this became *o il*, or *oïl*. In the province of the south, it became *oc*. Although France was effectively unified as an 'empire' under Charlemagne, different dialects and languages continued to be spoken throughout the Middle Ages. As was normal in medieval Europe, none of these languages had names other than the name of the place where they were spoken. In the north, three local dialects vied for dominance: Norman, Picard, and French (of the Franks of Paris). The battle was won by French, and the *langue d'oïl* became known as French. Meanwhile the southern language (also with its local variations) prospered in the territories of the county of Toulouse as both a court language and a common tongue, and during the age of the troubadours after the 11th century experienced a great flowering of literature. This era came to an abrupt end after the Albigensian Crusade (1229), when the county of Toulouse was forcibly taken over by the northern French: the name Languedoc was then used for the first time to denote that part of the French kingdom where the southern language was spoken.

In 1539 an edict made French the official language of the south, but not until the early 19th century when it was made illegal to speak the *langue d'oc* in schools (a law not repealed until 1951) did the language really go into decline. Efforts began to keep alive the literature of the *langue d'oc*: Frédéric Mistral's Félibrige (founded 1854) was a movement of writers using the old language. The name Occitan was invented in this period. The Escola Occitana (founded 1919) and the Institut des Études Occitanes (founded 1945) have worked to encourage an awareness of the southern tongue.

However, during the 20th century French has become the first language of almost all southerners, although the southern tongue does survive as the *patois* (as its speakers call it) current in some rural parts of upland Languedoc. Other traces of the *langue d'oc* can be found in the ringing, emphatic southern accent, which puts stress on the ends of words, and pronounces final letters left silent by northerners; and in vestigial southern spellings which make frequent use of, for example, 'lh' (sounded 'y', like a French double 'l'), or 'ou' (instead of the French 'o'). Personal and place names in the south often have typical *langue d'oc* endings -ou, -ous or -oux, or include *langue d'oc* elements, such as *puech* or *pech* (peak), *peyre* (rock), *mas* (a small building in the country), and many others.

permitting any journey on either bus or metro or both. If you're staying longer in Toulouse, and plan to make much use of public transport, a book of tickets works out even cheaper.

The Toulouse metro is well worth

Toulouse: the imposing façade of the Capitole, with the cross of Languedoc displayed above the entrance

seeing in any case, and has been de-scribed as the longest art gallery in France! Along its 17km, every station had its own commissioned architect and its own creative artist.

There's a good deal to see on a walk-ing tour of Toulouse and for much of the year the weather is hot (it is usually dry as well, but there can be quite a lot of rain from about March to May), so it is wise to take it slowly and make frequent stops. Depending on how leisurely (and/or comprehensive) a view of the city one would prefer, even the intro-ductory visit outlined here could take several days.

A good and sensible place to start would be place du Capitole, the large main square with the Renaissance façade (constructed in the 1750s) of the

huge Capitole (or Capitoul) along one side of it. Maybe this edifice is more im-posing than beautiful, but nonetheless it comes a surprise that the French writer Stendhal considered it 'the ugliest building you could imagine'! A large gateway, generally standing open to admit the public since this is now the city's Hôtel de Ville, leads behind the awesome front into a courtyard mainly dating from 1606. During the resur-gence of anti-northern feeling in the 17th century, the États du Languedoc — an independent parliament of the southern nobility — tried to bring about a separation from the Paris adminis-tration. At the same time there was a big move towards Protestantism going on in the city. While the ecclesiastical auth-orities took draconian measures against the religious reformers, Richelieu took decisive action to destroy the États du Languedoc, whose governor was executed in this courtyard in 1632. Inside the Capitole the rooms and monumental staircase have a palatial grandeur.

One end of the building is the city's theatre, or 'Opéra' as it is called, where there are seasons of music and drama. Normally banked with parked cars, on festive occasions place du Capitole comes into its own and reveals itself as a vast space and a grand setting for public events. The back of the Capitole (its rear façade is 19th-century) looks over square Charles de Gaulle, in which the Donjon du Capitole (or Tour du Donjon), an impressive fortified keep of 1529, now houses the tourist office. Beside it a pretty little public garden has fountains and flowers. Public gardens are one of the charms of Toulouse; there are said to be one hundred of them — small parks and squares with neatly kept grass and flowerbeds, fountains, benches, restful shade and greenery.

It's not obvious where to go first from here, as there are excellent things to see close to the Capitole in every direction. Perhaps it is best to go straight to one of the city's most remarkable and beautiful buildings, Les Jacobins. Take rue Gambetta from place du Capitole west (towards the river). Before turning right up rue Lakanal, go a few paces farther to see the superb vaulted arch, corridor and galleries inside the elegant courtyard of Hôtel de Bernuy (built 1503).

Rue Lakanal comes to the magnificent redbrick walls of Les Jacobins, powerful yet graceful, with an octagonal tower of arches, one of the landmarks of the city centre. The name Jacobins in this instance refers not to extremists of the Revolution but is a nickname for Dominicans; founded by St. Dominique personally in 1215, intended to be a rock of Catholicism against the rising sea of Catharism, this was the Dominicans very first monastic community. The surviving edifice, built over a period of more than one hundred years starting in 1230, was its church. (Dominique went on to found his second community next to the Porte St. Jacques in Paris, hence the name Jacobins). The interior is extraordinary: wide, spacious, uncluttered, with just a single row — running along the middle of the building — of seven simple pillars which support the whole roof by an intriguing system of interlocking ribbed vaults in a fantastic palm-tree pattern. Tall windows have good modern stained glass. At the centre of the building is, unexpectedly, the tomb of the theologian Thomas Aquinas (1225–74). It seems astonishing now, with all the beauty of the building uncovered, that after the Revolution it was divided into storeys and made into a warehouse, with stables on the ground floor. The restoration, which took almost as long as the original construction, was completed in 1974. Outside, beautiful and tranquil cloisters with dozens of arches supported by slender double pillars enclose neatly tended gardens. Off the cloisters a side chapel serves for piano concerts — a marvellous setting. If you only want to see one thing in Toulouse, it should be Les Jacobins and its cloisters.

Continue along rue Lakanal and turn right at the end into rue Romiguières to return to place du Capitole. On reaching the square, turn left into rue du Taur. Straight away the strange high redbrick façade of Notre-Dame de Taur comes into view.

The strange belltower of Notre-Dame du Taur

The interior of the church is oddly arranged, the 15th-century choir being wider and more elaborate than the simple 14th-century nave. There is good stained glass, and behind the altar several frescoes. The church's name (*taur* means bull) refers to the martyrdom of St. Saturnin (or Sernin) who attempted without success to convert the town to Christianity in the year 250. He was tied to a bull, which dragged him to his death. Sernin's remains used to be in the crypt of Notre-Dame du Taur, until they were transferred to the huge Basilique St. Sernin. Walk farther along rue du Taur; along this busy street, several big doors open onto the courtyards of grand redbrick mansions, now transformed into apartments. The courtyards are public areas, so it is quite in order to stroll into these yards and admire the architecture. Nos. 49 and 38, for example, are notable. Farther up on the

right, the former Chapelle du Carmel lies back from the street. It now belongs to the Bibliothèque Universitaire (University Library). The porter at 56 rue du Taur will allow you to see the admirable 18th-century interior.

Rue du Taur runs directly towards the bulk of the Basilique St. Sernin, largest Romanesque edifice in France and once an abbey church. A cleared oval area around the structure, now place St. Sernin, used to be densely packed with abbey buildings. At weekends a tatty and aptly described flea market sets up in this space. Also in the *place*, Musée St. Raymond (with historical and prehistoric collections) occupies an imposing mansion which was once part of the St. Raymond College, a charitable and theological institution founded in the 13th century and disbanded at the Revolution. It is named after the 11th-century St. Raymond Gayrard, who founded a charitable hospital on the site and was also responsible in part for the St. Sernin builing. The basilica, begun in about 1075 and finished about a hundred years later (and structurally hardly altered since), is a massive ornate redbrick edifice with a fine octagonal spire, the example *par excellence* of what came to be known as the Tolosan style, imitated over a wide area. The main doorway, the Porte Occidentale, is immense. The Porte Miégeville, the usual public entrance, is small with well-preserved tympanum and capitals. The closed Porte des Comtes de Toulouse, through which the Raymonds entered the church, has a touch of grandeur. The rear of the building — the curves of its apses and little chapels with their arches — is really beautiful, with the superb tower of arches soaring above.

Inside the building, there are an astonishing five aisles separated by a forest of pillars. The brickwork has a lovely soft pink colour. Although elaborate in its way, the structure is essentially simple in the Romanesque manner. A barrel-vaulted ceiling covers the narrow central aisle; a balcony extends over the other aisles. A dome covers the crossing. The choir is highly decorated, and has very fine elaborately carved Renaissance wooden stalls of 1670 (which could do with a good dusting). Holy relics arranged around the ambulatory include the Saturnin (or Sernin) tomb on bronze bulls. A guided visit of the balcony, which has a sort of indoor-cloisters feeling, gives a close-up view of the excellent capitals.

Take a walk by the river. From Basilique St. Sernin follow some rather ordinary Toulousain streets. Start with rue Cartailhac and continue along rue Lautmann and rue Valade, passing the remains of the Romanesque church of St. Pierre-des-Cuisines (on the steps of which Raymond IV stood and solemnly bade farewell to his city before embarking for the Holy Land, the Crusades, and his death) to reach the Garonne at place St. Pierre. This congenial little square beside pont St. Pierre has a good view of the domed Hôtel-Dieu hospital on the far side of the water. The Garonne has enjoyable strollable embankments; the broad river looks good from the walkways. Go south (upriver) from the square towards the next bridge. This takes you through the Daurade area, location of the original Gallo-Roman city centre. Beside place de la Daurade an 18th-century church (closed), Notre-Dame de la Daurade, was built by Benedictines. In the process they destroyed a much more ancient structure and important Gallo-Roman remains. It stands on the site of a large Roman temple; inside there are

The tower rising from one corner of the palatial Hôtel d'Assézat

what survived of its golden mosaics, which give the church and the area its name (Provençal *daurada*, golden). The beautiful bridge adjacent is the Pont Neuf: despite its name, it is the oldest of Toulouse's river bridges. It was officially opened in 1659 and was the only bridge to survive the severe floods of 1875.

Turn left into rue de Metz and go up just as far as Hôtel d'Assézat, set back on the left beside a little turning. This splendid mansion, one of the finest in Toulouse, prudently conceals its grandeur behind a plain exterior wall. Go through the vast outer doorway (closed 12–2) to discover the magnificent building arranged around a central courtyard. Built in 1555, it has a brick façade with pale Corinthian and Ionic pilasters. A curious tower rises above one corner. Arcades, covered with a heavy wooden panelled ceiling, run along one side of the courtyard. On the

197

second floor, there is a museum of medical history. In addition, the building now accommodates a number of learned and cultural societies, including the remarkable Académie des Jeux Floraux, literally the academy of the floral games. Until changed by Louis XIV in 1694, its title used to be le Compagnie du Gai Savoir — an enchanting name which probably sounds a trifle odd to modern ears whether French or English, as it means (approximately) the company of gay learning or gay science. In Provençal, poetry was often referred to as *gai saber*. Despite the gaiety, this is a most distinguished guild, the oldest literary society in Europe. It was founded in 1323 by seven *langue d'oc*-speaking poets a few years after the French seizure of the county of Toulouse. Prophetically fearing for the future of their language, the seven instituted an annual poetry-reading contest in *langue d'oc*. These *jeux*, games, as they were called, have been continuing ever since. They are held at the beginning of May, usually on the 3rd. Ever since the society began, the winners have been honoured with valuable and highly esteemed prizes of gold and silver violets and eglantines.

Go back a few paces along rue de Metz — unless it's time for some refreshment, in which case first go a little farther up rue de Metz to the brasseries in place Esquirol — and return to rue des Cordeliers. Turn left there. Stroll along to rue de la Dalbade. If you've plenty of time and energy and the weather is not too hot, it is enjoyable to saunter along this quiet back street admiring the elaborate façades of some

The magnificent tower of Basilique St. Sernin rises above the streets of Toulouse

exceptional buildings. This used to be a prestigious residential quarter (Quartier Parlementaire) with the homes of many of the members of Toulouse's elite parliament. At the start of the street, the church of Notre-Dame de la Dalbade, an imposing brick mass with large rose windows above, was completed in 1542; with a superb Renaissance portal added later and an extraordinary tympanum, it has an impressive exterior. On the opposite corner is a charming old timbered house, No. 32, the Hôtel des Chevaliers de St. Jean, or Grande Prieuré de Malte, dated 1688, was — as the name makes obvious — a possession of the Knights of St. Jean. No. 25, the Hôtel de Clary, or Hôtel de Pierre, dated 1613, is frankly incredible, a frenzied extravaganza of carving in wood and stone. There are no bricks in the façade (the use of stone in this region was an indication of enormous opulence), but within the doorway is a handsome courtyard around which the rest of the mansion is made of brick and is a good deal more normal looking! The courtyard of No. 22 is especially attractive.

Rue de la Dalbade emerges into the two unremarkable squares, place du Parlement and place du Salin, once the seat of the Catholic Inquisition. The Palais de Justice now occupies the site. Turn up rue Pharaon (also part of the Quartier Parlementaire) and continue straight across place des Carmes (with market hall) and along rue des Filatiers; turn right into rue de la Trinité. At the junction with rue du Languedoc (with the grand Palais Consulaire, or Hôtel de Fumel, straddling the corner), cross straight over into rue Croix-Baragnon. (A quicker, although arguably less agreeable route from place du Salin, would be to go straight up rue du Languedoc to rue Croix-Baragnon. Pause at Hôtel du Vieux-Raisin, 36 rue du Languedoc, on the corner of rue d'Aussargues. Built in 1573, this splendid Renaissance mansion has changed its name many times, and is now a 'dance workshop'. The enclosed spiral staircase in the far corner of the courtyard is atmospheric.) Rue Croix-Baragnon has more superb old mansions. The ground floors of some have been converted into chic pricey boutiques and jewellers.

The Cathédrale St. Étienne, at the end of the street, is a fine example of how not to build a cathedral. It looks like the result of a wild party for student builders. The chronology of its construction, stretching from the 11th to the 17th centuries, hardly bears telling. For all that, it has reached the present day with a certain quaint picturesqueness, and does contain some good work. At the earliest stage in the construction, part of the original nave was built in Romanesque style, and completed with Gothic rib-vaulting. No sooner was this completed than a new nave in a different Gothic style was begun in stages on a slightly different axis, but this too was left only half completed. Various other superfluous bits and pieces were built, and then in the 17th century, more vaults were added. The end result has a rather curious shape, with a broad aisleless nave (note the old tapestries in this part), joining a much wider nave with side aisles. The wider section meets the choir, with fine stalls, and ambulatory with side chapels. The ceiling is beautiful. In the Chapelle des Reliques, gold caskets are alleged to contain the remains of about 40 more or less obscure 'saints', although among the less obscure ones is St. Louis (King Louis IX).

Place St. Étienne separates the cathedral from rue de Metz, a major shopping street with which 19th-century developers sliced through the old town centre. Turn left into rue de Metz. If you fancy a rest, take a right turn, say into rue Boulbonne, quickly reaching place St. Georges, a relaxing tree-shaded central square, almost traffic-free, full of café tables and little areas of garden. Rue de Metz intersects another major commercial street of 19th-century construction, rue d'Alsace-Lorraine. On the corner (entrance in rue de Metz) stands the huge building of Les Augustins, looking rather neglected from outside. The largely 19th-century exterior encloses the admirable chapter house, sacristy, and church of a 14th-century priory. Inside, it contains an important museum of local antiquities and art, with some excellent Romanesque sculpture, and gives access to the superb Great Cloister.

Rue de Metz crosses rue d'Alsace-Lorraine and enters place Esquirol, where there are several cheap brasseries. At the far end of the square, rue des Changes turns away to the right. This continues into rue St. Rôme. The two together, both narrow ancient streets, make a single pedestrianised shopping throughfare with many impressive old brick and timber buildings. Go through the entrance marked 16 rue des Changes into an amazing courtyard with two wooden staircases. Note the carved lintels. Rue St. Rôme emerges into the spaciousness of place du Capitole.

Although there are some café-bars at the perimeter of the square, a much more popular and congenial spot for relaxing at outdoor tables is place Wilson, five minutes' walk away. Square Charles de Gaulle (behind place du Capitole) is bordered by busy rue d'Alsace-Lorraine. Cross straight over

Les Villes Roses

The Toulousain basin, lying between eastern Gascony and the hills of Haut Languedoc, and extending from the uplands of Quercy to the Pyrenean foothills, is one of only two regions in France which lack suitable stone for building (the other is Flanders). In this region, the towns are given a distinct character by their use of Roman-style bricks, which are narrower, wider, and made of softer material than modern bricks. Their colours vary across a pastel spectrum from yellow to pink, and give the towns an attractive rosy hue shown to brilliant advantage in certain lights. They are known as *villes roses* or *villes rouges*, pink or red towns. The pinkest is said to be Montauban, the reddest Toulouse (which happens to have a political parallel as well). From Roman times onwards, the Toulouse region manufactured bricks for the construction of its important edifices — the great civic and religious buildings. Humbler dwellings were made of wattle and daub on sturdy timber frames. After a great fire which destroyed much of Toulouse in 1363, wattle-and-daub timbered houses throughout the area were replaced by brick. The large-scale production of bricks, rooftiles, and cement has grown into an important local industry.

this main road and take rue Lafayette into the pleasant oval-shaped place Wilson. Its pavements have the tables and chairs of several bars all around, while in the middle of the *place* is a public garden dedicated to the 17th-century *langue d'oc* poet Goudouli (or Godolin).

Allées Roosevelt leaves place Wilson and immediately meets boulevard Lazare Carnot, one of the major roads which follow the course of the demolished city walls: this too is a lively corner and meeting point with popular eating and drinking places. Allées Roosevelt changes to allées Jean-Jaurès and keeps straight on (with a seedy red-light district off to the left) to the Canal du Midi and the even busier encircling boulevards which run parellel to it. Boulevard Lazare Carnot, heading south, passes rue de la Colombette, a useful and unfashionable street with

several cheap shops and restaurants; it leads to the peculiar-looking domed modern church of St. Aubin (circular altar, good stained glass), around which there's a popular market on Sunday mornings.

Boulevard Carnot continues towards the Grand Rond (or Boulingrin), a big roundabout enclosing a large pleasant park. Allées Jules Guesde, continuing the ring road, turns down directly for the river and Pont St. Michel. An extensive public botanic gardens, or Jardin des Plantes, lies on the left of allées Jules Guesde. For pedestrians, a footbridge connects the Grand Rond park to the Botanic Gardens. The Jardin des Plantes is a peaceful green area of lawns, fountains, and shaded paths. Toulouse's Museum d'Histoire Naturelle stands just inside the gardens. This was the site of the Château Narbonnaise, cornerstone of the city's defences.

Pont St. Michel then makes its way onto the Garonne's left bank and the ring road continues along allées Charles de Fitte. Left-bank Toulouse, between allée de Fitte and the river, has busy, lively streets of everyday shops and agreeable bars, a riverside park, and the striking Château d'Eau (water tower) in which there is now a notable photographic art gallery. Place St. Cyprien is the focal point on this side of the river.

The route nationale N124 starts at place St. Cyprien and makes its way out of town on the west side, heading first for the airport (in the neighbourhood of which are several important Gallo-Roman remains), then to Auch and across Armagnac towards Bordeaux.

All around Toulouse the landscape consists of areas of rolling farmland separated by broad flat river valleys. The valleys, heavily developed and industrialised in places, act as channels for the major roads and railways linking Toulouse with industrial centres. On the south side of town, the N20 follows the Garonne's west bank upriver, while on the river's east side a tangle of minor roads follows a more rustic course; one little road goes through **Vieille Toulouse**, but little survives there of a settlement of the Volques Celts. At the confluence of the river Ariège with the Garonne, the N20 takes the Ariège, while the N117 stays with the Garonne, both soon coming within view of the Pyrenees. **Muret**, now not an especially interesting town, was in 1213 the scene of a major battle of the Albigensian Crusade. Pedro II of Aragón had arrived in person with his army to give support to Raymond VI of Toulouse. The engagement at Muret was a disaster for the

southerners; the Spanish troops were completey routed by the northerners under Simon de Montfort, and Pedro II was killed. The battle site was just north of town.

The country east and south-east of Toulouse is called the Lauragais. A redbrick area, many of its towns have a certain amount of industry and are not particularly appealing. In this district more Cathars were concentrated than anywhere else. The reason was simply that the important main highway linking the two great Languedoc cities of Carcassonne and Toulouse ran through the middle of the area. Even today this corridor, busy with the autoroute A61, the N113, and the Canal du Midi, is a major link between Toulouse and the Mediterranean. Along the old highway preachers walked, pausing at villages and market towns to spread the new ideas, read the Gospels, and urge rebellion against the corrupt Catholic hierarchy. People of all classes converged on the markets to trade not only goods but ideas and news, which they then took back home with them into the countryside. Off the highway, the heresy spread fast until many small Lauragais towns were entirely Cathar, including not just local nobility but local priests as well. Most of the area was a possession of the Trencavel viscounts, and dealing with them, and with this area, was a first priority of the Albigensian Crusaders.

The other great feature of the Lauragais is *cassoulet*, the highly esteemed local pork and bean casserole. In Toulouse itself, and throughout Languedoc, *cassoulet* features on the menus of scores of restaurants whether cheap or expensive. The recipe for *cassoulet* is on the one hand immutable and known

Previous page: *Across the Tarn at Montauban — le Vieux Pont*

to every Languedoc housewife; on the other hand, the proportions are the subject of endless dispute. (An even more sensitive matter is the rightness or wrongness of including lamb.) Everyone agrees that the ingredients must all be obtained from this immediate vicinity and should be cooked in a traditional type of local earthenware dish called a *cassolo*. While restaurants and housewives pride themselves on their own home-made *cassoulet*, nearly all charcuteries of Lauragais towns and villages sell ready-made *cassoulets* for a quick family dinner. If you really want to find out about *cassoulet* at its best though, you'll have to carry on along the N113 to Castelnaudary, birthplace and capital of this regional favourite dish. Master *cassoulet* chefs of the Lauragais join a distinguished brotherhood called the Grande Confrérie du Cassoulet de Castelnaudary.

North-east of Toulouse, north of the Lauragais, is the vineyard country of Gaillac, the Frontonnais, and the Côtes du Tarn, producing good crisp whites and straightforward reds. Some of these wines are a bargain: ordinary and unpretentious, they are for all that highly enjoyable, very drinkable with local food. The slightly *pétillant* white Gaillac Perlé is a personal favourite among these remarkably inexpensive wines. The N88 drives straight through the area to Albi, another handsome *ville rose*, dominated by its immense brick cathedral.

The route nationale N20 and the autoroute A62 go north and north-west from Toulouse with the Garonne. After 30km the N20 curves away from the Garonne to meet the Tarn at **Montauban** (pop: 51,000). This large redbrick town, an important commercial centre and préfecture of the Tarn-et-Garonne

département, started life as a community around the nearby monastery of Montauriol. In 1144 Alphonso-Jordan, Count of Toulouse, constructed the *bastide* of Montauban. Ever since, it has been an indomitable stronghold of southern regionalism. The most savage treatment was meted out to it during and after the Albigensian Crusade, yet its seething defiance re-emerged in the 16th-century with a passionate, and almost universal, support for Protestantism. It successfully fought off sieges by Catholic forces during the Religious Wars, but in 1629, recognising that the end had come, it surrendered to the royalist forces. No great clemency was shown to its citizens. Yet they remained firm supporters of religious reform, and Montauban is largely Protestant to this day.

The interesting part of the town, the former *bastide*, climbs up from the right bank of the wide, handsome Tarn, which flows lazily through town between green slopes. The Vieux Pont, an attractive bridge of 1777, its sidewalks patterned with pebbles, gives good views of the river and stately buildings of the old town.

The bridge emerges at place Antoine Bourdelle, named after the noted sculptor (1861–1921) who was a native of Montauban. At one side of the square (entrance in rue de l'Hôtel de Ville), occupying the former Episcopal Palace of 1664, there is a museum dedicated to another distinguished 'Montalbanais', the artist Dominique Ingres (1780–1867). The museum contains several of his most outstanding paintings, as well as a selection from 4,000 of his drawings.

Overleaf: *Montauban: the arcades of Place Nationale*

Works by other artists, including some of Ingres's best-known contemporaries, David and Delacroix among them, are also shown. In addition there are archaeological collections. The building has interest of its own, and contains remnants of the second of two castles which have stood on this site, the first erected by the count of Toulouse, the second by the Black Prince after he had taken the town during the Hundred Years War.

Pavements patterned with black and white pebbles give charm to many Montauban streets and squares. The curiously named Côte des Bonnetiers, opposite the Ingres museum, rises from the square. It soon passes a town landmark, the Église St. Jacques, a weatherworn redbrick church with an octagonal tower in the distinctive Toulouse style and an unusual 'tympanum' made of tiles. The church's origins date back to the foundation of the town, but there has been a constant succession of later work to repair the damage inflicted by the centuries of violence, and it is now mainly Gothic. Turn right into the short rue Princesse, which goes into the majestic double arcades of place Nationale, the central market square of the *bastide*.

The square is not vast, but forms an impressive ensemble of redbrick architecture of the 17th century. The surrounding arcades are beautifully vaulted. Usually the square serves as a parking area, which does not show it to advantage; but the frequent open-air market gives it more colour, as do many shows and entertainments held here. Interesting old streets, some with good boutiques and food shops, lead off the *place*. A few of the shops give an opportunity to see inside the older buildings with their remarkable brick vaulting.

Moissac: a capital in the abbey cloisters

The streets still follow their original grid pattern but the town's enclosing ramparts have been replaced by main roads which take most of the traffic. Rue de la République, the narrow pedestrianised main thoroughfare of the old town, runs into carrefour (or place) des Martyrs, in the south-east corner of the *bastide*. This square is one of the focal points of the town, with café tables and fountains. Adjacent, the impressive white towers and façade of the cathedral make a striking contrast with the rest of the town's buildings. Its spacious interior too is tremendously imposing, in classical style, largely of pale stone, with monumental statues (in a state of collapse). Among the pictures is Ingres's The Vow of Louis XIII. Rue du Docteur Lacaze leaves the square and runs into rue de l'Hôtel de Ville, which descends again to place Bourdelle and the Tarn.

The D927 follows the river Tarn as it curves round to Moissac. An alternative would be to take the D958 due west to rejoin the N113 and the Garonne at industrial **Castelsarrasin** (where there is a 12th-century brick church). **Moissac**, prettily situated above the broad calm river Tarn not far from its confluence with the Garonne, was wrecked successively by the Albigensian Crusades, then the Hundred Years War, and then by the Religious Wars. On the whole, there's not much left here to hold one's attention. It does though have a name as a centre for high-quality fruit, as the orchards all around testify. Summer and autumn sees abundant fruit markets held in the town. Moissac is known especially as the capital of the Chasselas variety of white eating grape. But it is noted above all for what survives of the magnificent Romanesque church and cloisters of the 12th-century abbey of St. Pierre.

The church porch (1140) and, in particular, the highly carved portal (1115) are especially admirable. The remainder of the building is a 15th-century reconstruction. Inside, painted decoration extends over the walls and ceiling. There is expressive 15th- and 16th-century woodcarving and statuary.

The lovely cloisters, originally 11th-century, with 13th-century arches, have great simplicity, but the marble columns — alternately paired and single — are adorned with fine and unusual capitals. One depicts St. Laurent being roasted alive — hence he is the patron saint of *rotisseurs* (meat roasters). It seems impossible that in 1850 the local railway company intended to pull all this down during the construction of the main Toulouse–Bordeaux line. Local protests were heeded and the railway was laid behind the church and cloisters.

The Tarn pours into the Garonne just outside Moissac. Accompanied by the railway line and the N113 on the right bank and the A62 on the left, the Garonne flows west, skirting the Armagnac hills, and passing through the Gironde vineyards, to reach Bordeaux and the Atlantic ocean.

209

*The impressive 12th-century porch of the St.
Pierre abbey in Moissac*

Hotels and Restaurants

MONTAUBAN: Most places to stay are on the utterly charmless west bank, around the station.
Hôtel d'Orsay, opposite station (63.66.06.66), useful, well-equipped mid-priced hotel with excellent restaurant.
Grand Hôtel du Midi, 12 rue Notre Dame (63.63.17.23), centrally located on east bank, solid traditional establishment, moderate prices.

MOISSAC: Hôtel du Chapon Fin, pl des Récollets (63.04.04.22), central location on the market square, good regional cooking. Inexpensive.

TOULOUSE: Grand Hôtel de l'Opéra, 1 pl du Capitole (61.21.82.66), excellent location at the start of rue de la Pomme in one corner of pl du Capitole; prestigious luxury hotel, some rooms surprisingly inexpensive, set back in courtyard behind its two well-known eating places:
Les Jardins de l'Opéra, (61.23.07.76), the hotel's superb and highly acclaimed restaurant, where locally born chef Dominique Toulousy prepares magnificent food of a resolutely regional character, served with first-rate southern wines; prices are very reasonable for the quality.
Grand Café de l'Opéra (61.21.37.03), the hotel's fashionable brasserie, with good food at moderate prices.
Orsi (Le Bouchon Lyonnais), 13 rue de l'Industrie (61.62.97.43). In Lyon, a '*bouchon*' is a high-quality unpretentious little restaurant frequented mainly by locals; this is along similar lines, a good restaurant in an unprepossessing backstreet, with bearable prices.
Restaurant le Barreau, 10 rue Moulins (61.25.25.52), on the three floors of an old bakery, delightful restaurant in a lane in the old heart of the city, good cooking; the cheapest menu is a bargain.
Brasserie des Beaux-Arts, 1 quai de la Daurade (61.21.12.12), good *menus* at an ornate old favourite on a busy corner beside the river, prices reasonable.
Chez Émile, 13 pl St. Georges (61.21.05.56), excellent and agreeable little restaurant with meat upstairs and fish downstairs, not cheap.
La Frégate, 1 rue d'Austerlitz, corner of pl Wilson (61.21.59.61), popular restaurant with good *cassoulet* and other regional specialities, moderate price.
Mercure Wilson, 7 rue Labéda (61.21.21.75), large comfortable modern city-centre hotel, a bit pricey.
Other good eating places around town include **La Bascule** (14 av Hauriou, 61.52.09.51), bistro specialising in regional dishes; **Le Mangevin** (46 rue Pharaon, 61.52.79.16), lively wine bar of character with good cooking; **La Divine Comédie** (14 rue Industrie, 61.99.28.57), taking orders till 1am; and **Attila** (Marché Victor-Hugo, 61.29.83.59), excellent lunches, exceptionally low prices; **Hôtel President**, 43–45 rue Raymond IV (61.63.46.46), decent modern small hotel, within easy reach of sights, but only a short walk from the railway station. Not expensive.

The hotels **Victoria** (61.62.50.90), **Orsay** (61.62.71.61), and **Bordeaux** (61.62.41.09) all offer acceptable accommodation at a moderate price, all are by a busy road facing across the canal to the railway station, about 15 minutes' walk from the city centre. In addition, the **Mercure Matabiau** (61.62.84.93), attached to the railway station Gare Matabiau, is a reasonable if characterless large traditional hotel, well modernised, not expensive and a useful resource for rail travellers.

VIEILLE-TOULOUSE: Hôtel de la Flânerie, rte de Lacroix-Falgarde (61.73.39.12), 9km from Toulouse; quiet, comfortable, modern hotel, attractive building, extensive grounds, close to Garonne. Reasonable prices, no restaurant.

Loisirs-Acceuil (hotel booking service): HAUTE-GARONNE — 14 rue Bayard, 313000 Toulouse (61.99.44.00); TARN-ET-GARONNE — Hôtel des Intendants, pl Foch, 82000 Montauban (63.63.31.40; fax 63.66.80.36).

Museums

MOISSAC: Musée Moissagais. In former abbot's mansion, beside cloisters. Collections on local arts and tradition, and local historical items *10–12.30 all year; 2–5.30 Sept–Jun, 2–7.30 Jul–Aug. Closed Sun am, Tue, all of Dec, and some j.f.*

MONTAUBAN: Musée Ingres, corner of pl Bourdelle/rue Hôtel de Ville. In 17th-century Episcopal Palace. Fine art collections of above average standard, with emphasis on Ingres *10–12, 2–6. Closed Mon and j.f.*
Musée d'Histoire Naturelle et de Préhistoire, pl Bourdelle. Extensive collections devoted to worldwide ornithology, prehistoric specimens of animal life, other prehistoric items locally discovered *9.30–12, 1.30–6. Closed Sun am, Mon, and j.f.*

TOULOUSE: Musée St. Raymond, pl St. Sernin, beside Basilica (61.22.21.85). Important local archaeological museum *Mon–Sat, exc. Tue: 10–12, 2–6; Sun 2–6. Closed Tue, j.f. Free on Sun. In Jul–Aug, open also Tue 2–6, Sun 10–12.*
Les Augustins (61.22.21.82), rue de Metz. Art and sculpture from Middle Ages to 19th century. See text. *10–12, 2–6 (till 10 on Wed). Closed Tue, j.f.*
Capitole, pl du Capitole. Hôtel de Ville. See text. *8.30–5. Closed Sat, Sun, j.f.*
Musée Paul Dupuy (61.22.21.83), rue de la Pleau, off rue Ozenne. Interesting museum of skilled workmanship in arts and crafts from Middle Ages to present day *10–12, 2–6. Closed Tue, Sun am, j.f.*
Museum d'Histoire Naturelle (61.52.00.14), inside Botanic Gardens (Jardin des Plantes). Important collections of natural history and prehistory *2–6. Closed Tue.*
Les Jacobins (61.22.21.92), rue Lakanal. Superb church and cloisters. *10–12, 3–6.30. Closed Sun am.*
Musée du Vieux-Toulouse (61.13.97.24), in alleyway rue du May, off rue St. Rôme. Local history and crafts *Jun–Sep: 3–5 daily. Rest of year Wed 2.30–5.30 only. Closed Sun, j.f.*

Tourist Offices

CRT office (regional information): BP166 or 54 bd de l'Embouchure, Toulouse 31022 (61.13.55.55; fax 61.47.17.16).

CDT offices (information on the départements): HAUTE-GARONNE — 14 rue Bayard, 31000 Toulouse (61.99.44.00); TARN-ET-GARONNE — Hôtel des Intendants, pl Foch, 82000 Montauban (63.63.31.40).

OTSI offices (local information): CASTELSARRASIN — pl de la Liberté (63.32.14.88); MOISSAC — 6 pl D-de-Bredon, next to cloisters (63.04.01.85); MONTAUBAN — 2 rue du Collège (63.63.60.60); TOULOUSE — Donjon du Capitole, sq Charles-de-Gaulle (61.11.02.22; fax 61.22.03.63).
Where there is no tourist office, apply to the Town Hall (Mairie or Hôtel de Ville).

Sports and Leisure

CYCLE & MOPED HIRE: Locauto, 9bis pl Jeanne-d'Arc, Toulouse (61.62.47.60); 104, bd Lacapelle, Montauban (63.63.32.06).

CYCLE TOURING: from Toulouse: organised by Union des Cyclotouristes Toulousains, 54 rue des Trois-Troubadours, Toulouse (61.62.91.88); other cycle-touring associations in Montauban, Moissac, Castelsarrasin.

FLYING, GLIDING ETC: Toulouse — Les Ailes Toulousaines, Aérodrome de Lasbordes 31130 Balma (61.80.51.61). Castelsarrasin — Aéroclub de Moissac-Castelsarrasin, BP60, Castelsarrasin; Montauban — Aéroclub, Aérodrome de Montauban Ville (63.03.26.93).

GOLF: Two 18-hole golf courses within 10km of Toulouse (61.73.45.48 and 61.84.20.50), enquire at OTSI for details.

GO-KARTING: GNK, 4 rue du Roc, Toulouse.

RIDING: ARTE, 61 allée de Bruenne, 31069 Toulouse (61.21.94.60); Centre Équestre des Côteaux de Pech-David, Toulouse (61.52.21.45); ADTE, Mme Couderc, Gasseras 82000, Montauban (63.63.05.72).

SAILING and WATERSPORTS: several associations and clubs around Toulouse and Moissac, ask at OTSIs.

TENNIS: details of all facilities from FFT, M. Bimes, Résidence La Palmeraie, Immeuble Le Vendée, 226 av St. Exupéry, Toulouse, or from OTSI.

WALKING: GR653 goes from Toulouse to Auch; the GR65 passes through Castelsarrasin and Moissac.

INDEX